ROADTRIP AMERICA

Arizona *and*
New Mexico

25 Scenic Side Trips

IMBRIFEX

ROADTRIP AMERICA

RTA

Arizona *and* New Mexico

25 Scenic Side Trips

Rick Quinn

IMBRIFEX BOOKS

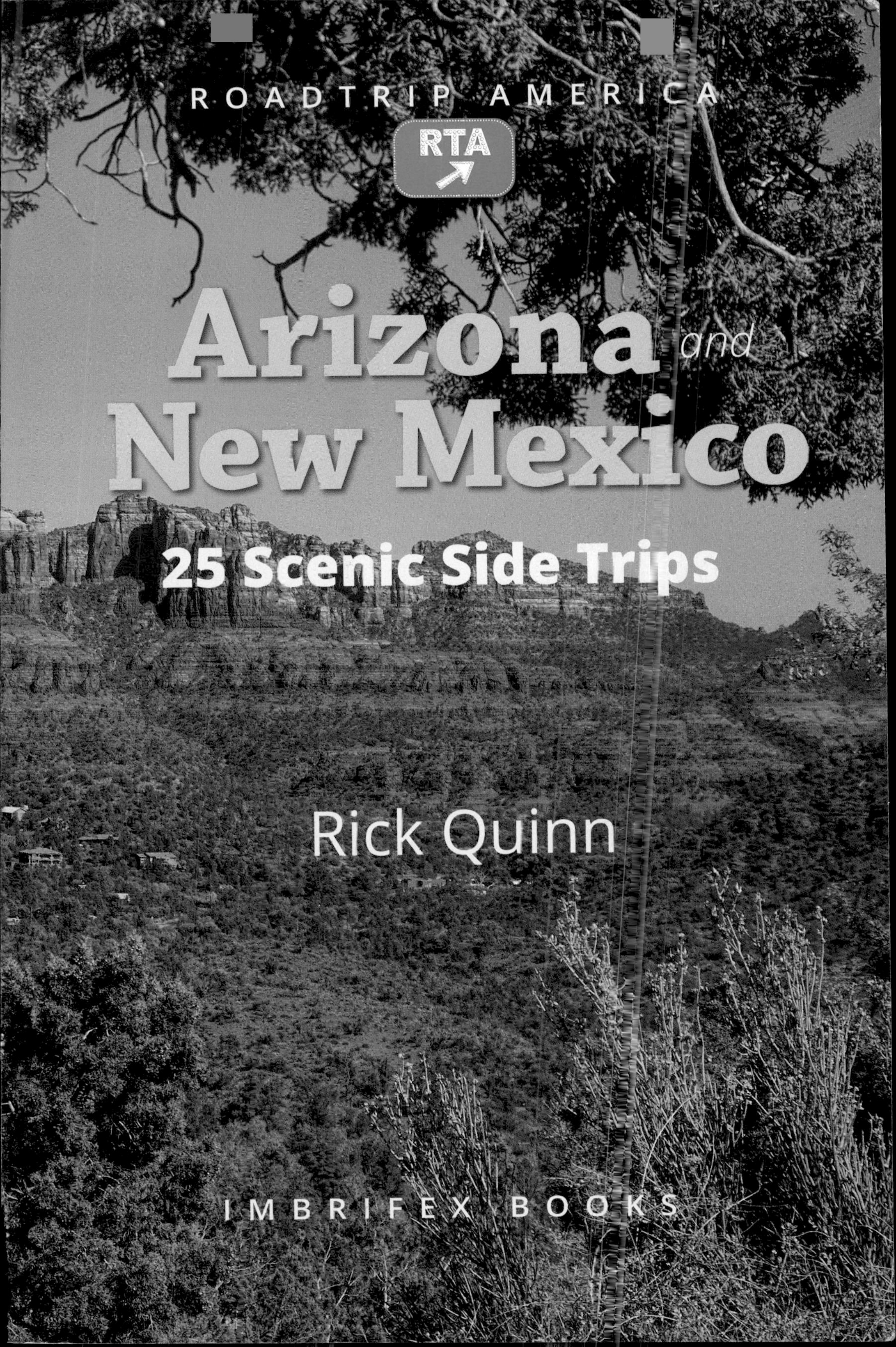

IMBRIFEX BOOKS
Published by Flattop Productions, Inc.
8275 S. Eastern Avenue, Suite 200
Las Vegas, NV 89123, USA

IMBRIFEX. BOOKS

Editor: Nancy Zerbey
Book and Cover Designer: Sue Campbell
Maps: Chris Erichsen
All cover and interior photos by Rick Quinn.
All photos from the tribal parks are used by permission, pursuant to permits secured by
the author.
Author Photo: Jill Quinn

IMBRIFEX® and ROADTRIP AMERICA® are registered trademarks of Flattop Productions,
Inc.

This publication is provided for informational and educational purposes. The information
contained in the publication is true to the best of our knowledge however no representations
or warranties are made with respect to its accuracy or safety, and the publisher and author
assume no liability for its use. Understand that driving and outdoor activities are always
potentially dangerous. Preparing yourself and your vehicle with the proper equipment and
skills will lead to the most enjoyable and safest experience. Know your vehicle and how
to drive and maintain it. Be aware of local road, weather, and terrain conditions. Obey
all posted rules and regulations. Respect Native American jurisdictions, use public lands
thoughtfully, and do not trespass on private lands. Things can change after a guidebook is
published: roads undergo construction, attractions and businesses close, jurisdictions change,
etc. All these things can affect the road trip routes described in this book. Check locally
whenever you can. Seasonal weather will have an effect on roads and routes described in this
publication. Corrections, updates and suggestions may be sent to the author at
Rick.Quinn@roadtripamerica.com.

ScenicSideTrips.com
Imbrifex.com
RoadTripAmerica.com

ISBN 9781945501050 (trade paper)
ISBN 9781945501111 (e-book)

Library of Congress Control Number: 2017934281
First Edition: April, 2018

Printed in the Republic of South Korea

For Quinn and Ollie, and
all our children's children

Contents

Foreword   xi

Introduction   xiii

Part 1: Scenic Alternatives to Interstate 10   21

1. Van Horn, Texas, to Las Cruces, New Mexico 23
Guadalupe Mountains National Park, Carlsbad Caverns National Park, Roswell UFO Museum, Lincoln Historic Site, Billy the Kid Scenic Byway, Sierra Blanca Mountains, White Sands National Monument, White Sands Missile Range Museum

2. Las Cruces to Lordsburg 37
Las Cruces Museum of Nature and Science, Hatch (Chile Capital of the World), Spaceport America, Geronimo Trail Scenic Byway, Trail of the Mountain Spirits Scenic Byway, Gila Hot Springs, Gila Cliff Dwellings National Monument, Pinos Altos, Historic Silver City, City of Rocks State Park, Chino Copper Mine

3. Lordsburg to Willcox, Arizona 50
Silver City, Catwalk National Recreation Trail, Mogollon Ghost Town, White Mountains of Eastern Arizona, Coronado Trail Scenic Byway, Blue Range Primitive Area, Morenci Mine, Clifton Townsite Historic District, Rex Allen Museum

4. Lordsburg to Phoenix 63
Duncan, Safford and Mount Graham, Globe/Miami, Superior and the Boyce Thompson Arboretum, Phoenix Mountain Parks, Arizona State Capitol Museum, Heard Museum, Desert Botanical Garden, Pueblo Grande

5. Willcox to Benson 75
Fort Bowie National Historic Site, Chiricahua National Monument, Douglas and Agua Prieta, Bisbee and the Copper Queen Mine, Tombstone, O.K. Corral and Boot Hill, St. David, Benson

6. Benson to Tucson 89
Kartchner Caverns State Park, Ramsey Canyon Preserve, Coronado National Memorial, Montezuma Pass, Parker Canyon Lake, Sonoita, Patagonia, Nogales, Tumacácori National Historical Park, Tubac Presidio, Titan Missile Museum

7. A Tucson Circuit 101
Sabino Canyon, Mount Lemmon, Saguaro National Park East, AMARG Boneyard, Pima Air & Space Museum, Mission San Xavier del Bac, Old Tucson, Arizona-Sonora Desert Museum, Saguaro National Park West, Gates Pass

8. Tucson to Phoenix 117
Biosphere 2, Pinal Pioneer Parkway, Tom Mix Memorial, Historic Florence, Casa Grande Ruins National Monument, LDS Mesa Temple, Tempe Town Lake, Old Town Scottsdale, Western Spirit Museum

Part 2: Scenic Alternatives to Interstate 17   129

9. Phoenix to Flagstaff, West Route 131
Wickenburg, Yarnell Hill, Prescott and Whiskey Row, Mingus Mountain and Jerome, Tuzigoot National Monument and the Verde Valley, Sedona and the Red Rocks, Oak Creek Canyon, Flagstaff

10. Phoenix to Flagstaff, East Route 143
Taliesin West, Fountain Hills, Payson and the Zane Gray Cabin, Mogollon Rim, Tonto Natural Bridge State Park, Pine and Strawberry, Montezuma Castle National Monument, Arcosanti, Schnebly Hill, Sedona, Oak Creek Canyon

11. Phoenix to Holbrook 157
Superstition Wilderness, Apache Trail Historic Road, Salt River Lakes (Canyon, Apache, and Roosevelt), Tonto National Monument, Globe, Salt River Canyon, Show Low, Petrified Forest National Park, Painted Desert, Holbrook

Part 3: Scenic Alternatives to Interstate 40   171

12. Kingman to Flagstaff 173
Historic Route 66, Oatman, Peach Springs and the Hualapai Reservation, Diamond Creek Road, the Colorado River, Grand Canyon Caverns, Seligman, Williams, Grand Canyon Railroad, Flagstaff

13. St. George, Utah, to Flagstaff 189
Zion National Park, North Rim of the Grand Canyon, Lee's Ferry, Lake Powell, Antelope Canyon, Horseshoe Bend, Flagstaff

14. Flagstaff and the Grand Canyon Loop 207
Cameron Trading Post, Grand Canyon National Park, Red Mountain Crater, Hart Prairie Preserve, Snowbowl (San Francisco Peaks), Museum of Northern Arizona, Flagstaff

15. Flagstaff to Holbrook 221
Walnut Canyon National Monument, Sunset Crater Volcano and Wupatki National Monuments, Coal Mine Canyon, Hopi Mesas, Little Painted Desert, Winslow, Holbrook

16. Holbrook to Gallup, New Mexico 233
Canyon de Chelly National Monument, Monument Valley, Navajo Route 13 and the Lukachukai Mountains, Shiprock, Gallup

17. Gallup to Grants 249
Gallup, Bisti Badlands, Aztec Ruins National Monument (Farmington), Chaco Culture National Historical Park

18. Gallup to Albuquerque 261
Gallup Historic District, Zuni Pueblo, El Morro National Monument, Ice Cave and Bandera Volcano, El Malpais National Monument, the Sky City of Acoma, Laguna Pueblo, Los Lunas, Rio Grande, Albuquerque

19. Grants to Socorro 275
Grants, El Malpais National Monument, Pie Town, the VLA, Plains of San Agustin, Bosque del Apache National Wildlife Refuge

Part 4: Scenic Alternatives to Interstate 25   287

20. Socorro to Albuquerque **289**
Historic Socorro, Sevilleta National Wildlife Refuge, Salinas Pueblo Missions
National Monument (Abo, Gran Quivira, and Quarai), Salt Mission Trail Scenic
Byway, Sandia Peak Tramway

21. Albuquerque Loop **301**
Indian Pueblo Cultural Center, Petroglyph National Monument, Corrales, Kasha-
Katuwe Tent Rocks National Monument, Turquoise Trail, Tinkertown Museum,
Sandia Crest

22. Albuquerque to Santa Fe **313**
Coronado Historic Site, Jemez Mountain Trail Scenic Byway, Jemez Historic Site,
Valles Caldera National Preserve, Fenton Lake State Park, Abiquiu, Bandelier
National Monument, Los Alamos, Bradbury Science Museum, Santa Fe

23. Santa Fe/Taos Loop, Part A **327**
Santa Fe, Low Road to Taos, Old Spanish Trail, Puye Cliff Dwellings, Rio Grande
del Norte National Monument, San Francisco de Asis Church, Taos, Taos Pueblo

24. Santa Fe/Taos Loop, Part B **339**
Taos, Enchanted Circle Scenic Byway, Taos Ski Valley, Wild Rivers Backcountry
Byway, Red River, Eagle Nest Lake, Vietnam Veterans Memorial State Park, Angel
Fire, High Road to Taos Scenic Byway, Las Trampas, Truchas, El Santuario de
Chimayo, Santa Fe

25. Santa Fe to Raton **355**
Santa Fe, Georgia O'Keeffe Museum, Abiquiu, Georgia O'Keeffe Home and Studio,
Ghost Ranch, Echo Amphitheater, Brazos Cliffs, Rio Grande Gorge Bridge, Taos,
Cimarron Canyon State Park, Cimarron, Raton

Acknowledgements   371

Index   372

Foreword

ROAD TRIPS THROUGH THE AMERICAN WEST ARE AMONG MY ABSOLUTE FAVORITE adventures. The western states, and particularly Arizona and New Mexico, have some of the most dramatic open space in the country. The wild history, the spectacular geography, and the mythical ethos of this region just make you want to gas up the car and go. What a pleasure, then, to discover a book that not only captures the magic and mystique of the terrain, but also reveals how to best enjoy it. Rick Quinn's infectious love of the open road and joy in driving make him an ideal narrator and travel companion.

In this day and age, when many people wonder if books still have a chance against the Internet, Quinn has delivered definitive proof that a good travel book deserves a place in the navigator's seat. The information presented here is compelling, multilayered, easy to navigate, and chock full of tips and details that will allow you to enjoy Arizona and New Mexico to their fullest. Quinn's research is meticulous, the maps are beautifully drawn, and Quinn's photography is simply wonderful. Paging through the book really makes you want to hit the road. Whether you have days to explore or only a few hours, these scenic routes will add unforgettable adventure to your Interstate journeys.

As a life-long avid road tripper, and the author of several travel books, I thought I knew everything about Tombstone, White Sands, the Indian Pueblos, and Sedona, not to mention many other sites in these areas. But Quinn has dug deep to uncover some wonderful and little-known stories that add color, depth, and intrigue to these destinations. And his descriptions of the roads linking these fascinating places take the book to new and impressive levels, capturing the energy and serendipity of a real road trip, with its many views and stops along the way. Reading Quinn's book is like having a smart and funny guide sitting in the seat next to you, always ready to share the best directions, practical information, and local lore.

Sunbaked, vast, and mysterious, Arizona and New Mexico are the wonderlands of the American West. Now, even with limited time and even if you've driven through this territory before, you can enjoy these places in new and interesting ways. With this book riding shotgun, you'll bring home many back-road memories and two-lane experiences that you might otherwise have driven right by.

I salute the spirit and accomplishment that Quinn has achieved in this fine book.

—Chris Epting

Chris Epting is an award-winning travel writer and author of 30 books including *James Dean Died Here* (Santa Monica Press) and *Roadside Baseball* (McGraw Hill).

Introduction

ROAD TRAVEL IN THE AMERICAN SOUTHWEST IS A PART OF EVERYDAY LIFE. Family gatherings, a new job or home, kids off to college, and hundreds of other reasons draw travelers to the Interstate Highway system to make a fast run across Arizona and New Mexico. This book was conceived as a way of introducing those destination-focused and time-pressed travelers to some of the incredible vistas, attractions, and natural wonders that the Interstates were designed to avoid. My goal was to identify 25 alternative routes—scenic detours that begin and end at Interstates—that can turn a boring speed run into a memorable road trip without adding very much time. They also make great day trips from the region's major cities.

I began my research by locking myself in a room full of maps and didn't come out until I had pinpointed every natural wonder, every site with historical or cultural significance, and every scenic stretch of highway in Arizona and New Mexico. Then I loaded up *La Reina Sucia*, "The Dirty Queen," my beloved and well-traveled Jeep Cherokee, and I hit the road. Over the course of the summer and fall of 2016, I drove 11,000 miles through Arizona and New Mexico, plus a bit of Texas and Utah, visiting all the places I've always loved, and a whole lot of places I'd always wanted to see. I took 7,000 photographs and compiled copious notes. The drives, the views, and the skies were magnificent; I saw more beauty and experienced more joy than I would have thought possible.

This book is the result of intensive research combined with a lifetime of experience and the passions that have driven me for more than half a century. Exploring all these roads and writing this book was some of the best fun I've ever had.

HOW TO USE THIS BOOK

There are two purposes to every road trip: transportation and exploration. If your top priority is to get from A to B as quickly as possible, find the nearest Interstate Highway, set your cruise control, and go, go, go! But if you're traveling for pleasure and the journey is part of the fun, then think of this book as your treasure map. In it you'll find 25 Scenic Side Trips, each designed to take you out of that river of 18-wheelers and into the landscape beyond. That's where you'll find the real Arizona and New Mexico, a place of world-class treasures and some wonderful hidden gems.

Route selection. The book is organized into four sections, providing scenic alternatives to the following segments of Interstate Highway:

1	**10**	Van Horn, TX	Phoenix, AZ	East to West	8
2	**17**	Phoenix, AZ	Flagstaff, AZ	South to North	3
3	**40**	Kingman, AZ	Albuquerque, NM	West to East	8
4	**25**	Socorro, NM	Raton, NM	South to North	6

The endpoint of nearly every Scenic Side Trip is the beginning of the next, so you always have the option to get back on the Interstate, or to keep going, exploring more of the wonders that lie just beyond the horizon.

Reversing course. The trips are described with the line of travel set in a particular direction (say, east to west). If you are going the other way, just begin at the end of the route and reverse the itinerary, using the attractions listed in **bold type** as your points of reference. To avoid confusion at turns, you may want to plot the reverse course on a map before you set out.

Maps. The route maps should be supplemented with detailed highway maps. Ideally, a designated navigator would use the narrative in the book, along with a current paper map or atlas, to alert the driver to turns, highway changes, and upcoming attractions. *Never rely entirely on a GPS*, especially in remote areas, but if you do use one, you'll find that most of the attractions set in **bold type** in the route descriptions will function as waypoints when you program your device.

Roads. Most of the roads on these routes are paved and in excellent condition, but if you're nervous about mountain driving, or if your vehicle is an oversized RV, some of these trips may not work for you; always read the trip description before setting out. A few unpaved segments are included on some routes. *If you are driving a rental vehicle, always check your contract before driving on unpaved roads*; many companies specifically prohibit such travel in their vehicles. It's always a good idea to check road conditions locally before traveling into remote areas; in Arizona: *az511.com*, in New Mexico: *nmroads.com*.

Travel time. The travel time listed at the beginning of each trip is an estimate based on normal weather, traffic, and road conditions. Anything out of the ordinary, including construction delays, will add to that estimate. A little extra time is built into each trip to allow for a relaxed pace and an occasional short stop, but anything over five minutes—whether to visit a national park or have a leisurely lunch—will add to your travel time. Longer routes include lodging suggestions at or near the midpoint, to allow for overnight stops. *Always keep track of where you are in relation to where you'd like to be at nightfall, and do not overestimate your ability to drive mountain roads in the dark.*

Vehicle Checklist

Have a competent mechanic check out your vehicle before you hit the road. Perform all scheduled maintenance and needed repairs, and check the following:

- Fluids: check engine oil, transmission fluid, coolant, brake fluid, power steering fluid, differential lubricant (both front and rear on four-wheel drive); flush and change if necessary
- All belts and hoses: check for leaks and wear
- Battery: load test
- Wiper blades should be reasonably new, washer fluid topped up
- Headlights, tail lights, turn signals, and brake lights
- Shocks, front end, and steering components: check for excessive wear
- Tires: check for even wear and proper inflation; rotate tires and realign the wheels if needed
- Spare tire: check pressure and condition; a spare more than 8 years old should probably be replaced, even if never used

Time zones. Both Arizona and New Mexico are in the Mountain Time Zone. *Note that Arizona does not observe Daylight Saving Time, except on the Navajo Reservation.*

BEFORE YOU HIT THE ROAD

Whether this is your first road trip or your hundredth, it's good to review the basics before you hit the road. Your first consideration is what vehicle to drive. On a road trip, comfort is more important than style, so make sure your vehicle is large enough to comfortably accommodate you, your passengers, and all of your stuff.

If you're taking your own vehicle on your road trip, have it inspected by a trusted mechanic before you hit the road *(see sidebar)*. Always exercise caution on unfamiliar roads, even—or especially—in a beefy SUV with full-time four-wheel drive, which may give you a false sense of security. Stay away from deep sand and mud, and make sure you have proper clearance in rocky terrain. Never try to drive across a flooded wash, or any fast-flowing water more than a couple of inches deep. Note that four-wheel drive will not substitute for snow tires or chains when winter conditions warrant their use.

Emergency preparedness. It's a good idea to travel with a cell phone, and to keep it charged, but know that cell coverage can be spotty; in many places

in the Southwest you will get no signal at all. If you experience an emergency in such an area, sit tight and stay with your vehicle; someone will be along, no matter how remote the road. Insurance that includes towing and other roadside assistance can prove invaluable, whether it's through a car rental agency, your personal auto insurance, or AAA. Note that AAA membership also includes access to free, up-to-date maps of every state and major city in the U.S. and Canada, as well as guidebooks and other traveler's assistance.

What to Carry

Here are some things you should carry in your vehicle when traveling in remote areas of the Southwest.

Mandatory: an ample supply of drinking water, some nonperishable ready-to-eat food, paper maps of the area, blankets, sleeping bags or warm clothing (nights are much cooler than days, especially at high altitudes), a working flashlight, a working vehicle jack, a lug wrench, and a first aid kit

Optional, but a good idea: emergency flares, proper coolant for your radiator, a tow strap or chain, jumper cables or a fully-charged jump-start device, a 12-volt tire pump, a basic set of tools (wrenches, screwdrivers, pliers, and a hammer), a small trenching shovel, and a hatchet

Traveling with kids. Nobody knows your kids like you do, so these are just general recommendations. If they're old enough, try to involve the kids in your trip planning; maybe have them read the trip descriptions in this book in advance of the trip, and let them take turns as navigator. Switch seats periodically and make frequent stops. Be sure to carry healthy snacks, like fruit and trail mix, and limit sugar. Set expectations about the use of smartphones and tablets, and have a plan to counter the inevitable protest, "I'm bored!" Books on tape, games, videos, and nap time will usually buy you an hour or two.

Seasonal considerations. Summers can be dangerously hot in desert regions. Always carry plenty of drinking water and keep an eye on your vehicle's temperature gauge. When climbing long mountain grades, you may need to turn off your AC and open your windows for fresh air. If the gauge hits the danger zone, pull over at a rest area and let your engine cool down. *Never remove your radiator cap while the engine is steaming hot.*

Summer also brings a lot of sudden, heavy rain to this region; locals call it the "monsoon season." Clouds tend to build over the mountains through the day, then unleash downpours in the afternoon. These storms usually blow up quickly, and end just as quickly. If you're caught in torrential rain, it is often best to pull off the roadway and wait it out. Never enter a flooded wash, and never drive around barricades. If you are caught on open high ground during a lightning storm, remain in your vehicle with your hands in your lap; touch nothing metal.

Despite the southern latitude, mountain areas can get plenty of snow in winter. All the usual winter driving precautions apply here: wait for the plow, watch for black ice, and know how to control skids. If snow tires or chains are advised, be sure to use them. Driving in snow and on icy roads is an acquired skill, and not altogether intuitive. *Never assume you know what you're doing if you've never done it before.*

Desert. You'll see a lot of desert in Arizona and New Mexico. This is not friendly terrain. If you go out walking among the cacti, watch where you put your feet, and don't touch anything! Not only are there rattlesnakes, there's cholla (*choy-ah*), a common cactus with tiny barbed spines that attach and will not let go. And, please, don't go off-roading in desert terrain. If there's not already a road, don't make a new one; these ecosystems are fragile.

Wildlife. You may encounter deer, elk, antelope, and other animals on the road, especially in forested areas. Give animals a wide berth; don't approach them; don't attempt to feed them. If you're on foot, and you encounter a bear or a mountain lion, avoid eye contact and back away slowly; don't kneel or crouch down, and never turn your back and run. If you are bitten by any creature larger than an insect, seek medical attention ASAP.

Border country. When traveling within 25 miles of the U.S. border with Mexico, expect to see agents of U.S. Customs and Border Protection on routine patrol. There are checkpoints on every major road, and all vehicles must stop; agents have the right to verify the immigration status of everyone in the vehicle, and to visually inspect the interior, even if you have not crossed the border. Everyone, but especially foreign nationals, should carry appropriate identification, such as a passport, when traveling in this area.

Indian lands. Indian reservations, regardless of size, are essentially sovereign nations; they have their own laws, their own courts, and their own Tribal Police forces, which have the same authority over travelers as any police force. All reservation land should be considered private property, and travel off the main roads is generally prohibited without a permit. Photography is prohibited in many communities; obey all posted directives.

National parks and monuments. Arizona and New Mexico are home to many wonderful national parks and monuments. In parks that charge an entrance fee, keep your pass on display inside your vehicle when it's parked. If you're visiting several national parks, you can purchase an America the Beautiful Annual Pass ($80 in 2017), which covers admission to every national park and monument in the U.S. for an entire year.

For a wealth of information about road trips, including trip advice, maps, and forums, visit the RoadTrip America website: RoadTripAmerica.com. All of the routes described in this book are available for downloading for free at roadtripamerica.com.

Enjoy the ride!

— Rick Quinn

Part 1: Scenic Alternatives to Interstate 10

Interstate 10 is the southernmost of the true cross-country expressways. West of the Mississippi River, the highway traverses the vast Texas plains and three deserts: empty, treeless terrain that's the color of dust and seems to go on forever. As it crosses through New Mexico and Arizona, the highway skirts south of the remnants of the Rockies, running parallel to the old Southern Pacific Railroad just north of the Mexican border. It's a fast road, with minimal grades and very few curves, which makes it a favorite of long-haul truckers.

Sightseeing vacationers might prefer one of the eight Scenic Side Trips in this section, which covers the 591-mile segment of I-10 from Van Horn, Texas, to Phoenix, Arizona. Each route leads off into the mountains that line the horizon, and on through the countryside beyond. These are some of the most beautiful back roads you'll ever drive, and they take in some amazing attractions. Each route finishes back on I-10, where you can continue on your way, or head off on another adventure.

In this desert region, you can expect hot, mostly dry weather from spring into fall, with temperatures commonly rising well above 100 degrees. If you're traveling between mid-June and mid-September, keep an eye on the sky; this is "monsoon" season, when warm, moist air flows north from the Gulf of California, brewing violent thunderstorms that can disrupt highway travel, but also deliver beautiful rainbows and sunsets.

Several routes have mountain segments where the road climbs as high as 9,000 feet, rising from cactus-studded desert into cool pine forest over the course of just a few dozen miles. On those roads, you might pass through several different ecosystems, each with a completely different climate, different vegetation, and different species of wildlife. These "sky islands," as they're called, are unique to this desert region.

Wildflowers bloom along these routes from spring through summer; the cactus blossoms in the Arizona deserts are especially lovely, and different species bloom at different times, beginning in mid-March. Autumn brings fall colors to the higher elevations and river valleys. Winter can bring snow to the high country, and sometimes road closures; check road conditions locally when in doubt. Note that some of the featured attractions on these routes are seasonal: some open only in summer, others only in winter.

The routes in this section are sequenced for drivers traveling east to west. If you are going the other way, just reverse the itinerary.

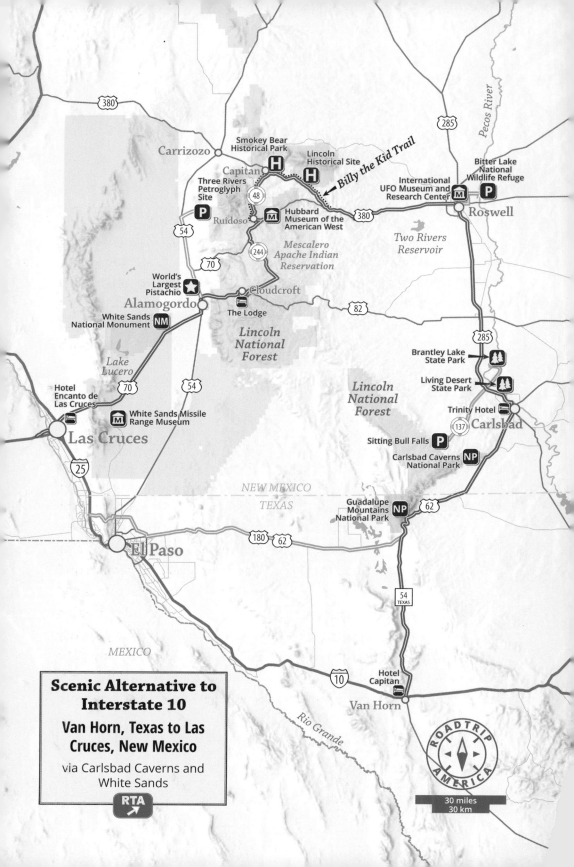

Van Horn, Texas, to Las Cruces, New Mexico

via Carlsbad Caverns and White Sands

432 miles, **9** hours **45** minutes
for drive time, more for optional
routes stops, and sightseeing

**To the Bat Cave, Billy the Kid!
The aliens are coming!**

IF YOU'VE COME BARRELING ACROSS TEXAS ON INTERSTATE 10—
and many travelers do, taking advantage of the 80 mph speed
limit—you will be ready for a change of pace by the time you're
within striking distance of El Paso. This seriously scenic detour
will add at least 250 miles to your journey between Van Horn
and Las Cruces, turning what would have been 3 more hours of
highway driving into a full-day adventure that will leave you both
exhausted and exhilarated.   ▶▶

LEAVING TEXAS

The route begins 120 miles east of
El Paso in the small ranching community of Van Horn. If you arrive
at the end of the day and want to
stay the night before starting this
drive, consider the historic **Hotel El
Capitan**, a nicely restored Spanish
colonial-style establishment with
decor dating from the 1930s.

After exiting the Interstate, follow
the frontage road to Cavern Street,
TX 54, and head north toward the
distant hills. This is West Texas desert ranchland, classic cattle country,
sparsely studded with creosote and
mesquite. There are no signs to mark
it, but after roughly 25 miles, all the
open country you'll see to the east
of the highway belongs to Jeff Bezos,
the billionaire CEO of Amazon. The
visionary entrepreneur purchased
290,000 acres here, and he's using
the land as a testing ground and
launch site for reusable rockets and
suborbital vehicles under development by **Blue Origin**, his privately
funded space-flight company. The
long-term goal is to promote space
tourism and to provide a launchpad

Coming from the West

If you're coming from somewhere west of El Paso, there's no need to go all the way to Van Horn to
begin this route. Instead, you can exit I-10 at Canutillo (Exit 34), about 30 miles east of Las Cruces.
Follow TX 375 through Franklin Mountains State Park until you reach US 62/180, then follow that road
east to join the route. This option is not only more scenic, it's shorter.

for commercial payloads headed into space. You won't see much indication of this activity from the highway; the project is closely guarded, and for now at least, the public isn't allowed anywhere near the place.

TX 54 merges with US 62/180 about 55 miles north of Van Horn. You are headed northeast now, straight into the heart of **Guadalupe Mountains National Park**, a beautiful tract of wilderness that includes 8,749-foot Guadalupe Peak, the highest in Texas. The visitors center is near the south entrance to the park, just off the highway; stop in if you'd like information about camping or hiking trails that ramble through the stunning terrain. One highlight is **McKittrick Canyon**, an oasis of green

that contrasts sharply with the earthen hues of the surrounding desert. Cacti and wildflowers bloom in the spring; in the fall, native oaks and maples create a brilliant autumn display. There are Texas madrones here, too, rare holdovers from an ancient time when this area was a rain forest. You'll recognize this "relict species" by it showy, peeling bark and the bright red berries that appear in the fall and winter. Early morning and late afternoon are best for roadside photos: stunning mountain views against the vast West Texas sky.

Texas Highlights

Hotel El Capitan
100 E. Broadway, Van Horn, TX 79855
(877) 283-1220
thehotelelcapitan.com

Blue Origin
blueorigin.com

Guadalupe Mountains National Park
400 Pine Canyon, Salt Flat, TX 79847
(915) 828-3251
nps.gov/gumo

US 180, Guadalupe Mountains National Park, Texas

Opposite, and above: The Big Room, Carlsbad Caverns National Park

CARLSBAD

Leaving Guadalupe Mountains National Park, continue northeast on US 62/180 and you'll soon cross into New Mexico. A few miles farther, you'll reach the turnoff for **Carlsbad Caverns National Park.** If you've never experienced the wonders of a major underground cave system, you should stop here. The caverns rank among the true wonders of the natural world, a jewel in the crown of the National Park system. The visitors center is about 7 miles back from the highway, after a beautiful drive on a very curvy road through an extension of the Guadalupe desert mountain range. Keep a sharp eye out for wildlife along this route, especially deer and pronghorn antelope.

If your time at Carlsbad Caverns is limited, head straight for the **Big Room**, one of the world's largest subterranean chambers. You can hike in from the cave's natural entrance, about a mile's walk along the trail used by the cave's earliest explorers, or you can use the

elevators in the visitors center, which drop you 750 feet straight down to the floor of the cavern in a minute flat. The best thing about those elevators? When you're done exploring, they lift you all the way back up again!

A self-guided tour will lead you along a very easy loop trail that takes about an hour; much of the loop is wheelchair-accessible. Go at your own pace past a wide variety of extraordinary formations—it's like a crystal-line forest of icicles magically turned to stone, all set aglow by concealed, low-intensity lighting. Ranger-led tours take small groups deeper into the vast system of caverns; tours are limited, so advance reservations are recommended. If you're in the park at dusk, you can watch from the small outdoor amphitheater as hundreds of thousands of bats emerge from the caverns, a primordial smoke-like swirl of living creatures, off on their nightly bug hunt. Alas, no cameras are allowed; the bats are disturbed by all things electronic.

Leaving the park, head north on US 62/80 to the town of Carlsbad. When you reach the intersection with US 285, stay left and follow US 285 through the downtown area. Just beyond it, you'll see signs for the **Living Desert State Park.** This nice zoo and botanical garden is like a microcosm of the surrounding Chihuahuan Desert, the second largest desert in North America, encompassing a major portion of the southwestern U.S. and much of northern Mexico. This is a fun stop for families; be sure to check out the art gallery, featuring the work of Maggie, the black bear who paints with her feet.

Just north of town is **Brantley Lake State Park**, a recreation area centered on an impoundment of the Pecos River, popular with local boaters and fishermen. If you're spending extra time in and around Carlsbad, consider a side trip to **Sitting Bull Falls,** a series of spring-fed cascades spilling 150 feet into a rocky canyon. It's not a huge volume of water, but lovely nonetheless. Getting to the falls requires a 60-mile round-trip on county roads; follow the signs off US 285 at Queen's Highway (NM 137). Allow at least 2 hours, and call ahead to confirm hours of operation and road conditions; in some seasons it is open weekends only. If you decide to overnight in Carlsbad, consider the beautifully renovated **Trinity Hotel**. It's small but well appointed, located in a historic bank building that dates to 1892.

Roswell

Leaving Carlsbad, you'll head north along the Pecos River, which enlivens an otherwise barren landscape, much of it dotted with oil wells and petrochemical facilities. Beyond the oil fields are irrigated fields, most of them devoted to grasses and alfalfa destined for animal feed; these are interspersed with stands of lush green pecan trees, all lined up in perfect rows.

Keep the Pecos on your right for 100 miles until you reach Roswell, the town that's famous throughout the world for something that probably never happened: the so-called Roswell Incident. Certainly *something* crashed on a ranch northwest of town on a dark night in 1947. Some locals claimed it was a flying saucer, while military investigators insisted it was a weather balloon. That official story didn't explain all the secrecy and military security that surrounded the crash site, and soon UFO rumors were rife, as were claims of a massive cover-up: There were multiple flying saucers; there were dead aliens; there were possibly even *live* aliens—*in the custody of the Air Force!*

Carlsbad Highlights

Carlsbad Caverns National Park
727 Carlsbad Caverns Highway, Carlsbad, NM 88220
(575) 785-2232
nps.gov/cave

Living Desert State Park
1504 Miehls Drive N., Carlsbad, NM 88220
(575) 887-5516

Brantley Lake State Park
33 E. Brantley Lake Road, Carlsbad, NM 88221
(575) 457-2384
Sitting Bull Falls

U.S. Forest Service, Guadalupe District Office
5203 Buena Vista Drive, Carlsbad, NM 88220
(575) 885-4181

Trinity Hotel
201 S. Canal St., Carlsbad, NM 88220
(575) 234-9891
thetrinityhotel.com

Image from outside wall of El Toro Bravo Mexican Restaurant in Roswell: "Are there aliens among us?"

The Roswell Incident has been officially debunked at least a dozen different ways. In fact, in 1994, the military finally admitted that the U.S. Army Air Forces had, in fact, covered up a crash—not of an alien spacecraft, but of a high-altitude, instrument-laden balloon that was being used to spy on Russian nuclear tests. Diehards don't believe that for a minute; it's pretty tough to quash a good conspiracy theory. If you're the sort who appreciates such things, check out Roswell's **International UFO Museum and Research Center**, located in the middle of town. The exhibits tell the whole crazy story with newspaper clippings, artwork, fiberglass models, and grainy photographs of objects purported to be flying saucers. There are no actual alien artifacts on display, nor any verifiable photographs of any *actual* alien spacecraft. But that doesn't mean it isn't cool. and it doesn't mean it didn't happen …

For bird lovers: Eight miles east of Roswell, off US 380, is the **Bitter Lake National Wildlife Refuge,** a swampy area along the Pecos. This is an important wetland habitat for migratory birds, including sandhill cranes and snow geese, and it's home to no fewer than 90 species of dragonflies and damselflies.

Roswell Highlights

International UFO Museum and Research Center
114 N. Main St., Roswell, NM 88203
(800) 822-3545
roswellufomuseum.com

Bitter Lake National Wildlife Refuge
4200 E. Pine Lodge Road, Roswell, NM 88201
(575) 622-6755
fws.gov/refuge/bitter_lake/

BILLY THE KID SCENIC BYWAY

Leaving Roswell, head west on US 70/380 toward a range of low mountains. After about 45 miles, you'll reach Hondo, where US 70 and US 380 split. This is the start of the **Billy the Kid Trail**, a National Scenic Byway. Stay on US 380, and after another 15 miles you'll roll into Lincoln. For aficionados of the history of the Wild West, this is a place of some significance: the site of the Lincoln County War, a famously deadly feud that took place in 1878 and featured Billy the Kid *(see sidebar).*

Lincoln hasn't changed a whole lot since Billy's day. The Lincoln County courthouse, the Tunstall store, the old mission church, and more than a dozen other buildings dating back to the late 1800s make up the **Lincoln Historic Site**, a state monument that includes six small museums and a cemetery where some of the Kid's victims were buried. Original 19th-century merchandise is still on display in the store. This is not a touristy commercial enterprise but a rather remarkable piece of preservation, and well worth the visit.

Ten miles beyond Lincoln is Capitan, the final resting place of another

Billy the Kid

Billy the Kid is one of the most iconic figures of the American West: a fearless young outlaw, cut down in his prime. His story is very well known, figuring in the plots of no fewer than 40 Hollywood movies, but it's not a heroic tale. The real-life Billy, whose given name was actually Henry, got his outlaw start in the little town of Lincoln during a hellacious outbreak of violence known as the Lincoln County War.

Two factions, each backed by gangs of hired guns, went at it in a fight for control of commerce in what was, at the time, a largely lawless territory. There were skirmishes and ambushes, raids, shoot-outs, and executions, and because each killing had to be avenged, an eye for an eye, the situation spiraled out of control. A gun battle raged in the streets of Lincoln for three days and nights. until Army troops, sent by the territorial governor, arrived on the scene with artillery.

Young Billy, who was fighting for the losing side, escaped out a back door. The Kid spent a couple of years on the run, rustled cattle, committed some robberies, and killed a blacksmith, a sheriff, and a couple of deputies. He famously escaped from jail after being sentenced to hang, but finally met his fate, shot in an ambush by Sheriff Pat Garrett, a man who had once been his friend.

Lincoln Town Cemetery, Lincoln Historic Site; "Final resting place of some of Billy the Kid's Victims."

Torreon (Tower), "A mini-fortress, built to defend early residents of Lincoln, New Mexico from Apache raiders."

American icon. In 1950, a black bear cub survived a devastating fire in the Lincoln National Forest and was rescued by firefighters. When he had recovered from his burns, he was sent to the National Zoo in Washington D.C., where he became a national celebrity: the original, real-life Smokey Bear, the symbol of fire safety for generations of American children. After Smokey died, in 1976, the zoo flew his body back to New Mexico and buried him here, near the place where he'd been found. **Smokey Bear's Gravesite** is located in a small park dedicated to his memory—and to his message: "Only YOU can prevent forest fires!"

Turn south from Capitan on NM 48, the continuation of the Billy the Kid Trail, and head for Ruidoso, 16 miles south, in the Sierra Blanca mountains. It's a wonderfully curvy road that's great fun to drive. Continue down the mountain to **Ruidoso Downs**, a famous venue for high-stakes quarter horse racing. In town, you can check out the **Hubbard Museum of the American West**, a terrific collection of sculpture, paintings, and 19th-century artifacts, including rifles, wagons, and assorted cowboy paraphernalia.

Leaving Ruidoso, you'll reconnect with US 70 for a quick 10 miles. When you reach the turnoff for NM 244, make a left onto the state highway, toward **Cloudcroft,** a favorite mountain getaway for New Mexico's desert dwellers. The route travels for 30 miles through forested mountains and meadows alive with wildflowers, across the Mescalero Apache Reservation, finally connecting with US 82 in this cool town in the tall pines. Stop here if you've had enough for the day. **The Lodge Resort** provides old-fashioned luxury in a sprawling Victorian-era lodge; it's very popular, so book ahead if you can. If you're not staying, continue on down the mountain. You're now just 20 miles (and 4,000 vertical feet) from Alamogordo, along another wonderful road that drops rapidly through a series of switchbacks and curves.

Lincoln County and Sierra Blanca Highlights	
Lincoln Historic Site On US 380, Lincoln, NM 88338 (575) 653-4082 nmhistoricsites.crg/ lincoln	**Hubbard Museum of the American West** 26301 US 70 W., Ruidoso Downs, NM 88346 (575) 373-4142 hubbardmuseum.org
Smokey Bear Historical Park 118 W. Smokey Bear Blvd., Capitan, NM 88316 (575) 354-2748	**The Lodge** 601 Corona Place, Cloudcroft, NM 88317 (800) 395-6343 thelodgeresort.com

ALAMOGORDO TO LAS CRUCES

When you reach US 54, turn south toward Alamogordo. If you like seriously quirky stuff, or if you just happen to like pistachios, turn north on US 54 instead and drive a couple of miles out of your way to McGinn's Pistachio Tree Ranch. You can not only purchase your fill of pistachios, but also check out the **World's Largest Pistachio,** a 30-foot-tall steel-and-concrete paean to nuttiness that stands in front of the business.

Alamogordo is the gateway to **White Sands National Monument**, an astonishing natural display of

pure-white gypsum crystals deposited in such quantity that they form a sea of shifting dunes that sparkle in the sunlight. Any time of day is great for photographs, but the sunsets are beyond superb. There is a 16-mile loop drive, with turnouts, and you can sled down the dunes on plastic saucers available for purchase from the gift shop. The visitors center is 15 miles southwest of Alamogordo off US 70.

Opposite: Rainbow over the Sacramento Mountains, south of Alamogordo

If you have some extra time to spend in this area, stop by the **Three Rivers Petroglyph Site,** where you can see the remains of an Ancestral Pueblo village and thousands of petroglyphs dating back 600 to 1,100 years. Three Rivers is one of the largest, most accessible sites of its kind, and well worth a visit for anyone with an interest in ancient cultures. It's a 60-mile round-trip from Alamogordo (north of Tularosa, just off US 54), so you should allow at least 2 hours.

Another nearby attraction is the **White Sands Missile Range Museum.** The missile range, which lies 30 miles beyond the national monument, is the largest military installation in the United States. Follow the signs to the military base, a few miles off US 70. Here you can explore some of the darker history of this remarkable

Alamogordo to Las Cruces Highlights

World's Largest Pistachio
McGinn's Pistachio Tree Ranch
7320 US 54/70, Alamogordo, NM 88310
(575) 437-0602
pistachioland.com

Three Rivers Petroglyph Site
301-453 3 Rivers Road, Tularosa, NM 88352
(575) 525-4300

White Sands National Monument
19955 Highway 70 West, Alamogordo, NM 88310
(575) 479-6124
nps.gov/whsa

White Sands Missile Range Museum
Holloman Air Force Base
Owen Road, White Sands Missile Range, NM 88802
(575) 678-3358

Hotel Encanto de Las Cruces
705 S. Telshor Blvd., Las Cruces, NM 88011
(575) 522-4300
hotelencanto.com

area. Established in 1945, in the closing months of World War II, the range encompasses the Trinity site, where the first atomic bomb was tested. Since then, White Sands has served as a testing ground for missiles and other modern weapons of war, many of which are on display at the museum.

Leaving the museum, follow US 70 the rest of the way to Las Cruces, where you can rejoin Interstate 10. The **Hotel Encanto de Las Cruces** is a great spot for a well-deserved rest; call ahead to book some time in the full-service spa.

Sunset at White Sands, New Mexico

Las Cruces to Lordsburg

via Gila Cliff Dwellings National Monument and Silver City

252 miles, **7** hours **30** minutes for drive time, more for optional routes, stops, and sightseeing

From the ancient past to outer space and back, on the Trail of the Mountain Spirits

THIS SCENIC DETOUR WILL ADD 130 MILES AND MOST OF A DAY to your journey between Las Cruces and Lordsburg. What would have been a rather monotonous 2 hours on a flat, straight freeway becomes an amazing expedition over magnificent mountain highways and a fascinating journey through time—with some very hot chiles thrown in. ➡➡

LAS CRUCES AND HATCH

Leave Interstate 10 at Exit 140 in Las Cruces, on the Avenida de Mesilla. While you're in town, check out Las Cruces' **Museum of Nature and Science**. It has, among other exhibits, fossilized footprints of animals that predate the dinosaurs in slabs of rock taken from nearby **Prehistoric Trackways National Monument,** which is possibly the world's richest source for this type of Permian Age fossil. Contact the BLM in Las Cruces if you'd like to tag along on a guided hike to the fossil beds, which contain tracks left by lizard-like critters, giant bugs, and sea

creatures anywhere from 250 to 300 million years ago.

Otherwise, head north on Valley Drive, NM 185, which will lead you through the agricultural area north of town. The highway runs through the valley of the Rio Grande, the same Rio Grande that marks the 1,200-mile border between Texas and Mexico. At Radium Springs, pull off the road for the **Fort Selden State Historic Site**, the crumbling adobe remains of a 19th-century Army outpost, a relic of the days when marauding bands of Apaches preyed on pretty much everyone who came near their territory. After the

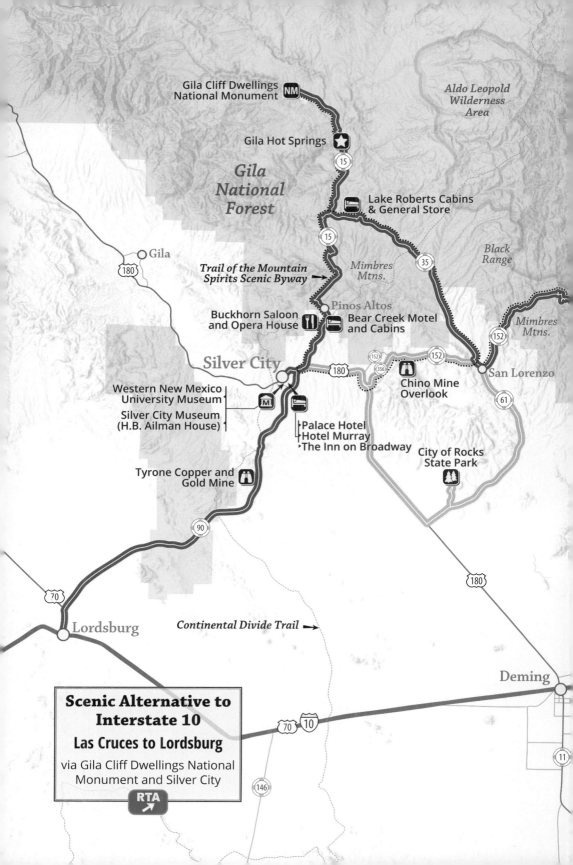

Gila Cliff Dwellings
National Monument **NM**

*Aldo Leopold
Wilderness
Area*

Gila Hot Springs ★

15

*Gila
National
Forest*

Lake Roberts Cabins
& General Store

15

*Black
Range*

35

Gila **180**

*Mimbres
Mtns.*

***Trail of the Mountain
Spirits Scenic Byway*** ➤

*Mimbres
Mtns.*

Pinos Altos

152

**Buckhorn Saloon
and Opera House** ⑈

Bear Creek Motel
and Cabins

Silver City

152 **152**

180 **356**

San Lorenzo

Chino Mine
Overlook

Western New Mexico
University Museum ⑂

M

61

Silver City Museum
(H.B. Ailman House) ⑂

Palace Hotel
Hotel Murray
The Inn on Broadway

City of Rocks
State Park

**Tyrone Copper and
Gold Mine**

90

180

Continental Divide Trail ➤

70

Lordsburg

Deming

70 **10**

11

Scenic Alternative to
Interstate 10
Las Cruces to Lordsburg
via Gila Cliff Dwellings National
Monument and Silver City

RTA ↗

146

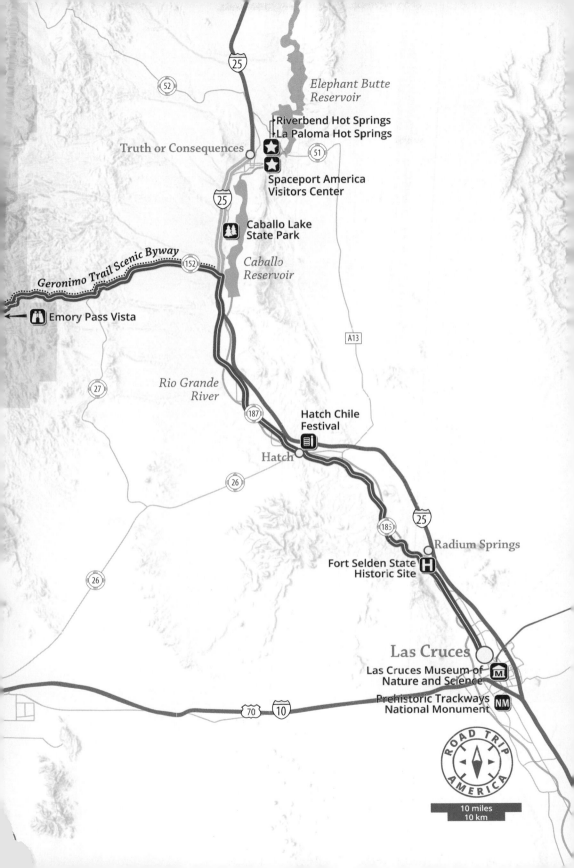

52

I-25

Elephant Butte
Reservoir

Riverbend Hot Springs
La Paloma Hot Springs

Truth or Consequences

51

I-25

Spaceport America
Visitors Center

Caballo Lake
State Park

Geronimo Trail Scenic Byway

152

Caballo
Reservoir

Emory Pass Vista

A13

27

Rio Grande
River

187

Hatch Chile
Festival

Hatch

26

185

I-25

Radium Springs

Fort Selden State
Historic Site

26

Las Cruces

Las Cruces Museum of
Nature and Science

M

Prehistoric Trackways
National Monument

NM

70   I-10

ROAD TRIP AMERICA

10 miles
10 km

last of the renegade Apache warriors were disarmed and herded onto reservations, small garrisons like Fort Selden were no longer needed; this post was decommissioned and abandoned in 1891.

Lovers of chile peppers will have something to celebrate when they reach the little town of Hatch, the official **Chile Capital of New Mexico** and site of the annual Hatch Chile Festival. The spicy food and music extravaganza is held each year over Labor Day weekend, and draws as many as 30,000 visitors. There's no question that the farms in this area produce some of the finest, hottest peppers you would ever dare to eat, and local shops do a brisk business. You can get the chiles fresh when they're in season, from August through mid-September; the rest of the year they're available dried, frozen, and pickled, along with every conceivable chile-related food product and curio. Favorite souvenirs include beautiful decorative wreaths made entirely of dried chile peppers, and traditional *ristras:* strings of dried chiles,

as much a staple of Southwestern décor as they are of Southwestern cooking.

From Hatch, drive 30 miles north on NM 187 to the intersection of NM 152,

Opposite and above: Ristras of Hatch Chiles, New Mexico

Spelling Lesson

In New Mexico, everything related to hot peppers is spelled *chile*, with an 'e,' not *chili*, with an 'i.' That's official, and they're serious about it. Per the New Mexico Legislature: Any citizen caught using the word *chili* will be deported to Texas.

near **Caballo Lake**, a large reservoir on the Rio Grande that offers all the usual boating, fishing, camping, and picnicking opportunities. The route heads west from here, but you might consider an optional side trip: 15 miles north is the town of Truth or Consequences, the official gateway to **Spaceport America**, the world's first "purpose-built, FAA-certified commercial spaceport." It's not an amusement park, and it's not a movie set. It's an actual spaceport, owned and operated by the State of New Mexico, with a 12,000-foot runway, launch pads for rockets, hangars for spacecraft, and a passenger terminal that boosters compare to the Sydney Opera House. When trips into outer space become available to paying passengers, this is where they'll fly from.

There's not a lot going on out at the Spaceport just yet, but if you'd like to take a look at the staging area for what could well become the Next Big Thing, you can take a tour, the "Spaceport America Experience"; it lasts about 4 hours, counting travel time. All tours leave from, and return to, the Spaceport America Visitors Center in downtown Truth or Consequences, and advance reservations are required. If you stay overnight in the area, take advantage of the natural hot springs for which Truth or Consequences has long been famous. Several of the local hotels, including **Riverbend Hot Springs** and **La Paloma Hot Springs**, have private thermal pools right on their properties.

Mural on the wall of the Hillsboro Cafe on the Geronimo Trail

GILA CLIFF DWELLINGS NATIONAL MONUMENT

Leaving Caballo Lake, head west on NM 152 up into an impressive wall of mountains known as the Black Range, or Sierra Diablo. If you like to drive, you'll love this road. This segment, known as the **Geronimo Trail Scenic Byway**, is widely considered one of the finest driving roads in the United States. You'll negotiate one S curve after another on a climb to almost 9,000 feet at **Emory Pass**, which marks the Continental Divide. Pull off the road at the scenic viewpoint for awesome vistas and some great photographs.

Seventeen gloriously curvy miles beyond the pass will drop you 3,000 feet to the Mimbres River, which runs along the base of the Black Range. When you reach the intersection with NM 35, in the small town of San Lorenzo, check your time. If you plan to visit the Gila Cliff Dwellings, be aware that the gate to the ruins closes promptly at 4 p.m.—no exceptions. The distance from San Lorenzo to the site is only 45 miles, but you should allow at least 90 minutes for the drive. Late afternoon is a wonderful time of day to photograph the ruins—just don't cut it too close.

The route to the cliff dwellings begins with NM 35, known as the **Trail of the Mountain Spirits Scenic Byway**. The highway follows the Mimbres River upstream, through the town of Mimbres. Twenty miles farther along is **Lake Roberts**, a small but quite beautiful lake popular with trout fishermen and bird-watchers. There are cabins and motel rooms for rent here, and a lovely campground. Four miles beyond the lake is the intersection with NM 15; turn right (north) and follow it all the way to the end, about 18 miles, to the **Gila Cliff Dwellings National Monument**. The road to the ruins is narrow and winding, very slow going, with some sheer drop-offs and many hairpin turns posted as low as 10 mph—and for good reason! At one point, the highway skirts the edge of a collapsed volcanic caldera. Timeworn, overgrown, but still plainly visible, the caldera is a graphic reminder of the region's violent geological past. Stop at Anderson Scenic Overlook for a breathtaking view of the Mogollon Range, the tallest mountains in southwestern

*Wildflowers,
Mimbres Valley,
New Mexico*

New Mexico, and Gila River Canyon, 2,000 feet below.

Continuing north on NM 15 you'll pass **Gila Hot Springs** a few miles before the end of the road. Much of this area is geothermally active and there are several natural hot springs nearby, some on public land, some private. There are a few campsites here, with access to the hot springs included.

At the National Monument visitors center, you can pick up maps and information about the ruins and the trails in the park. Even if you've seen your share of cliff dwellings, you'll find this one is special. The setting is a narrow, wooded canyon with a perennial stream. On the west side of the ravine there's a sheer cliff, and hollowed out from the face of it, high above the canyon floor, you can see a series of natural alcoves: interconnected caves that are open to the morning sun. In the late 13th century, a small group of perhaps 15 farming families from the Native American culture we now call the Mogollon moved into the caves and built an elaborate communal home there.

It was a perfect spot: protected from the elements, easily defended, close to water. A lot of craftsmanship went into the construction, and the wonderful organic structure that they created is still standing and largely intact. There are graceful, curving walls built of flat stones stacked like bricks, cemented with adobe mortar, and then plastered. The walls enclose more than 40 interconnected rooms that fill the alcoves: large common areas, smaller private living quarters, a granary. Many of the outward-facing walls had windows, and some sections were left open. Clearly, the builders appreciated their view!

There's a tour every day at 11 a.m., but you can hike to the ruins and explore them on your own any time between 9 a.m. and 5 p.m., when the park closes. It takes about an hour to see the ruins, including the 1-mile hike up and back.

Gila Cliff Dwellings National Monument

Gila River Valley, 2000 feet below New Mexico Route 15

Gila Cliff Dwellings Highlights

Lake Roberts Cabins & General Store
869 NM 35 N., Silver City, NM 88061
(575) 536-9929
lakeroberts.com

Gila Hot Springs Campground
HC 68, Box 80, Silver City, NM 88061
(575) 536-9944
gilahotspringscampground.com

Gila Cliff Dwellings National Monument
(575) 536-9461
nps.gov/gicl

Buckhorn Saloon and Opera House
32 Main St., Pinos Altos, NM 88053
(575) 538-9911
buckhornsaloonandoperahouse.com

Bear Creek Motel & Cabins
88 Main St., Pinos Altos, NM 88053
(575) 388-4501
bearcreekcabins.com

Leaving the ruins, head back the way you came in, on NM 15. When you reach the junction with NM 35, bear right, staying with NM 15, which continues south from here to Pinos Altos, at an altitude of more than 7,000 feet. The distance isn't great, just 30 miles from the national monument, but it will seem much farther. This is a wonderful corkscrew of a road, but it's very, very narrow, with poor shoulders, no center stripe, and very few signs, so you have to take it slow. Be extremely careful on blind curves, as there is little room to pass vehicles coming from the other direction. I would not recommend driving this stretch in the dark, so if you're not staying the night at Lake

Roberts or camping near the monument, be sure to be on your way south well before dusk.

Pinos Altos (Tall Pines), once a booming gold-mining town, was largely abandoned more than 100 years ago. It has found new life as a recreation area for the desert dwellers in Silver City and points south. The **Buckhorn Saloon and Opera House** is a restaurant and bar that offers live music several nights a week, and **Bear Creek Motel & Cabins** is a quite decent place to stay, if you're ready to call it a day at this point.

SILVER CITY

From Pinos Altos, it's less than 10 miles to historic Silver City, which stands at 5,900 feet. The pine trees disappear as you descend, and the surrounding area more closely resembles the sagebrush-and-juniper landscape you left behind earlier on this route. Silver City was a mining town first prospected in the 1870s, when New Mexico was still a territory. The **Silver City Museum**, located in a historic home in the old downtown area, has an interesting collection of artifacts and thousands of photographs from the early days of the town. The **Western New Mexico University Museum**, also in town, has an excellent collection of Mimbres pottery and baskets.

Mural. Silver City, New Mexico

City of Rocks and the Chino Copper Mine Loop

Before leaving the Silver City area, consider this optional loop, which will take you an extra 83 miles and requires about 2 hours. Follow US 180 south toward Deming. After 30 miles, at the junction with NM 61, turn left and follow signs to **City of Rocks State Park** (327 NM 61, Faywood, NM; 575-536-2800). The park is 5 miles east, set back a bit from the road. The main attraction is a wild display of standing

City of Rocks State Park, Silver City, NM

stones: massive volcanic boulders as much as 40 feet tall, carved by the elements over millions of years into an extraordinary variety of shapes and poses. If it had been created by man instead of nature, this place would be far more famous than Stonehenge. There's a cool campground with some campsites nestled among the rock formations, and there are hiking trails. Other popular activities include birding, stargazing, and rock climbing (free climbing only).

From City of Rocks, drive 22 miles north on NM 61, following the Mimbres River upstream to San Lorenzo. At the intersection with NM 152, turn west and drive another 10 miles to the northern edge of the Chino Copper Mine, an open pit that's a mile and three-quarters wide and a quarter of a mile deep. Pull over at the Chino Mine Overlook, where you can view the whole operation. The trucks working on the terraced slopes below look like toys from the rim of the pit. Up close? Each of those 80-ton ore haulers is nearly the size of a two-story house! This mine has been actively worked since the time of the Spanish conquistadores. The pit you see today was opened in 1910, making it the third-oldest, as well as the second-largest pit-mining operation in the world.

From the overlook, take NM 152 west to NM 356 and follow that road south past mountains of tailings from the pit. At Bayard, you'll rejoin US 180, back to Silver City.

Silver City is, without a doubt, the best overnight stopping place in this part of the state, considering all the great options for lodging: **The Palace**, a hotel dating to the late 1800s; **Murray Hotel**, an Art Deco-style establishment dating to the late 1930s; and **The Inn on Broadway**, a historic bed-and-breakfast in the heart of the old downtown.

Note. *If you're planning to take* **Scenic Side Trip 3** *immediately after this one, you should definitely stay in Silver City. You'll not only have a better selection of hotels, you'll save some time and distance, because that route, which* *starts in Lordsburg, comes right back through Silver City on its way north.*

To Lordsburg and Beyond

The end of this route is in Lordsburg, a small town with about 2,700 people, a Greyhound stop, and an Amtrak station. It lies 45 miles south on NM 90 *(for a description of this relatively flat stretch of road, see* **Scenic Side Trip 3***).* When you drive into the town from Silver City, you'll notice signs for Motel Drive. Don't be fooled. The street name refers to the string of old motor courts along that stretch of road, only a few of which are still operating. They're relics of a bygone era, and their singular virtue is being very inexpensive. Beware of that. When it comes to hotels, you generally get what you pay for. There's an assortment of newer, nicer, chain hotels clustered near the I-10 interchange at the center of town (off Main Street).

If you're continuing on to Phoenix or points west, the Interstate is certainly the fastest way to get there, but if you don't mind skipping Tucson, you should take a look at **Scenic Side Trip 4**. That route is actually a shortcut to Phoenix, and it passes through some amazing terrain. There are also three full-day scenic side trips between Lordsburg and Tucson, another full-day side trip that surrounds Tucson, and yet another that follows back roads from Tucson to Phoenix. Study the routes. Decide how much time you have to spare. If all you know of Arizona is what you've seen from the Interstates, you're going to be very pleasantly surprised!

Silver City Highlights

Silver City Museum (The Ailman House)
312 W. Broadway, Silver City, NM 88061
(575) 538-5921
silvercitymuseum.org

Western New Mexico University Museum
1000 W. College Ave., Silver City, NM 88061
(575) 538-6386
museum.wnmu.edu

Palace Hotel
106 W. Broadway, Silver City, NM 88061
(575) 388-1811
silvercitypalacehotel.com

Hotel Murray
200 W. Broadway, Silver City, NM 88061
(575) 956-9400
murray-hotel.com

The Inn on Broadway
411 W. Broadway, Silver City, NM 88061
(575) 388-5435

Lordsburg to Willcox, Arizona,

via Silver City, Alpine, the White Mountains, the Coronado Trail, and Morenci

374 miles, **9** hours **45** minutes for drive time, more for optional routes, stops, and sightseeing

There and back again on the Devil's Highway

THIS SCENIC DETOUR WILL ADD 290 MILES AND 8 AND A HALF hours of driving to a journey between Lordsburg and Willcox—a drive that would ordinarily take no more than an hour on the Interstate. This is a full-on adventure that includes US 191, the Coronado Trail, one of the twistiest and least traveled roads in the entire U.S. Highway system. An optional 90-mile loop through Arizona's White Mountains is reason enough to make this a two-day odyssey, with a cool night spent in a cabin or campground amid the world's largest stand of Ponderosa pines, under a bright canopy of stars. ➠

LORDSBURG, SILVER CITY, AND US 180

The route begins off Interstate 10 in Lordsburg at the Main Street exit. Follow Main Street northwest to the edge of this small town and pick up US 70/NM 90 toward Globe and Silver City. Just outside the town limits, follow NM 90 as it splits off to the right; as you travel north and east, the Burro Mountains rise up on your left.

After about 30 miles, you'll come to the **Tyrone Copper and**

Gold Mine, an open-pit operation on the site of what was once a quite beautiful mining town called Tyrone. The Phelps Dodge Corporation built Tyrone as a planned community, a "dream city" for employees of their mines in the area. Instead of brothels and saloons, Tyrone had good schools, a hospital, and an elegant train station with chandeliers and marble drinking fountains. But after World War I, when the price of copper plummeted, the mining company

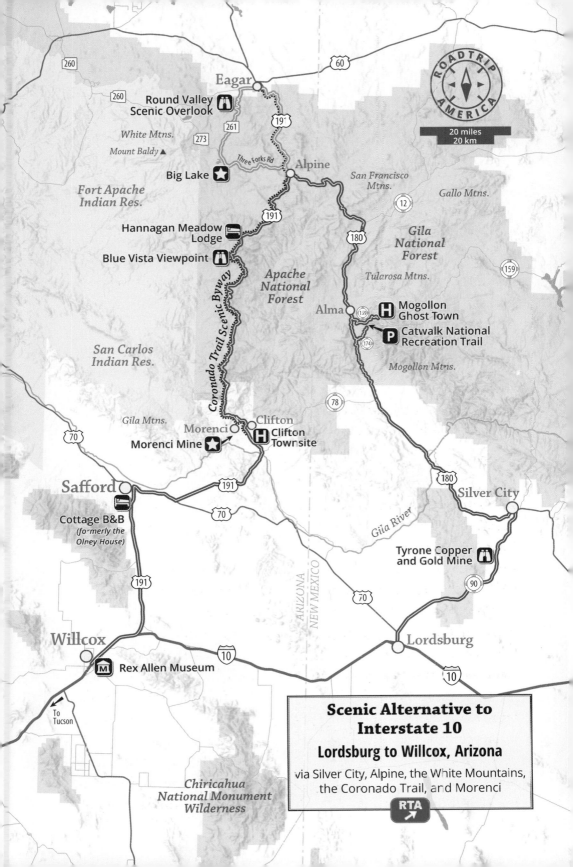

260

Eagar

260 **Round Valley Scenic Overlook**

White Mtns.

Mount Baldy ▲

273

261

19

Three Forks Rd

Big Lake ★

Fort Apache Indian Res.

Alpine

San Francisco Mtns.

Gallo Mtns.

12

191

Hannagan Meadow Lodge

Blue Vista Viewpoint

Apache National Forest

Coronado Trail Scenic Byway

180

Gila National Forest

Tularosa Mtns.

159

Alma

159

H **Mogollon Ghost Town**

P **Catwalk National Recreation Trail**

174

Mogollon Mtns.

San Carlos Indian Res.

78

Gila Mtns.

Morenci **Clifton**

Morenci Mine ★   H **Clifton Townsite**

70

Safford

Cottage B&B *(formerly the Olney House)*

191

70

180

Silver City

Gila River

Tyrone Copper and Gold Mine

90

191

Willcox

10

70

Lordsburg

10

M **Rex Allen Museum**

↖ To Tucson

Chiricahua National Monument Wilderness

ARIZONA
NEW MEXICO

ROADTRIP AMERICA

20 miles
20 km

Scenic Alternative to Interstate 10

Lordsburg to Willcox, Arizona

via Silver City, Alpine, the White Mountains, the Coronado Trail, and Morenci

RTA ↗

pulled out, and the dream city became an unusually elegant ghost town. In the mid-1960s, copper prices were up again, so Phelps Dodge started digging the pit mine that you see today. The remnants of the lovely ghost town were simply scooped up along with the rocks and the dirt to get to the riches underneath.

Silver City has its charms (*see* **Scenic Side Trip 2**), but if you don't plan to stop, you can take the truck bypass route to US 180 and avoid the traffic in town. From here, US 180 leads west toward a range of low mountains, then northwest along the base of that ridge. After 30 miles, just before the town of Cliff, you'll cross the Gila River as it comes down out of the higher mountains to the east, the forested peaks of the Gila Wilderness.

Twenty miles farther along, the road starts to climb up into the high country. After you pass through the rural communities of Pleasanton, then Glenwood, bear right onto NM 174, go about a mile, then turn right on Catwalk Road. Follow the signs for the **Catwalk National Recreation Trail** in Whitewater Canyon, a distance of about 4 miles.

From the picnic area, a very cool trail leads into the narrow canyon; part of it consists of a metal catwalk attached to the canyon wall, from which you can look down on the rushing waters 20 feet below. The original catwalk, which was built of wood, was installed to facilitate maintenance of a pipeline that carried water for mining operations and for the small town of Graham, at the mouth of the canyon. That rickety structure was never very safe, and it was wiped out more than once by floods roaring down the canyon. In the 1930s, when the pipeline was no longer needed, the catwalk was rebuilt for recreational purposes, and it was later upgraded to

Opposite: Catwalk National Recreation Trail, Gila National Forest

the sturdy structure you'll see today. This canyon is just 20 feet wide and the cliffs tower 250 feet overhead. From the trail, you get a thrilling perspective.

Leaving the recreation area, retrace your route back to US 180, turn right, and follow the road for 4 miles to NM 159, Bursum Road. Turn right again, and follow the twists and turns of what used to be a haul road for mule teams pulling ore wagons from the mines at Mogollon (pronounced *Muggy-ohwn*). The road is paved, and it's maintained, but it's not for the faint of heart. It's steep, it's narrow, there are sheer drop-offs, and it's barely wide enough for cars to pass one another going in opposite directions. If you elect to drive it, take it slow and be careful.

What's left of the once booming hamlet of **Mogollon**, some 6 miles farther along, is now a ghost town, with wonderfully dilapidated buildings that make great photographs. Some of the buildings have been restored and taken over by artists and craftsmen, sparking a revival of sorts for this remote community, and there are tours of the place offered on summer weekends.

Leaving Mogollon, drive back the way you came on NM 159 and keep going until you rejoin US 180.

Lordsburg, Silver City, and US 180 Highlights

Tyrone Copper and Gold Mine
NM 90 S. & Tyrone Mine Road, Tyrone, NM 88065
(505) 538-5331

Catwalk National Recreation Trail
5 miles from Glenwood, NM, at the end of NM 174 (Catwalk Road)
(575) 539-2481

Mogollon Ghost Town
mogollonenterprises.com

Note. *You can save about 25 miles and at least an hour of driving if you skip Catwalk Trail and the Mogollon ghost town. Simply stay on US 180 and keep going until you reach Alpine.*

ALPINE AND THE WHITE MOUNTAINS OF ARIZONA

US 180 runs north through pine-clad mountains for another 50 miles, through the small town of Luna, and then crosses into Arizona. The first Arizona town you'll come to is **Alpine**, set in beautiful mountains amid a stand of

Springerville Volcanic Field, White Mountain Scenic Loop

White Mountain Loop

Arizona's White Mountains are an oasis of green in a region best known for cactus-studded deserts and arid, rocky canyons. Pines and aspens cloak the mountainsides, while alpine meadows spread beneath a sky so bold and blue it seems close enough to touch. The mountains are cool in summer and there's snow in the winter; wildlife abounds, with herds of elk and antelope browsing alongside the roads. If you have the time, this optional 90-mile, 2-hour loop will show you some of the best this beautiful region has to offer.

Leaving Alpine, drive north on US 191. After about 2 miles, turn left onto Three Forks Road (Forest Road 249) toward **Big Lake.** The road, which was resurfaced after the Wallow Fire in 2011, is in excellent condition. Beyond the area that was burned in that fire, this scenic road passes through Williams Valley, which is like a sea of wildflowers in spring and summer. After about 16 miles, merge onto AZ 273, near the turnoff for Big Lake. There are Forest Service campgrounds here (928-521-1387, biglakeaz.com), and the fishing is some of the best in the state. Nights are cold, even in summer, as the altitude here is 9,200 feet.

From Big Lake, follow AZ 273 to the junction with AZ 261, White Mountains Scenic Drive. Looming on the horizon to the west is 11,421-foot **Mount Baldy,** the highest peak in the range. As the road starts back down into Round Valley, pull over at the overlook, and below you'll see a wide scattering of worn, conical hills on the high plain. These are remnants of the **Springerville Volcanic Field**, a 1,200-square-mile area comprising more than 400 extinct volcanoes. It is one of the most extensive concentrations of ancient volcanic activity in the U.S.

At the bottom of the hill, you'll connect with AZ 260. There are two small towns just east of here, Springerville and Eagar; both have lodging. Another option for lodging is the nearby **Apache Sunrise Resort,** on AZ 273, 19 miles east of Springerville off AZ 260 (855-735-7669). **Leaving Eagar**, drive another 27 miles south on US 191 to complete the loop back to Alpine.

If you're traveling this way in winter, be sure to check locally for road closures before setting out.

View of Morenci Mine from Coronado Trail

for 200 miles along the southern edge of the Colorado Plateau, a line of demarcation between the desert and these mountain forests. Thirty miles from Alpine you'll reach Blue Vista, a scenic viewpoint well above 9,000 feet. On a clear day you can see 100 miles or more, all the way to Mount Graham in the south and across the remote valley of the Blue River and trackless **Blue Range Primitive Area** to the east.

After you've taken a break to enjoy the view, push on, because you're only a third of the way along this infamous stretch of hairpins. Our Interstate Highways are marvels of engineering, as straight and as flat as roads can be, built for trucks and traffic, efficiently funneling vehicles from point A to point B—no surprises. But this road here, this Coronado Trail, or Devil's Highway, or whatever you'd care to call it—this is a road that's built for driving, and it couldn't be any less efficient if it had been designed that way on purpose. Because of all the

switchbacks, half the time you're looking straight ahead across a chasm at a place where you've already been!

Working pit, Morenci Mine, Arizona

By the time you get to **Morenci**, you will have descended over 4,000 feet and left the Ponderosa pines far behind. Morenci is, to put it bluntly, a hole—a very large hole: an open-pit copper mine that happens to be the richest copper mine in the United States, producing as many as 450,000 tons of the metal annually, with a value well in excess of $2 billion. Keep that in mind as you drive across the ridge that straddles two humongous scars in the earth. These open-pit mines are the largest of all the works of man, among the only works of man visible from outer space.

Most of the original town of Morenci has been swallowed by the big dig; the modern-day town is an ordinary suburban enclave for people who work for the mine. More interesting is **Clifton**, just beyond Morenci, which retains a bit of 19th-century mining

Coronado Trail, US 191, Arizona

Coronado Trail Highlights

Morenci Mine
4521 US 191, Morenci, AZ 85540

Clifton Townsite
510 Coronado Blvd., Clifton, AZ 85533
(928) 865-4146
cliftonaz.com

Rex Allen Museum
150 N. Railroad Ave, Willcox, AZ 85643
(520) 384-4583
rexallenmuseum.org

Cottage Bed and Breakfast (formerly the Olney House)
1104 S. Central Ave, Safford, AZ 85546
(928) 428-5118
cottagebedandbreakfast.com

town ambience, particularly in the **Clifton Townsite Historic District**. There you can see a number of original buildings, including the escape-proof **Clifton Cliff Jail**, whose cells were carved out of the granite cliff behind it by a local stonemason who became its first prisoner; it seems he celebrated his payday too exuberantly, and was arrested for shooting up the local dance hall.

Leaving Clifton, you'll come down out of the mountains into the broad Gila River valley, where you'll reach the town of Safford. The majestic Pinaleño Mountains loom sharply to the southwest, making a spectacular backdrop. Mount Graham, the most prominent peak, is one of the "Sky Islands" of southern Arizona, mountains that rise so high from the desert floor that their upper reaches contain isolated, island-like ecosystems in which unique plants and animals have evolved. *(For more on the Sky Islands, see the sidebar on page page 66).* You'll skirt the base of the Pinaleños as you make your way south from Safford on US 191 to Willcox.

The small town of **Willcox** owes its existence to the railroad. For a time, it was one of the busiest livestock depots in the U.S., shipping cattle to market by the trainload. Its biggest claim to fame in later years was its native-son cowboy star **Rex Allen**, one of the last of Hollywood's singing cowboys. Rex is gone now, but they celebrate him every year during Rex Allen Days in October and year round at the **Rex Allen Museum**, which has movie-star memorabilia and historical exhibits from the surrounding area. Interstate 10 passes through Willcox, and that junction marks the end of this route.

Both Safford and Willcox have lodging, with most of the national chains represented. In Safford, the **Cottage Bed and Breakfast** (formerly known as the Olney House), comes well recommended. It's a historic property that dates to 1890. *For more about Safford and Mount Graham, see* **Scenic Side Trip 4**.

WILLCOX AND BEYOND

From Willcox, you can travel straight on to Tucson, 80 miles away on Interstate 10. Or, if you have time, you can drive all, or portions of, **Scenic Side Trips 4 through 7**, each of which begins and ends on I-10; a fifth route, **Scenic Side Trip 8**, takes you from Tucson to Phoenix on the back roads. Allow a minimum of one full day for each of these trips.

Lordsburg to Phoenix

via Duncan, Safford, Globe, and Superior

237 miles, **5** hours **30** minutes for drive time, more for optional routes, stops, and sightseeing

A shortcut over the top of the world always takes a little longer

THIS SCENIC ALTERNATIVE ROUTE FROM LORDSBURG TO Phoenix is actually 29 miles shorter than the same drive on Interstate 10, and it bypasses Tucson and all that big-city traffic. Even so, allow a little bit of extra time; it may be a shorter distance, but there are mountain roads and beautiful views worth slowing down for. ⏩

LORDSBURG TO SAFFORD

Leaving Lordsburg, take Exit 22 off I-10, and follow Main Street north to Motel Drive. Turn left and follow the signs for US 70/NM 90, toward Globe and Silver City. When NM 90 splits off to the right, just beyond the town limits, stay on US 70.

Twenty-five miles or so outside of Lordsburg, the highway angles in toward a low range of mountains dominated by a jagged peak known as **Steeple Rock**. To get a closer look, take the back road to Duncan by turning off US 70 north onto NM 92, toward the tiny town of Virden. It's a small detour that will add 4 miles and 10 minutes to your travels, but hey—if you

were in a hurry, you'd still be on the Interstate! The views in this area are outstanding. NM 92 leads you down to the Gila River, right at the point where it crosses into Arizona. Stay on that road, called Virden Road on the Arizona side. It will take you all the way to Duncan and reconnect you to US 70.

Duncan has a little bit of history and a few picturesque old buildings. Founded in 1882, the small town continues to serve a region still largely dependent on ranching and farming. The Lazy B, a prominent ranch just south of town, was the family home of Sandra Day O'Connor, the Arizona cowgirl who became the first female justice

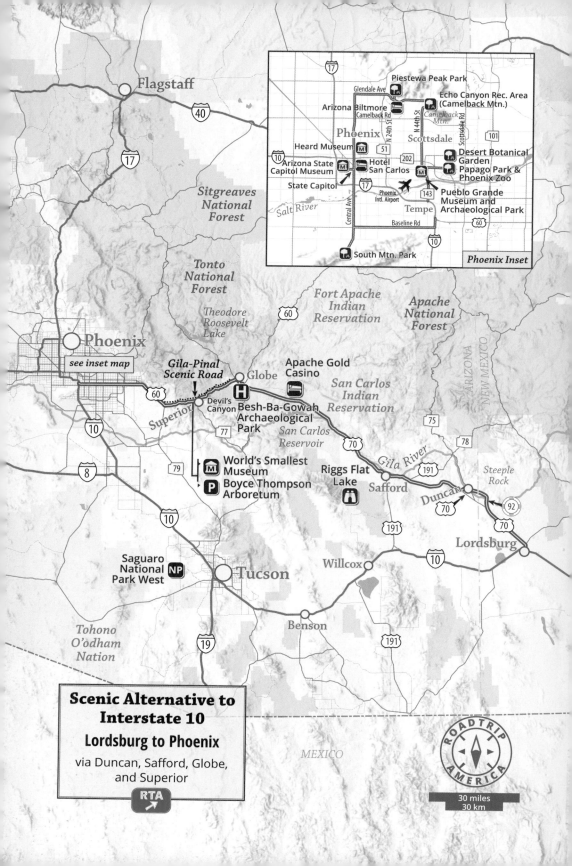

Flagstaff

40

17

Sitgreaves
National
Forest

Tonto
National
Forest

*Theodore
Roosevelt
Lake*

60

Fort Apache
Indian
Reservation

Apache
National
Forest

ARIZONA
NEW MEXICO

Phoenix

see inset map

*Gila-Pinal
Scenic Road*

Globe

Apache Gold
Casino

San Carlos
Indian
Reservation

75

60

10

Superior

Devil's
Canyon

Besh-Ba-Gowah
Archaeological
Park

77

*San Carlos
Reservoir*

70

Gila River

78

191

*Steeple
Rock*

8

79

World's Smallest
Museum

Boyce Thompson
Arboretum

Riggs Flat
Lake

Safford

191

Duncan

70

92

70

10

Lordsburg

Saguaro
National
Park West

NP

Tucson

Willcox

10

19

*Tohono
O'odham
Nation*

Benson

191

Phoenix Inset

17

Piestewa Peak Park

Glendale Ave

Echo Canyon Rec. Area
(Camelback Mtn.)

Arizona Biltmore
Camelback Rd

N 44th St

*Camelback
Mtn.*

Scottsdale Rd

101

Phoenix

Scottsdale

Heard Museum

N 24th St

51

Desert Botanical
Garden

10

Arizona State
Capitol Museum

Hotel
San Carlos

202

Papago Park &
Phoenix Zoo

State Capitol

Central Ave

17

143

Pueblo Grande
Museum and
Archaeological Park

*Phoenix
Intl. Airport*

Tempe

60

Salt River

Baseline Rd

10

South Mtn. Park

Phoenix Inset

Scenic Alternative to
Interstate 10

Lordsburg to Phoenix

via Duncan, Safford, Globe,
and Superior

RTA

MEXICO

ROAD TRIP AMERICA

30 miles
30 km

of the United States Supreme Court.

From Duncan to Safford you'll follow the Gila River as it makes its way toward a far-off rendezvous with the Colorado River, on Arizona's border with California. In the fields around Safford, water from the Gila is used to grow cotton, which, along with copper and cattle, has been a mainstay of Arizona's economy since Territorial days. The dominant feature of the local landscape is 10,700-foot **Mount Graham**, a "sky island" that rises well above the horizon to the southwest *(see sidebar)*.

If you want a closer look at Mount Graham, consider taking an optional side trip to **Riggs Flat Lake**, at 9,000 feet. The views are spectacular and the lovely reservoir

Duncan Bakery, Duncan, Arizona

Gila River Valley, near Safford, Arizona

Sky Islands

Some of the mountain ranges of southern Arizona are distinguished by one or more dominant peaks that rise well above their neighbors—to heights of 8,000, 9,000, even 10,000 feet. These taller peaks are big enough to disrupt the flow of warm, moist air through the atmosphere, stirring things up, generating clouds and localized rainfall.

The climate near the tops of those mountains is completely different from the climate at their base, and so are the flora and fauna. High on the mountain you'll find forests, streams, snow in the winter. Down below? You have the Sonoran desert, one of the hottest, driest climate zones in North America. The desert serves to isolate these high-altitude forests, one from another, in the same way that islands are isolated by the sea. These isolated peaks are called "sky islands," and there are no fewer than 40 of them in Arizona's Sky Island region, which extends into New Mexico and the northern Mexican states of Sonora and Chihuahua. Each sky island is unique.

Like many sea islands, most famously the Galápagos, Arizona's Sky Islands have evolved unusual species of plants and animals, some of which exist nowhere else on the planet. The Mount Graham Red Squirrel, for example, lives only on Mount Graham; the Rosemont Talus Snail, another unusual creature, lives only in the Santa Rita Mountains. Many other species, including frogs, flowers, birds, lichens, and many other small creatures are found exclusively on these sky islands.

The Sky Islands are considered the most biodiverse regions in North America, host to more species of birds and mammals, insects and trees than any comparable region outside the tropics. Some peaks encompass as many as eight climate zones. To put that in perspective, a drive to the top of Mount Lemmon, near Tucson, can be compared to a drive from the Mexican border all the way to Canada.

Lordsburg to Safford Highlights

Safford Ranger District Office
711 14th Ave., Safford, AZ 85546
(928) 428-4150

is stocked with trout. It is an 80-mile, 4-hour round-trip over a narrow, winding roadway, some of it unpaved; for directions, seasonal availability, and road conditions, check in at the Safford Ranger District Office.

GLOBE

Leaving Safford, the highway follows the Gila River to the northwest, across a portion of the **San Carlos Apache Reservation**. This is one of the poorest Native American communities in the U.S., a fact that will be apparent as you pass through the ramshackle town of Bylas, where 60 percent of the population lives below the poverty line, and 68 percent of the labor force is unemployed. At the western edge of the reservation, the **Apache Gold Casino** presents a stunning contrast with its opulent hotel, restaurant, gaming halls, and golf course. Owned and operated by the tribe, the casino provides jobs and welcome revenue for the community.

A few miles past the reservation border you'll be in the small city of Globe. According to legend, the town was founded by prospectors attracted by stories that local Indians were casting bullets from silver because it was easier to get than lead. Indeed, silver ore lay so near the surface it barely required digging. The silver deposits played out after just four years, but under the silver cap there was copper—so much copper that for a time Globe was one of the world's biggest producers of the metal. In fact, this entire region for hundreds of miles in nearly every direction continues to be among the richest copper-producing areas on earth.

The heart of the once bustling city is the **Downtown Globe Historic District**, which is on the National Register of Historic Places; it includes 18 buildings dating from the early 1900s, including the Post Office, the Gila County Courthouse, and several churches. The area's history as a mining center is apparent in the landscape, especially in the neighboring town of Miami, where you can still see the pit and the smelters, the tailings and leaching ponds—the bleak destruction that mining can inflict on the landscape. These mines aren't played out. The infrastructure is still intact, waiting for the price of copper to rise enough to make these diggings economically viable again.

While you're in Globe, consider a visit to **Besh-Ba-Gowah Archaeological Park**, a mile outside town atop a ridge overlooking Pinal Creek. There you can see ruins of a Salado pueblo dating to AD 1225. The pueblo was built of stacked cobblestones bonded with clay mortar, and it rose several stories high. In its heyday, as many as

Globe Highlights

Apache Gold Casino
5 US 70, San Carlos, AZ 85550
(928) 475-7800
apache-gold-casino.com

Besh-Ba-Gowah Archaeological Park
1324 S. Jesse Hayes Road, Globe, AZ 85501
(928) 425-0320
globeaz.gov/visitors/besh-ba-gowah

400 interconnected rooms surrounded the central plaza, like an ancient apartment building. The pueblo was built with great care, but the years have taken their toll. Part of what you see today is a restoration, and most of the walls have been stabilized, to prevent further deterioration. A small museum showcases artifacts found during the excavation, and there's a model of what the pueblo might have looked like before it was abandoned, around AD 1400. There was an extended drought around that time, which quite probably forced the people in this region to migrate north.

SUPERIOR

US 70 terminates in Globe, at the point where it merges with US 60, which you'll follow out of town as it swings toward the west. The portion of US 60 that runs from Globe to Superior is known as the **Gila-Pinal Scenic Road**, and the landscape along the way is stunning. After passing through the mining town of Miami, you'll wind your way up curves and switchbacks all the way to **Top-of-the-World**, so called because at 4,528 feet it's at the high point of this stretch of road. There's not a lot to see these days at Top-of-the-World—if you blink, you'll miss it—but back in the 1950s, it was a happening spot, with a guest ranch and ... let's call it a dance hall.

After Top-of-the-World you'll pass through **Devil's Canyon**, a jumbled maze of granite pillars lining the hairpin turns of the road. Beyond Devil's Canyon, you'll come to the quarter-mile-long Queen Creek Tunnel, which is immediately followed by the Queen Creek Bridge, a steel arch that crosses the deep gorge of **Queen Creek Canyon**. The completion of the bridge and tunnel in 1952 cut the time required for the journey between Globe and Superior in half, and made it considerably

Superior Highlights

World's Smallest Museum
1111 W. US 60, Superior, AZ
(520) 689-5800

Boyce Thompson Arboretum
37615 US 60, Superior, AZ 85173
(520) 689-2723
cals.arizona.edu/bta/

safer. The old "winding ladder" road can still be seen in the canyon below, slowly crumbling into ruin.

Like Globe, the town of **Superior** began as a silver camp and quickly turned to copper. The fabulously productive Magma Mine kept going longer than most, but it closed for good in 1996, forcing much of Superior's population to search elsewhere for work. Much of the old town is boarded up now, and very worn around the edges, giving it a gritty ambience.

There are a couple of things worth checking out. **The World's Smallest Museum**, which is contained entirely within a 134-square-foot shed adjacent to the Buckboard City Café, includes among its exhibits a 1984 Compaq computer, a Beatles poster, and other "artifacts of ordinary life."

Boyce Thompson Arboretum, Superior, Arizona
World's Smallest Museum, Superior, Arizona

A few miles outside town is something quite a bit more spectacular: the **Boyce Thompson Arboretum.** This world-class botanical garden, set on 320 acres, was created as a private garden and plant research center by William Boyce Thompson, the owner of the Magma Copper Company, who collected more than 3,000 species of both rare and common desert plants, including 800 different varieties of cacti. The arboretum, which attracts more than 200 species of birds, has walking trails and large greenhouses open to the public.

US 60 to Phoenix

Beyond the arboretum, US 60 becomes a divided road headed west. After about 10 miles it merges with AZ 79; 15 miles more and you're in Apache Junction, the official eastern edge of Metropolitan Phoenix. As you continue west into Mesa, US 60 turns into an urban freeway, soon opening up to six lanes in each direction. That should give you an idea of the volume of traffic carried by this major road during the morning and afternoon commutes. Since 1950, Phoenix has grown from the 99th-largest city in the U.S. to the 6th-largest, and it is on pace to become number 4 by 2020. That's big, and it happened in a hurry—over the course of a single lifetime.

Stay on US 60 until it merges with Interstate 10, bringing you back to the road you left in Lordsburg. If it's anywhere near the commuting hours (6-9 a.m. and 4-7 p.m.), you'll want to get off the freeway as quickly as possible, because all major routes leading into and out of the city center slow to a crawl during those times. If you have some time and you'd like a good look at what this vibrant city has to offer, consider the following optional loop.

PHOENIX: A SELF-GUIDED LOOP TOUR

This optional scenic loop takes you on a grand tour of Arizona's sprawling capital city. The total distance is about 60 miles, all on surface streets, so you should allow at least 2 hours just for driving it. If you stop at any of the many attractions, the reconnaissance mission can easily become a pleasant, full-day outing. Use the map for turn-by-turn guidance on this route; if you have a GPS, you can use the listed attractions as your waypoints. Just be sure to select the routing option that avoids major highways, or you'll end up touring the Phoenix freeway system.

From I-10, *take Exit 155 to West Baseline Road. Follow that west to Central Avenue, then head south to:*

1. South Mountain Park. At 16,000 acres, this is one of the largest urban parks in the world, and it features prominently on Phoenix's official "Points of Pride" list. Roads inside the park will take you to the summit of

View of downtown Phoenix from South Mountain

the highest peak, where you'll get a broad view of the city below.

From the park exit, *follow Central Avenue north for 6 miles, through the heart of downtown Phoenix, before turning west to:*

2. Arizona State Capitol Museum. Located on the grounds of the copper-domed Arizona State Capitol, this small museum has several worthwhile exhibits on the history of Arizona government dating back to the days of the Arizona Territory.

Arizona State Capitol, Phoenix

From the Capitol, *head back to Central Avenue and an even better museum:*

3. Heard Museum. Founded in 1929 by Dwight Heard, a rancher turned newspaper publisher, the museum has grown exponentially over the years, and is widely considered to house one of the world's finest collections of Native American art and artifacts.

From the Heard, *follow Central Avenue north about 4.5 miles to Glendale Avenue. At Glendale, turn right, and head for:*

4. Piestewa Peak Park (formerly Squaw Peak Park). A beautiful winding road takes you through an exceptionally lovely slice of natural desert, right in the middle of town. There's a trailhead here for an extremely popular hike to the top of the 2,600-foot peak. Parking is limited, so be prepared to wait for a space, or to park far away and walk. If it's too crowded, no worries, it's still worth driving in, because the drive back out offers stunning views, all the way across the city to South Mountain.

Leaving the park, *turn left on Lincoln Drive and travel 3.5 miles east, past the beautiful grounds of the **Arizona Biltmore Hotel** and golf course, to Tatum Boulevard. At Tatum, turn right and decide whether to end your day with a serious hike, or with a series of more touristy experiences. If you're a hiker, head to:*

5. Echo Canyon Recreation Area. From the parking lot just off Tatum and McDonald Drive, you can pick up a trail to the top of **Camelback Mountain**, the hump-shaped granite-and-sandstone behemoth looming above you, one of Phoenix's most prominent landmarks. Fair warning: Parking can be even more challenging than at Piestewa Peak. The hike is rated strenuous, so don't underestimate it. The payoff at the summit: some really great views, and marvelous photo opportunities.

For a less heart-racing but equally authentic Phoenix experience, take 44th Street south to:

6. Papago Park. This 1,500-acre park is home to the **Phoenix Zoo**, the **Desert Botanical Garden**, a great public golf course, and some wonderful rock formations, including the famous **Hole in the Rock**, a large eroded chamber that passes all the way through a sandstone hill—another great photo opportunity.

Leaving Papago Park, *take Galvin Parkway southwest to Van Buren. A mile or so west and a block south, on Washington Street, you'll find the:*

7. Pueblo Grande Museum and Archaeological

Park. This interesting ruin and display of artifacts tells the story of the Native American people who first settled the Salt River valley, some 2,000 years ago. These people, known as the Hohokam, built a sophisticated system of canals to shunt river water to their fields. In the late 1800s, long after the Hohokam were gone, European and American settlers co-opted the ancient irrigation system and enlarged it. That canal system still functions to this day.

There are many options for lodging in the Phoenix area. For a historic hotel, consider the **Hotel San Carlos**, an elegant downtown hotel that once hosted the likes of Marilyn Monroe and Humphrey Bogart. For a first-class resort, consider the **Arizona Biltmore**. Built in 1929, designed by Frank Lloyd Wright, and host to every U.S. president from Herbert Hoover to George W. Bush, the Biltmore is the epitome of class.

Phoenix Loop Highlights

Phoenix Points of Pride
phoenix.gov/pio/points-of-pride

South Mountain Park
10919 S. Central Ave., Phoenix,
AZ 85042
(602) 262-7393

State Capitol Museum
1700 W. Washington St.,
Phoenix, AZ 85007
(602) 926-3620
azlibrary.gov/azcm

Heard Museum
2301 N. Central Ave., Phoenix,
AZ 85004
(602) 252-8840
heard.org

Piestewa Peak Park
2701 E. Squaw Peak Drive,
Phoenix, AZ 85016
(602) 261-8318

**Echo Canyon Recreation Area
(Camelback Mountain)**
4925 E. McDonald Drive,
Phoenix, AZ 85018
(602) 261-8318

Papago Park
625 N. Galvin Pkwy., Phoenix,
AZ 85008
(602) 495-5458

Phoenix Zoo
455 N. Galvin Pkwy., Phoenix,
AZ 85008
(602) 286-3800
phoenixzoo.org

Desert Botanical Garden
1201 N. Galvin Pkwy., Phoenix,
AZ 85008
(480) 941-1225
dbg.org

**Pueblo Grande Museum and
Archaeological Park**
4619 E. Washington St., Phoenix,
AZ 85034
(602) 495-0901

Hotel San Carlos
202 N. Central Ave., Phoenix, AZ
85004
(602) 253-4121
hotelsancarlos.com

Arizona Biltmore
2400 E. Missouri Ave., Phoenix,
AZ 85016
(602) 955-6600
arizonabiltmore.com

Willcox to Benson

via Fort Bowie, Chiricahua National Monument, Douglas, Bisbee, and Tombstone

211 miles, **5** hours **45** minutes for drive time, more for optional routes, stops, and sightseeing

A Copper Queen trumps a Silver King in the town too tough to die

From Willcox to Benson on Interstate 10 is a distance of just 35 miles: a short, flat stretch that can be easily driven in half an hour. If you're not in too much of a hurry, consider this scenic alternative. It will cost you 150 extra miles, and anywhere from 5 hours to a full extra day, depending on how much time you spend enjoying the stops along the way. ⯈⯈

If you've already driven some of the other routes in this book, this one will be a change of pace. There isn't a single white-knuckle mountain road, just gentle, mostly empty highways, and the total distance is only about 200 miles. There's wonderful scenery, especially the amazing "hoodoos" in Chiricahua National Monument, but the primary attractions this time around are historical, with the vast, open countryside serving as context. Hike to the ruins of Fort Bowie, tour an underground copper mine, or watch a gunfight at the O.K. Corral. This is the Old West at its best, with some good fun for the whole family.

HERE
LIES
GEORGE
JOHNSON
HANGED BY
MISTAKE
1882

HE WAS RIGHT
WE WAS WRONG
BUT WE STRUNG
HIM UP
AND NOW HES
GONE

The Chiricahuas

Leaving Willcox, take the first exit off Interstate 10, Haskell Avenue, and follow it 4.5 miles to East Maley Street. This is the beginning of AZ 186, which will lead you out of Willcox to the southeast. The mountains looming in the distance are the Chiricahuas, so called because they were the territory of the Chiricahua Apaches. This rugged range is part of southern Arizona's archipelago of "Sky Islands," isolated peaks that support remarkably diverse ecosystems (*see sidebar, page 66*). Surrounded by semi-arid desert for miles in every direction, the Chiricahuas have pine forests in their upper reaches and are home to a wide

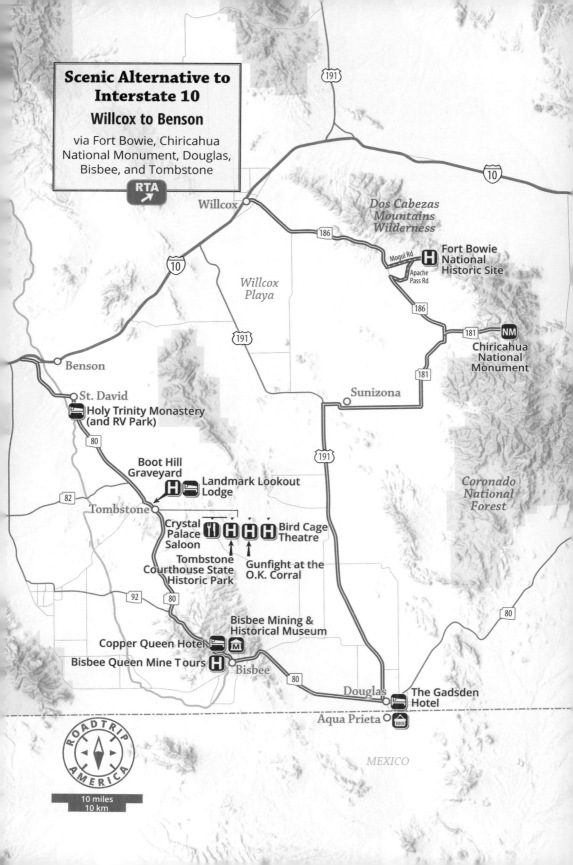

Scenic Alternative to Interstate 10

Willcox to Benson

via Fort Bowie, Chiricahua National Monument, Douglas, Bisbee, and Tombstone

RTA

Willcox

Dos Cabezas Mountains Wilderness

186

Mogul Rd

Fort Bowie National Historic Site

Apache Pass Rd

Willcox Playa

186

191

181

Chiricahua National Monument

181

Benson

Sunizona

St. David

Holy Trinity Monastery (and RV Park)

80

Coronado National Forest

Boot Hill Graveyard

Landmark Lookout Lodge

82

Tombstone

Crystal Palace Saloon

Bird Cage Theatre

Tombstone Courthouse State Historic Park

Gunfight at the O.K. Corral

191

92

80

80

Bisbee Mining & Historical Museum

Copper Queen Hotel

Bisbee Queen Mine Tours

Bisbee

80

Douglas

The Gadsden Hotel

Aqua Prieta

MEXICO

ROADTRIP AMERICA

10 miles
10 km

range of wildlife, including mountain lions, ocelots, bears, and even the occasional jaguar.

Back in the frontier days, the latter half of the 1800s, this area was the scene of some of the most vicious fighting in the Indian Wars. The Apaches were the last holdouts against western expansion, and they didn't let go easily. The two best-remembered warriors of that era, Cochise and Geronimo, were both Chiricahua Apaches, and both spent much of their lives in these mountains.

AZ 186 is a purpose-built highway with a single destination, the Chiricahua National Monument, but you can also see the **Fort Bowie National Historic Site** if you don't mind a slight detour along the way. Fort Bowie was the headquarters of the Army garrison charged with bringing the renegade Apaches to heel. The fort was well provisioned, well manned, and extremely well armed. Even so, it took the Army more than 20

The Mexican Border

In the old days (not so very long ago), a day trip to a Mexican border town was no more complicated than a trip to the mall, and it had the same essential purpose: shopping! Bargains were everywhere—everything from kitschy souvenirs to handcrafted furniture and fine jewelry—and all the prices were negotiable. Throw in some mariachi music and cheap tequila and you had a sure-fire recipe for a good time. For decades, U.S. travelers crossed over the border by the millions each year.

Sadly, times have changed. Between heightened security concerns on the American side of the border, and the rise of drug cartels on the Mexican side of the border, that carefree, fiesta, anything-goes atmosphere has been dampened. For a time, rival drug gangs and the Mexican military fought for control of the border country, and in cities like Juarez the violence was horrific. The immediate crisis has abated, but the U.S. Department of State continues to advise citizens to "defer non-essential travel" to the Mexican border states, to drive only on the main roads, and not to travel at night.

Should you make that trip across the border? That's up to you. Cautious travelers may wish to pass up the opportunity. Others may note that in Agua Prieta and Nogales, the two principal border towns accessible from Arizona, tourists have never been targets of cartel violence, not even during the worst of the troubles, and the border towns do have their charms. For a day trip, all you need is a valid passport. To keep things simple, leave your vehicle in a secure lot on the U.S. side of the border and walk across; that will speed your crossing, in both directions. (If you do drive across, be aware that travel by car in Mexico, anywhere beyond the border area, requires special permits, tourist cards, and Mexican auto insurance). If you do any shopping, purchases up to $800 per person are duty free; and patience is a virtue. The customs lines are often very slow.

years to accomplish its mission—strong testament to the cunning and persistence of the Apaches. Armies are adept at fighting other armies. But when the enemy is truly dug in, so at home they're like part of the landscape? That's another kind of fight altogether, and it was a tough one, for both sides.

To see the old fort, keep a sharp eye out for Mogul Road, about 20 miles out of Willcox. Turn left (east), and follow that unpaved road for about 7 miles, until it joins Apache Pass Road, where you'll find the parking area for Fort Bowie. The hike to the fort from here is about 3 miles round-trip and is rated moderate; interpretive signs will guide you. The fort, which was abandoned in 1894, is a fascinating ruin of crumbling adobe walls and foundations spread over a large area. Also on the site are a small museum and the ruins of the Butterfield Stage Coach stop, the target of many Apache attacks and the site of several bloody battles. As you hike back out through Apache Pass, imagine how it must have felt for the young soldiers who were stationed here 150 years ago. They were in forbidding terrain, surrounded by hostile Indians, and if there was trouble they couldn't handle, the closest reinforcements were too far away to save them.

Leaving the Fort Bowie parking area, head back west on Apache Pass Road; at the intersection with Mogul Road, stay left, and keep going until you rejoin AZ 186, just a bit south of where you left it. After 8.6 miles, AZ 186 intersects AZ 181. Turn left (east), and follow the signs into **Chiricahua National Monument**. The attraction here is the remarkable terrain: a wonderland of eroded pillars and spires called hoodoos, created by violent geological activity some 27 million years ago. Many of

Chiricahuas Highlights

Fort Bowie National Historic Site
3500 S. Apache Pass Road, Bowie, AZ 85605
(520) 847-2500
nps.gov/fobo

Chiricahua National Monument
E. Bonita Canyon Road, Willcox, AZ 85643
(520) 824-3560
nps.gov/chir

Opposite:
Chiricahua National Monument

the hoodoos are capped by seemingly balanced rocks that look like they might come tumbling down at any moment. Bonita Canyon Scenic Drive takes in many of the monument's most interesting features along its 8-mile paved route. (Note that the road is 16 miles round-trip; it is not a "loop" road as some guides suggest.) There are many pullouts and access to trailheads for those who want to explore the park's interior more fully. The 12,000-acre wilderness area, which has been protected since 1924, was sacred to the Apache people, who called it "the land of standing-up rocks."

Chiricahua National Monument

Douglas and Bisbee

Leaving Chiricahua National Monument, follow AZ 181 out of the park. Stay on it as it turns south, and then west, before terminating at US 191 in the small farming community of Sunizona. Bear left, and drive due south on US 191 about 40 miles, through Elfrida and McNeal, until you come to the town of Douglas, on the Mexican border. **Douglas** was founded in 1902 as the smelter town for the copper mines at Bisbee. In the early 1980s, as the price of copper plummeted worldwide, a bitter mineworkers strike broke out, disrupting production in Bisbee's Lavender Pit for nearly three years. That one-two punch was a knockout. The mines in Bisbee were closed, and with them the two smelters in Douglas.

Despite that blow to the local economy, Douglas still prospers, largely because of its proximity to Mexico. While you're here, you might consider a visit to Agua Prieta, just over the border in the Mexican state of Sonora. This city of 80,000, while much bigger than neighboring Douglas, has a small-town feel and the unmistakable ambience of Old Mexico, and it is considered one of the safest of the Mexican border towns. There are bargains to be had in the shops, not to mention duty-free tequila (see sidebar page 77).

While in Douglas, stop in at the **Gadsden Hotel**, one of 17 old Douglas buildings listed on the National Register of Historic Places, and certainly the most opulent. Built in 1907, and rebuilt in 1929 after an extensive fire, the Gadsden is the ultimate in Old World luxury. The lobby features a massive white Italian marble staircase (the only part of the original hotel to survive the fire), as well as four marble columns trimmed with 14-karat-gold leaf. Above the staircase, an exquisite 42-foot Tiffany stained-glass mural depicts a Southwest scene. Douglas

Lobby with Tiffany, stained glass, Gadsden Hotel, Douglas, Arizona

may seem an odd location for such a display of elegance, but in its heyday, the Gadsden was a meeting place for wealthy ranchers, mine executives, and international businessmen. In fact, in 1928, Douglas opened the nation's first international airport (literally international, because the runway was bisected by the border). Douglas was an especially popular destination during Prohibition, because travelers could soak up the Arizona sunshine and then quench their thirst with some Mexican moonshine. It's said that a tunnel from the basement of the hotel was used to keep guests surreptitiously supplied with their favorite beverages.

Leaving Douglas, take AZ 80 west and then north into the Mule Mountains, where you'll find the charming old mining town of **Bisbee**. More than any other town in Arizona, Bisbee retains its 19th-century frontier ambience. So many of the old buildings have been restored and refurbished that it's almost like a movie set, its brightly painted storefronts climbing the sides of Tombstone Canyon, Moon Canyon, Miller Hill, and Brewery Gulch—all part of the original townsite laid out in 1880. The terrain is so steep in some places that Bisbee High School has a ground-floor entrance on each of its four levels.

Bisbee hung on as a copper town until the mid-20th century, but when the mines shut down, real estate *Bisbee, Arizona*

values plummeted. The housing crash attracted a new wave of residents: artists, craftsmen, and counterculture types seeking camaraderie and a cheap place to live. Bisbee became nationally known as the "Best Historic Small Town in America," among other accolades, prompting yet another influx, this time of retirees and investors, who took the restoring and refurbishing to a whole new level.

Today, Bisbee is beautiful to look at, and a very cool place to visit. You can spend a pleasant afternoon browsing in the shops and galleries, sampling the saloons in Brewery Gulch, and walking along the many public staircases and pedestrian walkways that were built in the 1930s, as a New Deal project of the Works Progress Administration. A favorite place to stay is the beautifully restored **Copper Queen Hotel**, which dates back to 1902. The small but quite interesting **Bisbee Mining and Historical Museum** is just across from the hotel. Serious mining enthusiasts can take a tour of the inactive **Queen Mine** outside town, where a small train takes visitors 1,500 feet into the underground tunnels.

Douglas and Bisbee Highlights

The Gadsden Hotel
1046 G Ave., Douglas, AZ 85607
(520) 364-4481
thegadsdenhotel.com

Copper Queen Hotel
11 Howell Ave., Bisbee, AZ 85603
(520) 432-2216
copperqueen.com

Bisbee Mining & Historical Museum
5 Copper Queen Plaza, Bisbee, AZ 85603
(520) 432-7071
bisbeemuseum.org

Bisbee Queen Mine Tours
478 Dart Road, Bisbee, AZ 85603
(520) 432-2071
queenminetour.com

TOMBSTONE

Leaving Bisbee, head north on AZ 80. After about 23 miles, you'll roll up on Tombstone, "The Town Too Tough to Die." This place is an American original, a rough-and-tumble silver mining camp, founded in 1879, one of the last of the Wild West boomtowns. Tombstone was the stomping ground of Wyatt Earp and his brothers, their pal Doc Holliday, and Doc's gal, Big Nose Kate, as well as the gang of no-good cattle rustlers that called themselves The Cowboys—Ike and Billy Clanton and the McLaury brothers. These were the principals in the infamous Gunfight at the O.K. Corral; a bloody, 30-second shootout in the streets of Tombstone that still reverberates after more than 135 years. That brief portion of Tombstone's history has been immortalized time and again in movies and on television, and is as much a part of American popular history as Paul Revere's Ride or Custer's Last Stand.

The old part of Tombstone is very walkable, and visitors are quickly immersed in its story. Actors in period costumes hang around the downtown area wearing six-shooters, long coats, and dusty boots. In the **Crystal Palace Saloon**, you'll be greeted by comely dance-hall girls in bustiers and fishnet stockings. A re-enactment of the **Gunfight at the O.K. Corral** is staged daily, on Allen Street; the first show starts at noon. The original town newspaper, *The Tombstone Epitaph* ("Every Tombstone needs an Epitaph"), is still in operation; you can tour its offices and purchase souvenir editions. The **Tombstone Courthouse** is now a museum and historical park presenting many fascinating exhibits, including a set of well-used gallows out back of the building. **The Bird**

OK Corral, Tombstone, Arizona

Cage Theatre, once billed as "the wildest and wickedest night spot between Basin Street and the Barbary Coast," is open for tours, including a nightly ghost tour whose participants seek contact from the wandering spirits of the many unfortunates who departed this world violently during Tombstone's heyday.

Today Tombstone is a caricature of its former self, but in a good way. All that stagecraft provides a window into a complicated historical event (it wasn't all good guys and bad guys) in the very place where the whole thing happened, and with enough context to make it seem real. That's a good trick, and if you like that sort of thing, it really is great fun.

On your way out of town, stop by **Boot Hill**, the Tombstone graveyard from the earliest days of the town. It's a real graveyard, deserving of dignity and respect, but some of the headstones are pretty wacky, like this one: *Here lies George Johnson, hanged by mistake, 1882; He was right, we was wrong, but we strung him up, and now he's gone.* There are many others in a similar vein, more than 250 marked graves in all, all dating between 1878 and 1884. A short distance farther up the highway, atop a hill with a view of the distant Dragoon Mountains, is the **Landmark Lookout Lodge**, a nice hotel with all the essential amenities.

"Here Lies Lester Moore...," Boot Hill Grave Yard, Tombstone, Arizona

Tombstone Highlights

Crystal Palace Saloon
436 E. Allen St., Tombstone, AZ 85638
(520) 457-3611
crystalpalacesaloon.com

Gunfight at the O.K. Corral
ok-corral.com

Tombstone Courthouse State Historic Park
223 E. Toughnut St., Tombstone, AZ 85638
(520) 457-3311

Bird Cage Theatre
535 E. Allen St., Tombstone, AZ 85638
(520) 457-3421
tombstonebirdcage.com

Boot Hill Graveyard
408 AZ 80, Tombstone, AZ 85638
(520) 457-3300

Landmark Lookout Lodge
781 AZ 80, Tombstone, AZ 85638
(520) 457-2223
lookoutlodgeaz.com

ST. DAVID AND BENSON

Leaving Tombstone, continue on AZ 80. After about 16 miles you'll pass through the small community of St. David, an oasis of green trees along the banks of the San Pedro River. There's an unusual RV park here, on the grounds of the **Holy Trinity Monastery**, a Christian retreat founded in 1974 that is now home to a small community of Benedictine monks. Visitors are welcome on the grounds, as well as in the chapel, the library, museum, thrift shop, and bookstore. Most of the guests in the RV park are regulars who stay through the winter and volunteer their labor on the monastery grounds and in the adjacent pecan orchard; they are called the "Holy Hobos." A 70-foot-tall Celtic cross commemorating the Irish Famine is just visible from the highway. Feel free to pull in if you'd like to take a closer look at it.

Seven miles beyond St. David you'll reach the town of Benson and the intersection with I-10 that marks the end of this route.

> **St. David Highlights**
>
> **Holy Trinity Monastery (and Rv Park)**
> 1605 S. St. Mary's Way, St. David, AZ 85630
> (520) 720-4642
> holytrinitymonastery.org

BENSON AND BEYOND

If you're in a hurry to get to Tucson, head west on 1-10 and you'll be there in less than 45 minutes. If you've got some time and you'd like to see a bit more of this fascinating border region, consider **Scenic Side Trip 6,** which will take you from Benson to Tucson by way of a series of stupendously beautiful roads through the Huachuca Mountains.

Next page: 70-foot-tall Celtic cross, Holy Trinity Monastery, St. David, Arizona

Benson to Tucson

via Kartchner Caverns, the Huachucas, Patagonia, Nogales, and Tumacácori

213 miles, **7** hours **30** minutes for drive time, more for optional routes, stops, and sightseeing

What do hummingbirds, tequila, and Titan missiles have in common? Scenic Side Trip 6

FROM BENSON TO DOWNTOWN TUCSON IS A MERE 40 MILES. Traveling at the 75 mph speed limit, you could be there in about half an hour, but what's your hurry? This side trip will take you 170 miles out of your way, and will take you most of an extra day. What will you get in exchange? Some of the prettiest countryside in Arizona, and one heck of a beautiful drive. ➡️

KARTCHNER CAVERNS

From Interstate 10, take Exit 302 on the west side of Benson and merge onto AZ 90 headed south. After 9 miles, you'll reach the entrance to **Kartchner Caverns State Park**, one of the most extraordinary attractions in the Southwest: the most unspoiled major cave system ever made accessible to the public.

The cavern was discovered in 1974 when two caving enthusiasts came upon a crevice just 10 inches wide at the base of the Whetstone Mountains. This crack in the earth was "breathing," exhaling a flow of moist air redolent with the distinctive scent of bats—a sure sign of a cave. The two men squeezed through the crevice and wormed their way through a series of narrow passages, emerging into an extraordinary,

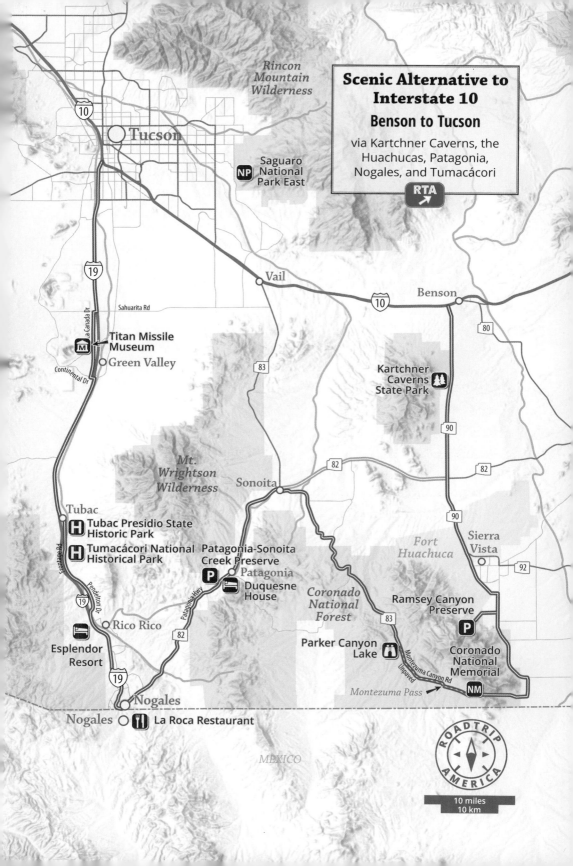

Scenic Alternative to Interstate 10

Benson to Tucson

via Kartchner Caverns, the Huachucas, Patagonia, Nogales, and Tumacácori

RTA

Rincon Mountain Wilderness

10 Tucson

NP Saguaro National Park East

Vail

Benson

10

80

19

Sahuarita Rd

La Canada Dr

Titan Missile Museum

M

Green Valley

Continental Dr

83

Kartchner Caverns State Park

90

Mt. Wrightson Wilderness

82

82

Sonoita

90

Fort Huachuca

Sierra Vista

92

Tubac

H Tubac Presidio State Historic Park

H Tumacácori National Historical Park

Patagonia-Sonoita Creek Preserve

P

Patagonia

Duquesne House

Esperanza

Pendelton Dr

Coronado National Forest

Ramsey Canyon Preserve

P

19

Esplendor Resort

Rico Rico

82

Patagonia Hwy

Parker Canyon Lake

83

Montezuma Canyon Rd

Unpaved

Coronado National Memorial

NM

19

Nogales

Montezuma Pass

Nogales O ⑂ La Roca Restaurant

MEXICO

ROADTRIP AMERICA

10 miles
10 km

undisturbed cavescape where no human had ever set foot before. The limestone chambers were filled with exotic cave formations called *speleothems*—fantastic accretions 200,000 years in the making. The best part? The cave was still growing, drop by drop, from water seeping through the desert floor above.

The cavers kept their find a secret, telling only the property owners, James and Lois Kartchner, who were completely unaware of the cavern beneath their land. The story of how the secret cave became a state park reads like a spy novel. State officials were blindfolded before being driven to the site. State funding was requested to acquire property that couldn't be described. A land swap was quietly arranged behind closed doors. The cave finally opened to the public in 1999—25 years after its discovery, and only after the state of Arizona had spent $28 million on air-lock doors, temperature and humidity controls, and a security system to protect the pristine condition of the cave.

To see the caverns you have to join a Ranger-led tour, and for that you'll need a reservation. Same-day reservations are possible, but only 800 people are allowed inside the caverns per day, so if you don't plan ahead, you could be turned away. Strict rules protect the cave; most notably, you can bring nothing into the caverns with you, including purses, strollers, water bottles, cameras—even cell phones. The **Throne Room Tour**, a half-mile walk that takes 90 minutes, is offered year round. The **Big Room Tour**, a little shorter, is offered from mid-October to mid-April (the rest of the year this part of the cave is used as a nursery roost for a thousand mother bats and their young). Headlamp-only tours are occasionally offered as well.

Kartchner Caverns Highlights

Kartchner Caverns State Park
2980 S. AZ 90, Benson, AZ 85602
(520) 586-4100
azstateparks.com/kartchner/

THE HUACHUCAS

Leaving Kartchner Caverns, return to AZ 90 and drive 19 miles south, into the town of Sierra Vista. On your right you'll pass **Fort Huachuca**, a military base that was established here in 1877 and is currently the home of the U.S. Army Intelligence Center and headquarters of the NETCOM team that controls the Army's computer network and cyber defense. Beyond the base, AZ 90 swings east. Keep right to stay on Buffalo Soldier Trail and continue driving south, about 6 miles, to the intersection with AZ 92. Turn right, and drive 2 miles west to Ramsey Canyon Road, which will lead you up into the mountains. The road is paved all the way to the end, a distance of about 3.5 miles. That's where you'll find the entrance to the **Ramsey Canyon Preserve**.

The Huachucas are another of southern Arizona's Sky Island chains *(see sidebar, page 66)*. All of the Sky Islands are known for their biodiversity, but Ramsey Canyon is truly extraordinary. The forested preserve,

Bare sycamore, Ramsey Canyon, Hereford, Arizona

which is managed by the Nature Conservancy, is located right at the point where the Rocky Mountains, the Sierra Madre Mountains, the Sonoran Desert, and the Chihuahuan Desert all come together. The unique conjunction of habitats attracts an astonishing variety of creatures, particularly birds: no fewer than 170 species, including 15 species of hummingbirds—the stars of the show—and dozens of visiting species from Mexico. That puts Ramsey Canyon high on the bucket list of many serious birding enthusiasts.

Hiking is another popular activity in the preserve. Massive sycamores and maples line the steep-walled canyon and fill it with color in autumn Trails meander for miles through the mountains here, but be mindful of any posted warnings. There are bears in the Huachucas, and also coyotes: both the four-legged kind, which prey on lizards and house cats, and the two-legged kind, who smuggle illegal immigrants from Mexico. This is border country, so it's best to stay off those trails after dark.

Leaving Ramsey Canyon, head back to AZ 92 and drive west, about 10 miles, to Coronado Memorial Road, and follow it south and then west into the **Coronado National Memorial**, a 4,750-acre Park Service property that commemorates the 1540-1542 expedition of Spanish explorer Francisco Vásquez de Coronado. Here you'll find a visitors center, picnic areas, an open-access cave, and 8 miles of hiking trails.

This next part of the route requires a judgement call: whether to go over the mountains to

Parker Canyon Lake (*see below*), or to go around (*see sidebar*). **Montezuma Canyon Road** climbs up and over 6,575-foot Montezuma Pass, then takes you on to the lake, a total distance of 18 miles. The first mile of this route is paved. The next 17 miles are not. The road is suitable for passenger cars, but there are tight switchbacks leading up to the pass, so vehicles over 24 feet long are prohibited. (As always, if you're in a rental vehicle, check your contract before taking the vehicle on unpaved roads). The unpaved portion of this road is graded, but it's a washboard. It's also steep and narrow, and there are precipitous drops, without guardrails. The road is not for the faint of heart, but if you drive carefully and at an appropriate speed, you'll be fine. The reward? The drive is absolutely *beautiful*, and the views from the overlook at the top of the pass are stupendous. Five stars, for real.

Montezuma Pass, Huachuca Mountains, Arizona

If you've come this far, the roughest part of the road is already behind you, so by all means continue down the other side of the pass to Parker Canyon Lake. It's slow, but quite lovely. The road is not well marked; if you come to a fork, follow the route that looks most well-traveled. It will take you about an hour to reach the lake from the Coronado Memorial.

Huachucas Highlights

Ramsey Canyon Preserve
27 Ramsey Canyon Road,
Hereford, AZ 85615
(520) 378-2785

Coronado National Memorial
4101 E. Montezuma Canyon
Road, Hereford, AZ 85615
(520) 366-5515
rps.gov/coro

A few words of caution. *This area is remote. There is little traffic, no services, and cell coverage is spotty at best. Before starting out, make sure you have plenty of fuel and water, that your tires are properly inflated and in good condition, and that you have a usable spare. Be aware that you are very close to the border; it's likely you'll encounter Border Patrol officers, who may stop and question you. If you encounter other people, smile—but be cautious.*

Parker Canyon Lake is a great spot: tranquil and uncrowded. Campsites are available, and the fishing is good for trout, bass, sunnies, and catfish. There is also a 5-mile shoreline trail for walking and bird-watching. The road north from the lake, AZ 83 to Sonoita, is like a dream, one of the best drives in Arizona: a gently curving, all-but-empty highway that dips and flows across a landscape of lush grassland rimmed by old green mountains weathered smooth by the ages. Wildflowers are abundant, even late into the season. Continue on to Sonoita, where the road intersects with AZ 82.

The Other Way to the Lake

If the drive up and over Montezuma Pass doesn't sound like your idea of fun, or if you're worried that your vehicle isn't suited for the road, you can take the long way around to Parker Canyon Lake. It will add 50 miles and an extra hour of driving to your journey, but it's 100 percent paved and has no steep grades. From the Coronado Memorial visitors center, retrace your route to Sierra Vista. Head north, back along AZ 90 to AZ 82, then drive west on AZ 82 to Upper Elgin Road. Take Elgin Road south, through Elgin, toward Canelo. When you reach the intersection with AZ 83, bear left and follow AZ 83 south to Parker Canyon Lake. You'll double back on this section of road on your way to Sonoita, but it's a beautiful run, well worth seeing twice.

Arizona Route 83, south of Sonoita

SONOITA, PATAGONIA, AND NOGALES

The grass-covered hill country around Sonoita is perfect for raising cattle. More recently, it has become home to the growing southern Arizona wine industry. Between Sonoita and Elgin, there are 10 wineries, most with tasting rooms. Just look for the signs.

Leaving Sonoita, follow AZ 82 west then south toward Patagonia and Nogales. **Patagonia** is a lovely little town and arts center that offers a slow pace of life in a seriously tranquil setting. Nearby, you can visit **Patagonia Lake State Park**, south of town off AZ 82, or the **Patago-nia-Sonoita Creek Preserve**, on the northern outskirts of town off Blue Heaven Road. The preserve is a riparian habitat manged by the Nature Conservancy; it is another great spot for hiking and bird-watching. If you decide to stick around in Patagonia, try the **Duquesne House B&B,** which has comfortable suites converted from an 1890s boarding house for miners. The homey residence is filled with an eclectic collection of colorful art, and is surrounded by beautiful gardens.

From Patagonia, AZ 82 continues south to **Nogales**, the largest of Arizona's border towns. The rolling green hills make for a beautiful setting. Houses climb up the slopes, and neighborhoods hug the contours of the land, spilling through the valleys in between. It's all very picturesque, but not what you'd call upscale; poverty is pervasive here, on both sides of the border.

Nogales is a busy port of entry. Upwards of $30 billion worth of goods pass through the commercial lanes each year, much of it produce bound for dinner tables all across the U.S. The lanes for private vehicles are also busy, and so are the gates for pedestrians, but if you'd like to take a quick trip into Mexico, it's easy to do. Nogales does have its share of bad neighborhoods, so unless you know your way around, stick to the main shopping district

nearest the pedestrian gate. There are some great bargains on handicrafts here, the tequila is duty-free, and **La Roca Restaurant**, right by the border crossing, is a terrific place to get seriously authentic Sonora-style Mexican food. *(For more information about Mexican border crossings, see sidebar page 50).*

Waiting for the bus in Patagonia, Arizona

If you plan to stay the night in the area, your best bet is the suburb of

Sonoita, Patagonia, and Nogales Highlights

Patagonia-Sonoita Creek Preserve
150 Blue Heaven Road, Patagonia, AZ 85624
(520) 394-2400

Duquesne House
357 Duquesne Ave., Patagonia, AZ 85624
(520) 394-2732
theduquesnehouse.com

La Roca Restaurant
Plutarco Elías Calles, Buenos Aires, 84010 Heroica Nogales, Sonora, Mexico
+52 631 312 0760
larocarestaurant.com

Esplendor Resort
1069 Camino Caralampi, Rio Rico, AZ 85648
(520) 281-1901
esplendor-resort.com

Rio Rico, about 14 miles north of Nogales (on the U.S. side). Take I-19 to the Rio Rico Drive exit. The **Esplendor Resort**, formerly the Rio Rico Resort, is located on a hilltop; it has wonderful views and excellent amenities.

ALONG INTERSTATE 19

Leaving Rio Rico, take the Rio Rico Drive exit off Interstate 19 east to Pendleton Drive, which runs roughly parallel to the freeway. Follow Pendleton Drive north to Palo Parado, and follow that to the I-19 frontage road. Continue north. After about 3.5 miles, you'll come to **Tumacácori National Historical Park,** the site of a Spanish mission that was founded by the Jesuit missionary and explorer Eusebio Francisco Kino in 1691 and abandoned 157 years later, in 1848. The mission church was never completed, and it remains largely unrestored, but there have been significant efforts to preserve the weathered adobe walls. There's a small museum on the site, a heritage orchard, and a spooky little cemetery in the mission courtyard.

Tumacacori National Historical Park

Arizona's Spanish Missions

Most of southern Arizona was once the northern frontier of New Spain. The Spanish had claimed this territory, which they called the Pimería Alta, without actually conquering it, and they weren't in any great rush to put it to use. It was remote and generally forbidding country, full of hot, dry deserts and rugged mountains. Home to the Pima Indians, humble desert agriculturalists with no resources of interest to Spain, it was largely controlled by the Apaches, bad-tempered marauders who refused to be dominated.

The Spanish had a method for dealing with difficult locals. First, they sent in their soldiers, who wielded their fine Toledan steel swords to devastating effect. Then they sent in their missionaries, whose work converting the population to Christianity was the key to holding the conquered territory. In the Pimería Alta, the process was a little different. The first man in was Eusebio Francisco Kino, a Jesuit, who first traveled there in 1687, more than 150 years after Spain asserted its claim to the area. In 1691, he founded Mission San Cayetano de Tumacácori, predecessor of the mission church that you can visit today, the first of 20 missions he would build over 24 years in the region. Each mission was strategically placed near a native village, usually near a river. The missions were surrounded by fields and orchards, and were self-sustaining communities.

Father Kino's task wasn't easy. The Apaches saw the missions as easy pickings, and they raided the surrounding villages with fierce regularity. For that reason, the missions were built like fortresses, providing both refuge and spiritual guidance to the local faithful.

Two of Kino's Arizona missions are still standing: Tumacácori, in the National Historical Park *(see above)*, and San Xavier del Bac, which still serves the community outside Tucson *(see page 111)*.

Three miles north, **Tubac Presidio State Historic Park** showcases the remains of a Spanish fort that was established there in 1752 to control restive native tribes and provision Spanish expeditions headed north from the New Spain frontier. There's not a lot left of the presidio, just remnants of adobe walls and foundations, but a small museum provides a good overview of the history. The park also preserves some structures from 19th-century Territorial days, including a schoolhouse and a church. Nearby, the modern town of Tubac has a small shopping district reminiscent of Mexico, with crafts and ceramics from across the border (albeit at slightly higher prices).

For a look at a very different form of territorial defense, head to the **Titan Missile Museum**. To get there, take I-19 north to Green Valley and exit at Continental Road. Turn left (west) and go one block to

South La Cañada Drive; follow that north for about 3 miles to West Duval Mine Road. From there, follow the signs to the museum. This is the only place in the United States where you can see one of the most graphic icons of the Cold War: an ICBM, an intercontinental ballistic missile, decommissioned but completely intact, still in its underground silo. At one time there were 54 of these missiles in locations all around the U.S., several in the Tucson area. For more than 20 years, the missiles were armed and ready to go, their crews on high alert 24 hours a day. Given the command to launch, these missiles could be in the air and on their way in 58 seconds. A Titan missile, the largest missile in the U.S. arsenal, was capable of delivering a 9-megaton nuclear warhead to a target 6,300 miles away, the approximate distance from Tucson to Moscow, in 30 minutes—less time than it takes to get a pizza delivered. Such was the world we lived in, until not so very long ago.

Leaving the museum, return to Duval Mine Road and follow it east, back to Interstate 19, and head north. After about 24 miles, I-19 merges with Interstate 10, marking the end of this remarkable route and heading you straight into Tucson. If you're not pressed for time, consider **Scenic Side Trip 7**, a 165-mile drive that will take you on a circuit of the "Old Pueblo."

Interstate 19 Highlights

Tumacácori National Historical Park
1895 E. I-19 Frontage Road,
Tumacacori, AZ 85640
(520) 377-5060
nps.gov/tuma

Tubac Presidio State Historic Park
1 Burruel St., Tubac, AZ 85646
(520) 398-2252
azstateparks.com/tubac/

Titan Missile Museum
1580 W. Duval Mine Road, Green Valley, AZ 85614
(520) 625-7736
titanmissilemuseum.org

A Tucson Circuit

165 miles, **7** hours and **15** minutes   **A tour around the Old Pueblo**
for drive time, more for optional
routes, stops, and sightseeing

LIKE ALL THE ROUTES IN THIS BOOK, THIS ONE BEGINS AND ENDS
on an Interstate Highway, but in every other way, it is unique. It's
the only route that stays near a single urban center for its entire
length, and all the points of interest are close to one another. You
can start or stop anywhere you'd like, and you can skip past any
that don't interest you, with no harm done.   ▶▶

Known as the Old Pueblo, Tucson
was founded as a Spanish military
outpost in 1775. More than any other
city in Arizona, Tucson has deep multicultural roots. For a traveler passing
through, it offers an opportunity
to sample some fascinating history,
natural wonders, and extraordinary
scenic drives—all in a daylong circuit
of the city.

SABINO CANYON

A good place to begin is at the Ina
Road exit off Interstate 10, in the
northern outskirts of the city. Follow
Ina due east for 7 miles until it curves
right (south) and turns into Skyline
Drive; keep right as Skyline merges
into Sunrise, and stay on Sunrise for
8 miles until it ends at Sabino Canyon
Road. Follow the signs to **Sabino
Canyon Visitors Center,** where
you'll find parking, informative

exhibits, access to trails, and a tram
that will take you up the canyon to
see the waterfalls.

Waterfalls? In the desert? Yes.
Sabino Canyon is a riparian oasis
tucked into a rocky fold of the Santa
Catalina Mountains, just a few miles
northeast of downtown Tucson.
These mountains are the key to life
here. The peaks breed clouds, the
clouds condense into rain, and the
rain feeds springs, which merge
into streams, which in turn charge
the aquifers—the source of at least

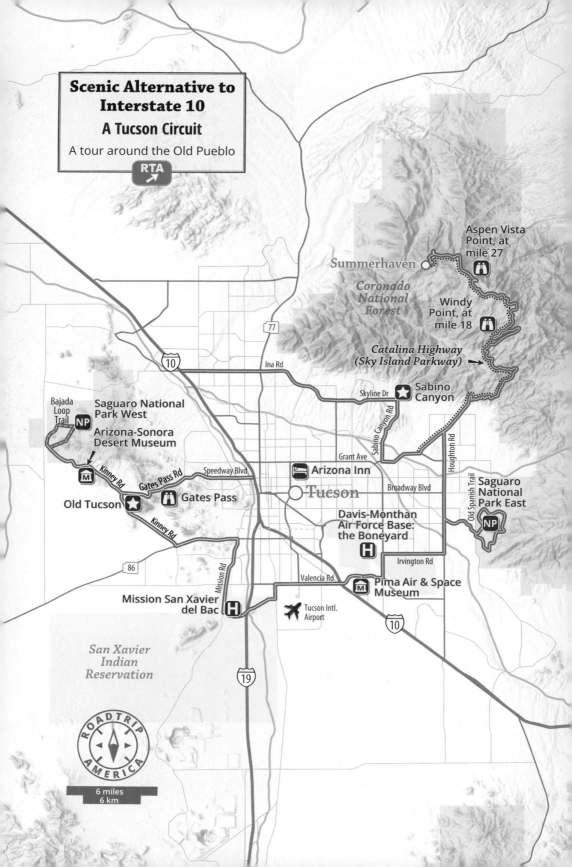

Scenic Alternative to Interstate 10

A Tucson Circuit

A tour around the Old Pueblo

RTA

Aspen Vista Point, at mile 27

Summerhaven

Coronado National Forest

Windy Point, at mile 18

Catalina Highway (Sky Island Parkway)

77

Ina Rd

Skyline Dr

Sabino Canyon

Bajada Loop Trail

Saguaro National Park West

NP

Arizona-Sonora Desert Museum

Kinney Rd

Gates Pass Rd

Speedway Blvd

Grant Ave

Sabino Canyon Rd

Houghton Rd

Old Spanish Trail

Saguaro National Park East

NP

M

Old Tucson

Gates Pass

Tucson

Arizona Inn

Broadway Blvd

Kinney Rd

Davis-Monthan Air Force Base: the Boneyard

H

86

Mission Rd

Irvington Rd

Mission San Xavier del Bac

H

Valencia Rd

Pima Air & Space Museum

M

Tucson Intl. Airport

10

San Xavier Indian Reservation

19

ROADTRIP AMERICA

6 miles
6 km

Catalina Highway, Mount Lemmon, Tucson, Arizona

half of the water that sustains this sprawling city in the desert. One of those streams forms a series of pools connected by tumbling cascades, the **Seven Falls**. The surrounding habitat is quite lovely, and it supports all manner of creatures—including bobcats, Gila monsters, dozens of species of birds--and a spectacular variety of lush desert vegetation.

As Tucson grew, Sabino Canyon became an increasingly popular destination for recreation; it got so crowded that private cars were banned on the canyon road. Since 1978, the only way to visit the recreation area has been on foot, on horseback, on a bicycle (during limited hours), or on one of the trams that run from the visitors center. A private company operates the trams, and there are fees for day use. Is it worth the trouble to visit? Absolutely. When Seven Falls is running strong, the deeper pools rank among the best swimming holes anywhere. The hike to the falls is just half a mile from the tram stop (or 2.2 miles if you walk the whole way from the visitors center). Sadly, the springs that feed the falls tend to dry up in the summer months, from June to September.

CATALINA HIGHWAY TO MOUNT LEMMON

Leaving the visitors center, follow Sabino Canyon Road 5 miles south to Tanque Verde; turn left and drive east 2.6 miles to Catalina Highway. Turn left again and head into those rainmaking mountains, the Santa Catalinas, which loom above the city to the northeast. The highest peak in the range is 9,100-foot Mount Lemmon, one of Arizona's famous Sky Islands (*see sidebar, page 66*); the mountain supports an ecosystem quite distinct from the surrounding desert, with tremendous biodiversity. There's a road to the top, paved the entire way, with an excellent surface, good shoulders, banked curves, and guardrails. There are scenic pullouts every few miles, and on a clear day you can see all the way to Mexico.

Sabino Canyon, a cool oasis in the desert near Tucson, Arizona

This 30-mile stretch of mountain road, variously known as the **Catalina Highway**, the Sky Island Parkway, or simply, "the road up Mount Lemmon," is among the finest short drives in the state. More than a million visitors travel it every year, including many bicyclists. The 27-mile uphill slog to the top has long been a favorite training ride for many of the world's top bicycle racers, especially during the cooler months of the year. When Lance Armstrong was training for the Tour de France, he would rent a cabin at the top of Mount Lemmon and end his daily workout around Tucson by pedaling back home, uphill all the way.

If you have a smartphone, you can download

a free app from the University of Arizona called **Mt. Lemmon Science Tour**. Launch the app when you start your drive up, and you'll hear an audio lecture that synchs with your location as you go (provided you drive at the speed limit). The narrative provides a fascinating overview of the history and geology of the area, and of the various climate zones you travel through. A drive to the top of Mount Lemmon has been compared to a drive from the Mexican border all the way to Canada, passing through desert, grassland, and mixed forests on the way up to an alpine region at the summit. There are many scenic pullouts along the route, but two in particular that you shouldn't miss: **Windy Point**, at mile 18, where you'll get a stupendous view of Tucson and the Santa Cruz valley, and **Aspen Vista Point**, at mile 27, near the top of the mountain, where you'll get extraordinary

Catalina Highway, Mount Lemmon, Tucson, Arizona

Next page: Wildflower season in Saguaro National Park

views looking off to the north toward the towns of San Manuel and Mammoth and the mountains beyond. The road ends at **Summerhaven,** a popular vacation retreat from the summer heat in the desert below.

Just before Summerhaven, you can take a right on Ski Run Road, which takes you a bit farther up the mountain to **Mount Lemmon Ski Valley**. The skiing in winter is hit or miss, but the lift operates year round, and you'll get great views from the top of the run. As you drive back down the mountain, watch your speed and keep a sharp eye out for cyclists, as many of them like to ride the centerline as they fly down the hill.

> ### Catalina Highway Highlights
>
> **Mt. Lemmon Science Tour App**
> visittucson.org/mtlemmonsciencetour
>
> **Mount Lemmon Ski Valley**
> 10300 Ski Run Road, Mount Lemmon, AZ 85619
> (520) 576-1321
> skithelemmon.com

Saguaro blossoms, Saguaro National Park, Tucson, Arizona

SAGUARO NATIONAL PARK EAST

At the bottom of the mountain, continue on Catalina Highway until you reach Houghton Road. Turn left and follow Houghton about 6 miles south to Old Spanish Trail. Turn left again, and the road will lead you straight into the eastern section of **Saguaro National Park.**

Established in 1933, the park now encompasses more than 91,000 acres of pristine desert habitat where 25 species of cacti flourish, including tens of thousands of saguaros. The park is divided into two sections 30 miles apart and on opposite sides of Tucson. At 67,000 acres, this eastern section, called the Rincon Mountain District, is the larger of the two; it is also at a slightly higher elevation,

The Saguaro Cactus

The majestic saguaro cactus, with its upraised arms, standing sentinel against the desert sky, is one of the most enduring symbols of the Southwest. Some of the big ones are 200 years old; they can grow to a height of 70 feet or more and weigh as much as 8 tons. Their shallow root systems soak up the infrequent rain like gigantic sponges, swelling the accordion-like pleats of the trunk and branches to store precious moisture against lean times, when the desert can go months with no rain at all. In May and June, each upright arm produces a cluster of large, creamy-white flowers; the resulting sweet, red fruit is an important food source not only for wildlife, but also for the Native Americans.

For the Tohono O'odham, the desert people, the annual harvest of the saguaro fruit is still one of the most important events of the year. Using a tool made from the ribs of dead saguaros, they pluck the fruit from clusters high overhead. The best specimens are eaten on the spot; the pulp from the rest is scraped into buckets and hauled back to the village, where it is boiled and strained and rendered into syrup. Once the seeds are removed, the dried pulp is added back into the syrup to make jam. The seeds are sweet when chewed, almost like candy; they can also be used as chicken feed or ground into meal. Some of the syrup is made into saguaro fruit wine, which is imbibed in ceremonies marking the onset of the monsoon rains in early July. The Tohono O'odham believe the saguaros were once human. When you've seen enough of them, each so different from every other, it's easy to see how that belief came to be.

The range of these mighty cacti is limited to portions of the Sonoran Desert in Arizona, northern Mexico, and southeast California; they grow best in and around Tucson.

Desert in bloom, Saguaro National Park, Tucson, Arizona

cooler, and wetter, and the cacti are a bit more spread out. Follow Cactus Forest Drive, an 8-mile loop through some of the most extraordinary desert vegetation on the planet. If you come in the spring, from March until about mid-May, you'll see the desert come alive with wildflowers, a tapestry in yellow, gold, scarlet, and pale blue.

THE AERONAUTICS CORRIDOR

Leaving Saguaro National Park, follow Old Spanish Trail back to Houghton Road, and turn left. When you reach Irvington Road, turn right, and take that to Kolb Road. Here, you're passing through **Davis-Mon-than Air Force Base**, headquarters of

"Cactus Conversation," Saguaro National Park, Tucson, Arizona

AMARG Aircraft Boneyard, Davis Monthan AFB, Tucson, Arizona

the 355th Fighter Wing and the home of AMARG, the Aerospace Maintenance and Regeneration Group, otherwise known as "The Boneyard." On both sides of the road, you'll see aircraft of every description lined up in rows that go on for miles. This is the place where military aircraft go to die, or perhaps to be reborn, rebuilt, or recycled as parts. The dry desert climate preserves them perfectly.

Take Kolb south to Valencia Road, turn right, and after a couple of blocks you'll come to the **Pima Air & Space Museum**. This 80-acre site has more than 300 old aircraft on display, from a Wright Flyer to a 787 Dreamliner and almost everything in between. There are fighter jets with belligerent monikers like Super Sabre, Fury, Thunder Flash, and Vigilante. There are workhorse helicopters like the Army Mule and the Flying Box Car. Among the favorite exhibits: one-of-a-kind wonders like the Hoppicopter, a prototype for a one-man backpack helicopter that, sadly, was never produced.

A limited number of bus tours start at the museum and cross the road to the military base, where they drive through portions of the AMARG Boneyard. It's a dream come true for serious aviation buffs.

Aeronautics Corridor Highlights

Pima Air & Space Museum
6000 E. Valencia Road, Tucson, AZ 85756
(520) 574-0462
pimaair.org

SAN XAVIER DEL BAC

Leaving the museum, travel west on Valencia, crossing under Interstate 10. Just past the airport, turn left (south) on Sixth Avenue, which will become San Xavier Road. You'll see the white stucco mission in the distance well before you reach it.

Eusebio Francisco Kino, the Jesuit missionary and explorer, founded the first Catholic mission in the lands of the present-day Tohono O'odham Indians (formerly called the Papago), in 1692. The original building, on the banks of the Santa Cruz River, was razed by marauding Apaches in 1770. The church built to replace it, the church you can still see today, was completed in 1797, built entirely by native laborers and craftsmen from the surrounding community. Known as the White Dove of the Desert, San Xavier del Bac is widely considered the finest example of Spanish Colonial architecture anywhere in the United States. The church and mission have been extensively restored, beginning with the brightly colored, ornate interior. Work on the exterior of the building is ongoing, and is nearly complete.

Saint Kateri Tekakwitha, San Xavier del Bac Mission

There is no charge to enter the church, which contains many fine examples of religious statuary, including a wooden figure of Saint Kateri Tekakwitha, the first Native American saint in the Roman Catholic Church. The

San Xavier Del Bac Highlights

Mission San Xavier del Bac
1950 W. San Xavier Road, Tucson, AZ 85746
(520) 294-2624
sanxaviermission.org

interior walls are covered with frescoes and other paintings depicting saints and angels and scenes from the Bible. The mission is still very much in use by the local native community, and is an important pilgrimage site for Catholics throughout the region; enter with respect, and note that photography is not allowed during services.

The White Dove is as photogenic as a building could ever be, especially during the summer monsoons, when the sky behind the church is filled with fabulous clouds. There are several stories explaining why the east tower of the church is unfinished; some say a tornado blew

San Xavier Del Bac Mission, Tucson, Arizona

the top off, others cite a tax advantage for unfinished buildings. The real reason is simpler: the original builders ran out of money, and later generations elected to just leave it undone.

THE WESTERN DESERT AND MOUNTAIN ROADS

Leaving the mission, continue west on San Xavier Road to South Mission and turn right. Take Mission 5 miles north to AZ 86, Ajo Way, and follow that 4 miles west to South Kinney Road. Turn right, and after another 5 miles you'll come to **Old Tucson.**

This reconstruction of an Old West town started out as a movie set, built in 1939 for the Hollywood film *Ari-*

zona, starring William Holden. Since then, more than 300 movies and television shows have been filmed here, including John Wayne's classic *Rio Bravo* and the classic TV series *Death Valley Days*. When it's not being used as a stage set, the operators offer living-history presentations, historical tours, and Western-themed entertainment. Check locally for hours and days of operation; you're most likely to find it open on weekends, particularly during the winter tourist season.

Leaving Old Tucson, return to Kinney Road and continue northwest, 3 more miles to the **Arizona-Sonora Desert Museum.** The "museum" is actually a world-class zoo and botanical garden that also houses an aquarium, a natural history museum, and an art gallery—all focused on the wildlife and vegetation of the Sonoran Desert. Walking trails take you through the 98-acre complex, which has exhibits showcasing 230 species of animals and more than 1,200 varieties of plants. This is no ordinary zoo. There are few cages. Instead, the animals live in habitats built to mimic their native ecosystems. There's a walk-in aviary, where you'll get an up close look at roadrunners, cactus wrens, and nearly 40 other species of native birds. There's a separate aviary just for hummingbirds; you can get close enough to feel the whir in the air from their wings, like a whisper against your cheek. The museum is set in one of the most beautiful tracts of desert in Arizona, lush with saguaros, ocotillos, prickly pears, chollas, and barrels.

Leaving the Desert Museum, continue on Kinney just a few more miles to the western portion of **Saguaro National Park**, a 24,000-acre preserve. The giant saguaros are more crowded here, covering the hillsides like a forest of leafless trees. Follow the **Bajada Loop**, a series of graded, unpaved roads that lead you on a

counterclockwise tour through the park. If it's near the end of the day, take the opportunity to photograph a classic scene: saguaros standing tall against a fiery desert sky, with those majestic mountains on the horizon, casting purple shadows in the twilight.

Leaving the national park, head back the way you came on Kinney Road (look sharp—you'll need to make a quick left off Sandario to get back on Kinney after you exit the Bajada Loop). Retrace the route you came in on for 6.7 miles to **Gates Pass Road**, just north of Old Tucson. Turn east here and head back toward Tucson.

Gates Pass Road crosses through the Tucson Mountains. There's a scenic overlook with a parking area close to the top of the pass. From there, you'll have an expansive view of the open desert and distant mountains to the west. When that sky is filled with clouds, the setting sun sets the whole scene ablaze. If night has already fallen, you'll see a panorama of city lights in the east.

Western Desert Highlights

Old Tucson
201 S. Kinney Road, Tucson, AZ 85735
(520) 883-0100
oldtucson.com

Arizona-Sonora Desert Museum
2021 N. Kinney Road, Tucson, AZ 85743
(520) 883-2702
desertmuseum.org

Saguaro National Park West
2700 N. Kinney Road, Tucson, Arizona 85743
(520) 733-5153
nps.gov/sagu

TUCSON AND BEYOND

Leaving the overlook, drive east back into the city. Gates Pass Road will turn into Speedway, one of Tucson's major crosstown boulevards. Speedway will return you to Interstate 10, ending this route just 10 miles from where it began.

Tucson is a major destination, with many choices for dining and lodging. One nice hotel is the **Arizona Inn**, which offers casita-style rooms and suites on 14 landscaped acres in a quiet residential area. The property dates to the 1930s, and it is elegant without being pretentious.

If you're headed on to Phoenix and points north,

Interstate 10 will get you to the city in less than 2 hours; alternatively, you can take **Scenic Side Trip 8** through Florence. If you're traveling on to New Mexico and points east, you can take I-10 east all the way; alternatively, you can reverse the itinerary for **Scenic Side Trip 6**; that will take you down along I-19 to the Mexican border and through the Huachuca Mountains before bringing you back to I-10 in Benson.

Saguaro National Park, Tucson, Arizona

Tucson Highlights

Arizona Inn
2200 E. Elm St.,
Tucson, AZ 85719
(520) 325-1541
arizonainn.com

Tucson to Phoenix

via Biosphere 2, Pinal Pioneer Parkway, Casa Grande, Mesa, Tempe, and Scottsdale

160 miles, **5** hours and **15** minutes for drive time, more for optional routes, stops, and sightseeing

Mixing it up on the Pinal Pioneer Parkway, the fastest road in the West

THERE'S A LONG-STANDING FANTASY IN ARIZONA, A VISION OF A future in which Phoenix and Tucson, the state's two largest population centers, one day grow so big that they merge into one huge megalopolis spread out along the Interstate 10 corridor. There are several reasons why that will never happen, but the deal breaker is the scarcity of water in the desert region that lies between the two cities. ⏩

This isn't the most beautiful part of the state, certainly not since the big, wide freeway came through and flattened all the surrounding vegetation, but the worst thing about the 90-mile stretch of Interstate between Tucson and Phoenix is the traffic. It's not stop-and-go congested, not when you're out in the open country, but it's one of the busiest commercial transportation corridors in the state, with a constant stream of 18-wheelers running in both directions, 24 hours a day. It can also be deadly. In fact, in terms of traffic deaths per mile, I-10 through Arizona is one of the most dangerous highways in the United States.

Is there a better route? Of course. This one will double the miles and triple the time required, but if you've never been this way before, you'll find it well worth your while.

BIOSPHERE 2

The first stop is perhaps the strangest: the futuristic science experiment called **Biosphere 2,** located about 32 miles north of Tucson outside the town of Oracle. To get there from Interstate 10, take the Miracle Mile exit in central Tucson and go east 1 mile to Oracle Road (AZ 77). Turn left on Oracle and stay on it, north through the city, past the Catalina foothills and on through the sprawling suburb of Oro Valley. When you

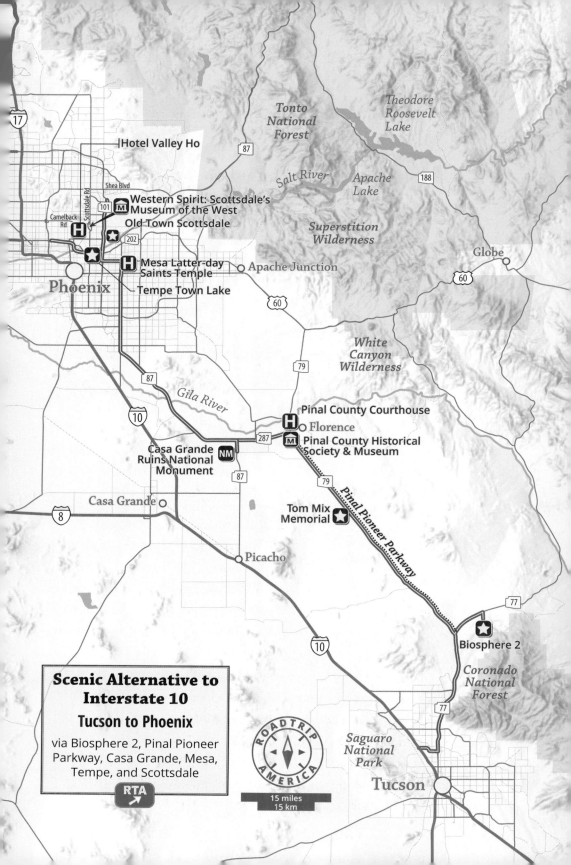

17

Hotel Valley Ho

Shea Blvd

Western Spirit: Scottsdale's
Museum of the West

101

Old Town Scottsdale

Camelback
Rd

H

Scottsdale Rd

202

H

Mesa Latter-day
Saints Temple

Phoenix

Tempe Town Lake

Tonto
National
Forest

87

Salt River

Apache
Lake

Theodore
Roosevelt
Lake

188

Superstition
Wilderness

Globe

Apache Junction

60

60

White
Canyon
Wilderness

87

Gila River

79

10

287

Pinal County Courthouse

H

Florence

M

Pinal County Historical
Society & Museum

Casa Grande
Ruins National
Monument

NM

87

79

Casa Grande

8

Tom Mix
Memorial

Pinal Pioneer Parkway

Picacho

77

10

Biosphere 2

Coronado
National
Forest

Scenic Alternative to Interstate 10

Tucson to Phoenix

via Biosphere 2, Pinal Pioneer
Parkway, Casa Grande, Mesa,
Tempe, and Scottsdale

ROADTRIP
AMERICA

RTA

Saguaro
National
Park

77

Tucson

15 miles
15 km

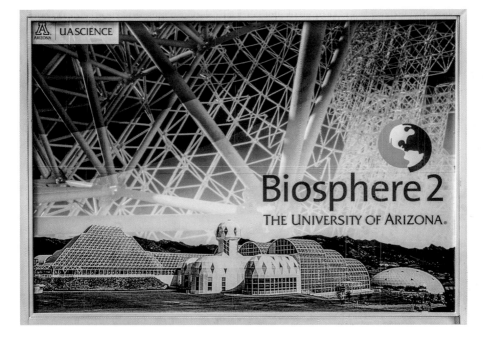

reach Oracle Junction, continue on AZ 77 about 5.5 miles to Biosphere Road. The Biosphere 2 complex is tucked in behind some hills, out of sight and well back from the highway. Follow the signs to the parking area.

Biosphere 2 was quite a bold experiment when it was first proposed, back in the late 1980s. An outfit called Space Biospheres Ventures, a private research firm backed by investors with very deep pockets, built a 3-acre complex of interconnected geodesic domes and greenhouses and sealed it, airtight, to create a "closed environment." The big idea: to create a self-sustaining habitat completely isolated from the outside world, simulating the challenges that colonists would encounter on another planet, such as Mars. A small team of scientists would conduct research inside the facility, cut off from the outside world for months or years at a time, recycling all the station's air and water, and producing all the food and energy the team and the resident plants and animals required for the duration of the experiment.

Biosphere 2 was the largest closed system ever constructed, and it was extraordinarily complex, supporting several miniature life zones including farmland, grassland, a mangrove swamp, a fog desert, a rainforest, and a tiny ocean with a coral reef—all of it interconnected and intensively monitored, providing a wealth of data to researchers. In 1992, a team of eight scientists was sealed into the complex and began Mission 1, which ran two full years. Mistakes were made, some of them critical, and the results were too equivocal to be of any real value. A second mission, begun in 1994, ended in disarray after just six months, and the investors pulled the plug. Rather than tear down the facility, the owners leased it to Columbia University for research into global warming. In 2007, they sold it outright to the University of Arizona, which now conducts research here on climate change and the terrestrial water cycle—very important work in the drought-plagued desert Southwest.

Biosphere 2 is open daily for tours, and since it's no longer a closed system, you can see it all. If you're on a budget or a tight schedule, you can skip the tour and watch an interesting video at the visitors center, free of charge. And, of course, you can see Biosphere 1 any time you'd like, also free of charge. Biosphere 1 is our very own Planet Earth.

Biosphere 2 Highlights

Biosphere 2
32540 S. Biosphere Road, Oracle, AZ 85623
(520) 838-6200
biosphere2.org

PINAL PIONEER PARKWAY

Leaving Biosphere 2, retrace your route to Oracle Junction, where AZ 77 intersects AZ 79. Bear right to take AZ 79 toward Florence. This section of road, officially designated the **Pinal Pioneer Parkway**, is more generally known as "the back road" from Tucson to Phoenix. It runs roughly parallel to I-10, just a few miles farther east, but it offers quite a different experience. The desert here

is neither overgrazed nor flattened, but rather lush with
mesquite and paloverde trees, creosote and brittlebush,
tall saguaros, and at least a dozen other varieties of cacti.
Rimmed by distant purple mountains, this is some of the
nicest desert terrain in the state, and AZ 79 is the perfect
route for cruising through it—flat, straight, and smooth,
with little traffic. If you find yourself tempted to push
that 65 mph speed limit, you won't be alone. In 2011,
the fastest 5 percent of the vehicles using this stretch
were clocked at an average speed of
88 mph, making the Pinal Pioneer
Parkway, during that time period at
least, the fastest road not just in the
West, but in the entire country.

   A word of warning. If you
stop alongside this road, don't go

*Pinal Pioneer
Parkway, Arizona*

Pinal Pioneer Parkway Highlights

Pinal County Courthouse
135 N. Pinal St., Florence, AZ 85132

Pinal County Historical Society & Museum
715 S. Main St., Florence, AZ 85132
(520) 868-4382
pinalcountyhistoricalmuseum.org

Cholla cactus, Saguaro National Park, Tucson, Arizona

Tom Mix Memorial, Arizona Route 79

anywhere near the cacti called **cholla** (pronounced *choy-ah*). There are several species, all bearing clusters of small branches covered with seemingly delicate white spines. You'll see a lot of broken-off bits of it lying on the ground. They call this stuff "jumping cactus." You don't want to find out why. That goes double if you're traveling with a dog.

Between mile markers 115 and 116, you'll come to the **Tom Mix Memorial** on the west side of the highway. Back in the silent-film era, Tom Mix was the ultimate screen cowboy, star of more than 300 Western movies and, at one time, the highest-paid actor in Hollywood. On an October day in 1940, when Mix was 60 years old, he was driving his yellow Cord Phaeton convertible down this road at a high rate of speed. Even in those days, it was a fast road. The Cord blew past a construction barricade, and Mix failed to stop it before it flew into a sandy wash and rolled. The legendary cowboy died at the scene. His memorial consists of a stone pillar crowned by a riderless horse. As with many metal signs in the desert Southwest, the black iron silhouette of Tom Mix's horse has been shot full of holes by vandals using it for target practice.

Pinal Pioneer Parkway terminates in **Florence**, a historic Arizona town founded in 1866 on the banks of the Gila River, back in the days when there was still water flowing in it this far west. The rich diggings at the nearby Silver King Mine spurred settlement of the area, but it was the river—and the water it supplied to irrigate crops—that prompted settlers to stay. There's still a little bit of farming and ranching going on in Florence, but these days the big business in town is incarceration. Today Florence is home to two state-run prisons, four privately operated prisons, and a county jail. As you drive into town from the south, you'll see miles of tall fencing topped with razor wire, a grim testament to 15,000 lives gone wrong. The silver lining: decent-paying jobs for hundreds of corrections workers facing a tough local economy.

The old downtown area of Florence is very cool, with 25 buildings of historical significance, including the **Pinal County Courthouse**, a well-preserved Victorian building dating to 1891. Just don't set your watch by the clock in the tower. When they were building the court-house, they ran out of money, so instead of installing an actual clock, they just painted a clock face on each side.

Pinal County Courthouse, Florence, Arizona; "It's still 11:44 in Florence."

Time has stood still ever since. More than 100 years later, it's still (and always will be) 11:44 in Florence.

Also of interest: the **Pinal County Historical Museum**, which has a number of intriguing exhibits related to the history of the area.

CASA GRANDE

Leaving Florence, head south on Main Street to the intersection with AZ 287, the Florence-Coolidge Highway, and follow that west for 8 miles to Arizona Boulevard. From there, follow the signs for **Casa Grande Ruins National Monument**, the first U.S. archaeological site to be protected as a historical preserve. Here you will see the timeworn, unreconstructed remains of a compact four-story structure built about 700 years ago from blocks of caliche, a dense, mineral-rich soil that is tougher than adobe. In 1932, the Park Service erected a large steel canopy over the ruin, supported by four big concrete pillars, to protect it from further erosion. It's such an incongruous combination: the obviously ancient building rising from the desert floor, and squatting above it, looking for all the world like an alien spacecraft

*Casa Grande
Ruins National
Monument*

on stilts, is this massive metal roof. Few people living today have ever seen the Casa Grande without that roof, which has by now become as much a part of the national monument as the ruin it was built to protect.

Casa Grande is the last surviving Hohokam "Great House," a ceremonial center built by the desert-dwelling people who lived here along the Salt and Gila rivers from about AD 300 to AD 1450. Their culture was complex and far-reaching. The people built an extensive system of canals, wells, and cisterns that brought water to their crops, sustaining life in this arid region where months can pass without rain. They traded goods to tribes in California and south into Mexico; they built a ball court for a game that originated in Mesoamerica; and they made sophisticated celestial calculations. Openings in the walls of the Great House align with the sun and moon during important celestial events, including the solstices, just as they do in many ancient pyramids in Mexico and Central America.

These early Sonoran Desert people abandoned the area several hundred years before the Spanish arrived on the scene. They built few lasting monuments, had no system of writing, and their oral traditions faded with their culture, making the Casa Grande a very important piece in a prehistoric puzzle. Archaeologists have been working for many decades to unlock its secrets. A small museum at the visitors center provides an interesting overview of what little we know for certain.

West of the national monument, AZ 287 becomes AZ 87. You'll pass the road to Sacaton, a small town at the center of the Gila River Indian Reservation. These are the ancestral lands of the Akimel O'odham, the River People, formerly known as the Pimas, who many believe are descended from the ancients who built the Casa Grande.

Casa Grande Highlights

Casa Grande Ruins National Monument
1100 W. Ruins Drive, Coolidge, AZ 85128
(520) 723-3172
nps.gov/cagr

THE EAST VALLEY: MESA, TEMPE, AND SCOTTSDALE

Beyond the Sacaton turnoff, follow AZ 87 north. Just over the reservation border, you enter the Phoenix metropolitan area. The change is dramatic. On one side of the road there's open desert, and on the other, 9,000 square miles of suburban neighborhoods and strip malls, home to 4.5 million people.

Stay on AZ 87 for 15 more miles, through the East Valley community of Chandler and on into **Mesa**. Founded by Mormon pioneers from Utah, sent here by their church in 1877, Mesa is now the third-largest city in Arizona. The Mormon Church still has a strong presence in the city, and its **Mesa Temple**, completed in 1927, is an important religious monument, one of the first Mormon temples built outside Utah. If you'd like to see the lovely neoclassical building, turn right off AZ 87 at First Avenue. The temple is a mile east, at LeSueur Street; note that only qualified Mormons may enter the temple itself.

Go back to AZ 87 (Country Club Drive), turn right, and drive north into the town of **Tempe**. At University Drive, turn left and head west across the sprawling campus of **Arizona State University**. When you reach Rural Road, turn right, and follow it north to Rio Salado Parkway. From there, follow the signs to **Tempe Town Lake.** Here a 2-mile-long section of the normally dry Salt River has been dammed and filled with nearly a billion gallons of water. This 220-acre reservoir, which averages 12.5 feet deep, is a happening place, the centerpiece of an urban recreational area offering bike paths, picnic areas, a baseball stadium, an amphitheater, boat and paddleboard rentals, and playgrounds for kids. The lake is stocked with

East Valley Highlights

Mesa Latter-day Saints Temple
101 S. LeSueur St., Mesa, AZ 85204
(480) 833-1211
ldschurchtemples.org/mesa/

Tempe Town Lake
tempe.gov

Old Town Scottsdale
Scottsdale Road between Osborn Road and Camelback Road
downtownscottsdale.com

Western Spirit: Scottsdale's Museum of the West
3830 N. Marshall Way, Scottsdale, AZ 85251
(480) 686-9539
scottsdalemuseumwest.org

LDS Mesa Temple,
Mesa, Arizona

rainbow trout (license required for fishermen 14 and older).

Head north over the bridge that crosses the lake, and you'll be in **Scottsdale**, the community that's synonymous with high-end Southwest living. Back in the 1950s, Scottsdale was a sleepy Phoenix suburb. To draw in more of the winter tourist trade, the city billed itself as "The West's Most Western Town," promoting a cowboys-and-Indians ambience that included boardwalks and cheesy Western souvenir shops. That early phase of Scottsdale history can still be seen in **Old Town Scottsdale**, the area along Scottsdale Road from Osborn north to Camelback Road, though the shops are quite a bit more upscale now than they used to be. Along Fifth Avenue, in the heart of Old Scottsdale, you'll find dozens of art galleries and studios offering paintings and sculptures by famous Southwestern artists. Also in this area is **Western Spirit: Scottsdale's Museum of the West**, which opened in 2015. Western Spirit mounts rotating exhibits of art and artifacts related to the culture and

history of the entire American West.

The rest of Scottsdale, which extends for many miles to the north, is a community that prides itself on good living, fine dining, and world-class resorts. Since it was incorporated in 1951, the population of the West's most Western town has increased more than 100-fold to more than 230,000 today. Many are wealthy snowbirds from the East and Midwest who left the snow and ice one winter and never went back. Not *everyone* in the town is wealthy, but the per capita income in Scottsdale is nearly double the statewide average. And it's the only city in Arizona with a Rolls Royce dealership.

PHOENIX AND BEYOND

Leaving Scottsdale, take Scottsdale Road south to the Red Mountain Freeway, Loop 202. Turn right, and follow the Loop west to Interstate 10, and the end of this route.

Prices for lodging in the Phoenix area, particularly in Scottsdale, can easily double during the high season, November through April, when the weather comes close to perfection. During the rest of the year, May through October, daytime temperatures rarely dip below 100 degrees. If you can handle that kind of heat, you can get off-season bargains at most Phoenix-area resorts. One historic Scottsdale resort to consider, at any time of the year, is the **Hotel Valley Ho,** located in the arts district of Old Town, a property that dates to the 1950s and has that '50s charm.

Traveling north from Phoenix you have three routes to tempt you. **Scenic Side Trip 9** will take you to Flagstaff on a stupendous route through Arizona's canyon country west of I-17. **Scenic Side Trip 10** will take you to Flagstaff through the mountains east of I-17. Last but not least: **Scenic Side Trip 11** will take you to Holbrook, along the Apache Trail and through the Salt River Canyon.

Scottsdale Lodging

Hotel Valley Ho
6850 E. Main St.,
Scottsdale, AZ 85251
(480) 376-2600
hotelvalleyho.com

Part 2: Scenic Alternatives to Interstate 17

Interstate 17 connects I-10 with I-40 through central Arizona, beginning in Phoenix and ending in Flagstaff. Along the way, the road gains nearly 6,000 feet in elevation, rising from hot, dry desert to cool pine forest over the course of 146 miles. There are stunning mountain views and wide-open vistas along this highway, one of the prettiest stretches of Interstate anywhere in the country. Why would anyone want an alternative to such a beautiful road? One word: traffic!

Arizona and New Mexico have a combined population of 9 million people and *half* of them live in metropolitan Phoenix. During the hot months, which is nearly half the year, the high country around Flagstaff is 30 degrees cooler than Phoenix, and that's an attraction almost as powerful as gravity. Throughout the long summer, heat-exhausted desert dwellers pile into their cars by the tens of thousands and head north to escape the sizzle. The favorite escape route? Interstate 17. Like all Interstate Highways, the road was built to handle a high volume of traffic, but there are very few exits along most of this route, so if anything at all goes wrong—an accident, or even a breakdown that blocks a lane--chaos ensues.

Here are three Scenic Side Trips you can take instead. None of the roads are secret, so you won't miss the traffic altogether, but with so many amazing sights to see, you'll enjoy taking a slower pace. Two of the routes run roughly parallel to I-17, passing through the beautiful countryside and small towns that lie to the east and west of the highway. Both routes include sections of the Red Rock country outside Sedona, and both end at I-40 in Flagstaff. The third route follows rugged desert canyons north to the Petrified Forest and the Painted Desert, ending at I-40 in Holbrook.

All three routes put you in the way of "monsoon" thunderstorms from mid-June to mid-September, and the higher elevations are prone to snow in the winter; check road conditions locally before setting out. Along the Salt and Verde Rivers, and in Oak Creek Canyon, you'll see the golds and reds of autumn on prominent display in October and early November; in the desert valleys and mountain meadows, you'll see beautiful wildflowers in spring and summer, especially at higher elevations.

These routes are all sequenced for drivers headed north from Phoenix. If you are traveling the other way, just reverse the itinerary.

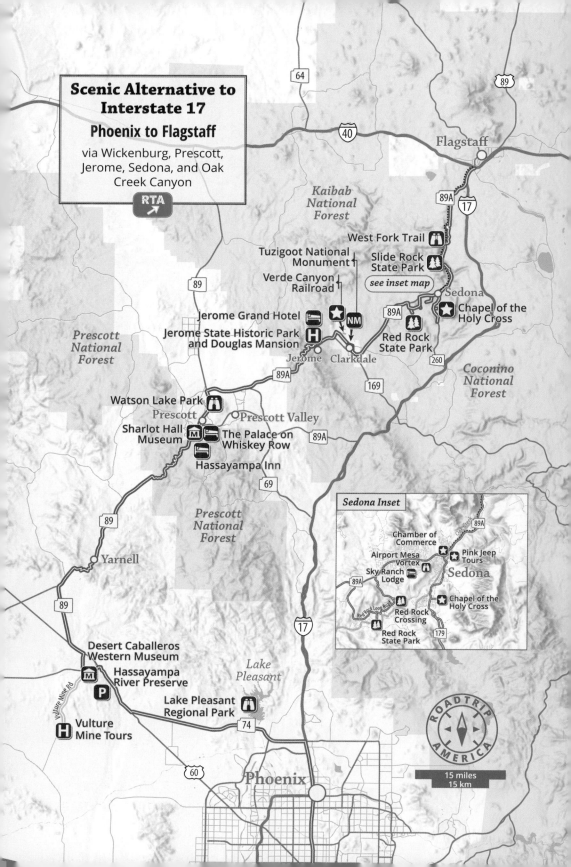

Scenic Alternative to Interstate 17

Phoenix to Flagstaff

via Wickenburg, Prescott, Jerome, Sedona, and Oak Creek Canyon

RTA

64

40

89

Kaibab National Forest

Flagstaff

89

89A

17

West Fork Trail

Tuzigoot National Monument †

Slide Rock State Park

Verde Canyon Railroad †

see inset map

Sedona

Jerome Grand Hotel

NM

89A

Chapel of the Holy Cross

Jerome State Historic Park and Douglas Mansion

Jerome   Clarkdale

Red Rock State Park

260

Prescott National Forest

169

Coconino National Forest

89A

Watson Lake Park

Prescott

Prescott Valley

Sharlot Hall Museum

M

The Palace on Whiskey Row

89A

Hassayampa Inn

69

Prescott National Forest

89

Sedona Inset

Oak Creek

89A

Chamber of Commerce

Airport Mesa Vortex

Pink Jeep Tours

Sky Ranch Lodge

Sedona

89A

Red Rock Loop Road

Chapel of the Holy Cross

Red Rock Crossing

Red Rock State Park

179

89

Yarnell

89

17

Lake Pleasant

Desert Caballeros Western Museum

M

Hassayampa River Preserve

P

Vulture Mine Rd

Lake Pleasant Regional Park

Vulture Mine Tours

74

ROADTRIP AMERICA

60

Phoenix

15 miles
15 km

Phoenix to Flagstaff

via Wickenburg, Prescott, Jerome, Sedona, and Oak Creek Canyon

257 miles, **8** hours and **15** minutes for drive time, more for optional routes, stops, and sightseeing

The wickedest town in the West is going downhill, fast!

THE FASTEST, MOST DIRECT ROUTE BETWEEN PHOENIX AND Flagstaff is the straight shot north on Interstate 17. This is one of the most beautiful sections of Interstate Highway in the entire Southwest, but it's also one of the most heavily traveled. Luckily, travelers with a few hours to spare have an incredibly scenic alternative. This route adds 75 miles and 4 hours to a trip between Phoenix and Flagstaff, but the drive north through Sedona and Oak Creek Canyon to the base of the San Francisco Peaks is well worth the extra time and distance. ➡➡

WICKENBURG

Leaving Phoenix, head north on I-17. Twenty-five miles north of the city center, take Exit 223B, the Carefree Highway (AZ 74), and head west. The landscape opens up rapidly here. Low, scrubby vegetation blends into desert, and Arizona's signature saguaro cacti appear, dotting the landscape. You'll pass the turnoff for Lake Pleasant Regional Park, a popular spot for picnicking, swimming, boating, and fishing. This stretch of road is heavily patrolled, so watch your speed as you drive 19 miles farther to the intersection with US 60, just north of Morristown. Turn right (north) toward Wickenburg.

Founded in 1863, **Wickenburg** dates back to the early days of the Arizona Territory, when a German prospector named Henry Wickenburg struck gold on a claim that later became the Vulture Mine, the richest gold mine in Arizona. Wickenburg's strike attracted other prospectors, and before long the area was overrun with gold seekers. The grasslands along the nearby Hassayampa River were perfect for grazing cattle, and there was water for crops, so cattlemen and farmers joined the prospectors and miners. By the end of the Civil War, Wickenburg was already a prosperous, rapidly growing community.

In 1913, a rancher looking for extra income opened the Garden of

Allah, a rustic hotel in a valley south of town that offered a real Wild West experience to city slickers. The guests slept in bunkhouses, ate meals cooked over a campfire, rode horses, and even herded cattle in the company of real cowboys. The concept was wildly popular and started a bit of a craze. Before long there were more than half a dozen of these establishments surrounding the town, and Wickenburg proclaimed itself to be "The Dude Ranch Capital of the World."

The Garden of Allah is long gone, but part of the old ranch is now the **Hassayampa River Preserve**, which features a spring-fed lake and a visitors center run by the Nature Conservancy. The Hassayampa flows underground beneath the desert for more than 100 miles, emerging at this spot, a riparian desert oasis popular with migratory birds and bird lovers; the preserve lists 291 species on its bird checklist, nearly a third of all species in the U.S. The turnoff is at mile marker 114 on US 60.

In downtown Wickenburg, the **Desert Caballeros Western Museum** offers an interesting glimpse into the history of the area, and the **Vulture Gold Mine**, which suspended commercial operations back in the 1940s, is open for tours.

Leaving Wickenburg, merge onto US 93 toward Kingman. At the junction with AZ 89, bear right toward Congress and Prescott. Beyond the town of Congress, the road starts to climb up into the Weaver Mountains. Known locally as the White Spar Highway, this stretch is one of the most popular motorcycle routes in Arizona. The highway is divided through the section that includes Elephant Curve—a good thing as motorists need to keep to their lane through the road's extraordinary twists and turns.

Wickenburg Highlights

Hassayampa River Preserve
49614 US 60, Wickenburg, AZ 85390
(928) 684-2772

Desert Caballeros Western Museum
21 N. Frontier St., Wickenburg, AZ 85390
(928) 684-2772
westernmuseum.org

Vulture Mine Tours
36610 N. 355th Ave., Wickenburg, AZ 85390
vultureminetours.com

Past the tiny town of Wilhoit, you will navigate some wild hairpin curves as the road climbs up Yarnell Hill. As you come up on the town of Yarnell, you will enter a tragic landscape. Look left and you will see scars from the 2013 wildfire that claimed the lives of 19 members of the Granite Mountain Hotshots, an elite firefighting crew that was overrun by the blaze. Look right and you'll see nothing out of the ordinary—and yet, this too was the scene of a disaster. In 1890, the Walnut Grove dam collapsed near here, unleashing 9.8 billion gallons of water, killing scores of farmers, ranchers, and camp workers in the valley downstream. Fire and water are potent forces in Arizona, and you'll often see their effects as you travel these roads. Beyond Yarnell, the road climbs far above the desert floor, into a mountainous ecosystem of temperate pine forests. Prescott, a town of nearly 40,000, stands at 5,400 feet, where the average temperatures are 20 degrees cooler than in Phoenix.

PRESCOTT

Named for historian W. H. Prescott, **Prescott** served as the first territorial capital, when Arizona formally separated from New Mexico in 1863. Wonderful old brick buildings ring the town square, and many beautifully restored Victorian-era homes grace the older neighborhoods.

The Yavapai County Courthouse has stood, essentially unchanged, for more than 100 years, anchoring the Courthouse Square at the center of town. On the west side of that square is Whiskey Row, a section of Montezuma Street that's been known for its raucous bars since frontier days. **The Palace**, once patronized by the likes of Wyatt Earp and Doc Holliday, is the oldest

Yavapai County Courthouse

continuously operating saloon in Arizona. The long, carved wooden bar is the original, and the artwork on the walls is worth the stop. If art and history are of interest, head to the **Sharlot Hall Museum**, one of the best history museums in Arizona, located on Gurley Street, just two blocks west of the square. The historic and still elegant **Hassayampa Inn** is a great hotel if you elect to stay overnight.

Leaving Prescott, follow Gurley Street east from the Courthouse Square, keeping left to stay on AZ 89 when it splits to the north from AZ 69. Just outside Prescott, scenic **Watson Lake Park** offers boating, fishing, hiking, and picnicking. It's part of a larger natural area known as the Granite Dells, a unique setting of granite boulders

Prescott Highlights

The Palace on Whiskey Row
120 S. Montezuma St., Prescott, AZ 86303
(928) 541-1996
historicpalace.com

Sharlot Hall Museum
415 W. Gurley St., Prescott, AZ 86301
(928) 445-3122
sharlot.org

Hassayampa Inn
122 E. Gurley St., Prescott, AZ 86301
(928) 778-9434
hassayampainn.com

Watson Lake Park
3101 Watson Lake Road, Prescott, AZ 86301
(928) 777-1122

surrounded by water that's a favorite of photographers; you can rent a canoe or kayak to get just the right shot. After about 4 miles, take a right onto AZ 89A, the Pioneer Parkway. AZ 89A will be your route all the rest of the way to Flagstaff, so when it splits from Pioneer Parkway toward Jerome, stay on it.

JEROME

Once known as "The Billion Dollar Copper Camp," Jerome was built on the site of one of the richest copper ore deposits that has ever been found. It's high up on the slopes of Mingus Mountain, and to get to it you'll have to negotiate hairpin switchbacks that make the curves on Yarnell Hill seem tame. The higher you climb, the better

Watson Lake Park

the view of Verde Valley, almost 2,000 feet below, but if you're doing the driving, keep your eyes on the road!

The town comes at you all at once. You drive around one last curve, and there it is: four parallel streets carved like steep stair steps into the side of Cleopatra Hill. Today, Jerome is a ramshackle perch of a ghost town. Some of it has been restored, and people do still live here, but most of the place is falling into ruin. Some structures in the lowest street, including the old town jail, are actually sliding, very slowly, down the mountainside, giving rise to the popular civic motto: "Jerome, a town on the move!"

Jerome wasn't abandoned until the mine closed for good in 1952, but the boom times were almost half a century earlier, in the early 1900s, when as many as 15,000 people lived and worked here. Space was at such a premium that miners slept three to a tiny single room, in rotating shifts of 8 hours each. To serve the needs of all those hardworking men, downtown Jerome was

Highway 89A on Mingus Mountain near Jerome

a festering mess of brothels, saloons, and gambling halls—so many that the *New York Sun* declared Jerome to be "The Wickedest Town in the West." Meanwhile, up the hill, mine owner James ("Rawhide Jimmy") Douglas courted investors in his adobe mansion, which boasted a wine cellar, a billiards room, steam heat, and a central vacuum system. Newly restored in celebration of its 100th anniversary, the Douglas Mansion is open to visitors in **Jerome State Historic Park**.

Today, with a population of less than 500, Jerome is far more sedate. It's long been a magnet for free-spirited artists and craftsmen, and the downtown is filled with an eclectic mix of boutiques, galleries, shops, and restaurants that cater to the tourist trade. A favorite place to stay is the **Jerome Grand Hotel**, which is widely believed to be haunted. The hotel hosts a popular evening ghost tour, which includes the use of infrared cameras and other ghostbuster equipment, along with fascinating commentary about the wicked ways of the old mining town.

Jerome Highlights

Jerome State Historic Park and Douglas Mansion
100 Douglas Road, Jerome, AZ 86331
(928) 634-5381
azstateparks.com/jerome

Jerome Grand Hotel
200 Hill St., Jerome, AZ 86331
(928) 634-8200

VERDE VALLEY

Leaving Jerome, follow AZ 89A down the mountain to the Verde Valley communities of Clarkdale, Cottonwood, and Cornville, all worth a closer look. Clarkdale has the **Tuzigoot National Monument**, an interesting pueblo ruin atop a hill just above the town. The pueblo was built by the Sinagua people, Spanish for "without water," in reference to the arid terrain in which they thrived for nearly a thousand years. Built in AD 1125, Tuzigoot was home to a clan of peaceful Sinagua farmers for nearly 300 years.

Clarkdale is also the home of the **Verde Canyon Railroad**, a heritage railroad with restored vintage rail cars. The railroad runs on 20 miles of track through a

Verde Valley Highlights

Tuzigoot National Monument
25 Tuzigoot Road,
Clarkdale, AZ 86324
(928) 634-5564
nps.gov/tuzi

Verde Canyon Railroad
300 N. Broadway,
Clarkdale, AZ 86324
(800) 582-7245
verdecanyonrr.com

remote and pristine canyon, a place where this railroad is the only road. The round-trip journey takes about 4 hours, and offers a range of accommodations, from First Class to Caboose. If you're a wine lover, stop in Cornville, the center of the fledgling Verde Valley wine industry and the site of more than a dozen vineyards and wineries, most with tasting rooms. Several are clustered on Page Springs Road.

SEDONA

Verde Valley is the gateway to the red rock country of Sedona, second only to the Grand Canyon in popularity with visitors to Arizona. Surrounded by reddish-orange sandstone buttes with names like Coffee Pot, Bell Rock, Snoopy's Belly, and Courthouse Rock, Sedona has a landscape like none you've ever seen. The red color comes from a high concentration of iron in the sandstone—so much of it that the rocks are literally rusting. For an up close view of the beautiful formations, check out **Red Rock State Park**, easily accessible off Red Rock Loop Road, which intersects AZ 89A on its way into Sedona

Red Rock Crossing, Sedona

from Cottonwood. The park has a visitors center and access to several popular hiking trails. A couple of miles farther along Red Rock Loop Road, follow the signs to Red Rock Crossing and the **Crescent Moon Picnic Area**, a green and tranquil spot with several nice walking trails. Kids will enjoy splashing in the creek, and the view of Oak Creek

Red rock country, Sedona

Veni, Vidi, Vortex

The red rocks of Sedona have long been an inspiration to artists and photographers, but in more recent years, Sedona has developed a reputation as a haven for seekers of another sort. Devotees of the New Age movement have flocked to the area, convinced that there are forces at work here that enhance spiritual awareness. If you're curious about that, consider visiting one of the four nearby "vortex" sites: concentration points for a rare form of energy, said to impart a unique sense of well-being.

   Stop at the Sedona Chamber of Commerce for information and to purchase a **Red Rock Pass**, which you'll need to park your car anywhere in the area (even alongside the road). Then take AZ 89A back toward Cottonwood and follow the signs for the tiny **Sedona Airport**, located atop flat-topped Airport Mesa at the edge of town. As you drive up the hill, look for a parking area on your left, about a half mile up from the highway; you'll need that Red Rock Pass to park there. A short trail leads to Airport Overlook, a great scenic viewpoint. Another trail leads farther upward, to the **Sedona Airport Vortex**, a flat area in the saddle of the red rock ridge, just behind the parking area. The vortex energy has been variously described as a resonance, a subtle tingling, and "Earth breathing"— always with a calming effect. Whether you feel any of that or not, the spectacular view is well worth the short climb.

   Another popular drive: Take AZ 179 from downtown Sedona to the Village of Oak Creek, then turn around and come back. You won't regret driving this mostly divided road twice; the scenery along the 7-mile stretch is stunning. Of special interest: the **Chapel of the Holy Cross**, a Roman Catholic church built into the red rock buttes, and **Bell Rock**, another spectacular formation and the site of another energy vortex. The entire area around Bell Rock is said to be positively charged!

Chapel of the Holy Cross, Sedona

Sedona & Oak Creek Canyon Highlights

Red Rock State Park
4050 Red Rock Loop Road, Sedona, AZ 86336
(928) 282-6907
azstateparks.com/red-rock

Sedona Chamber of Commerce
331 Forest Road, Sedona, AZ 86336
(928) 282-7722

Chapel of the Holy Cross
780 Chapel Road, Sedona, AZ 86336
(888) 242-7359
chapeloftheholycross.com

Pink Jeep Tours
204 AZ 89A, Sedona, AZ 86336
(844) 225-7465
pinkjeeptourssedona.com

Sky Ranch Lodge
1105 Airport Road, Sedona, AZ 86336
(928) 282-6400
skyranchlodge.com

with Courthouse Rock in the background is a classic photo opportunity.

Modern Sedona is the pinnacle of upscale Arizona, with luxurious resorts, spas, retreats, gourmet restaurants, and high-end shopping to meet the needs of the most discerning travelers. If you'd rather get away from all that, try a **Pink Jeep Tour**. This long-established outfitter will take you off-roading in the back-country through terrain that's rugged enough to impress even the most experienced outdoorsman.

If you plan to stay the night in the Sedona area, consider **Sky Ranch Lodge**, a moderately priced motel with amazing views, located just up the road from Airport Overlook, near the little airport.

OAK CREEK CANYON AND BEYOND

Leaving Sedona, stay on AZ 89A toward Oak Creek Canyon. This next stretch of highway is a real treat. Like its better known cousin, the Grand Canyon, Oak Creek Canyon was formed by flowing water cutting through the layers of the Colorado Plateau over millions of years. The Grand Canyon is far bigger, of course, but Oak Creek has a unique advantage: you can drive through it. The heavily forested canyon floor ranges from 2.5 miles wide at the mouth to less than a mile at the top end, with a depth of 2,000 feet from the creek to the tops of the highest sheer red cliffs. This wonderful road, built in 1929, runs the entire 13-mile length of it.

Along the way you'll pass **Slide Rock State Park**, a popular creekside swimming hole with a natural water slide. There are several U.S. Forest Service campgrounds and picnic areas in the canyon as well as several resorts, with accommodations ranging from basic cabins to super-luxurious vacation homes. About 3.5 miles beyond Slide Rock, keep a sharp eye out on your left for the **Call of the Canyon picnic area**, where there is a parking lot. This is the trailhead for the beautiful **West Fork Trail**, a 6-mile round-trip that requires about 3 hours and is considered one of the finest day hikes in Arizona. At the north end of the canyon, AZ 89A makes a rapid, zig-zagging ascent through a series of sharp switchbacks. Stop at the scenic viewpoint at the top of the hill to see where you've been. One word: Wow! From here, the road enters into the tall pines of Coconino National Forest at an altitude of close to 7,000 feet. After a couple of quick turns, you will merge back onto Interstate 17, just before it ends at the intersection with Interstate 40.

You're now in Flagstaff, Arizona's mountain playground, at the base of the majestic San Francisco Peaks—a fitting end point for this scenic and remarkable route. For detailed information about scenic attractions in and around Flagstaff, see **Scenic Side Trip 14**.

> **Oak Creek Canyon Highlights**
>
> **Slide Rock State Park**
> 6871 N. Highway 89A, Sedona, AZ 86336
> (928) 282-3034
> azstateparks.com/slide-rock

Next page: Oak Creek Canyon in autumn

Phoenix to Flagstaff

via Taliesin West, Payson, the Mogollon Rim, Montezuma Castle, and Sedona

219 miles, **6** hours **30** minutes for drive time, more for optional routes, stops, and sightseeing

From Taliesin to Tonto, Mogollon to Montezuma, the long way around goes straight through the heart

LIKE **SCENIC SIDE TRIP 9**, THIS ROUTE RUNS FROM PHOENIX TO Flagstaff, but while the former route takes you through the mountains west of Interstate 17, this one takes you through the mountains to the east. Both routes have the same fabulous finale—the 30-mile stretch from Sedona north to Flagstaff—but everything else about them is delightfully different.   ➡

NORTH SCOTTSDALE & FOUNTAIN HILLS

Often called the Valley of the Sun, metropolitan Phoenix occupies mostly flat ground, but it is edged in every direction by small mountains whose summits rise as much as 2,000 feet above the valley floor. As the city grew outward, threatening to engulf those mountains, legislation was passed protecting several of the more prominent peaks and their surrounding foothills from further development. To that end, five large swaths of desert terrain, a total of 33,000 acres, were incorporated into a system of parks known collectively as the **Phoenix Mountains Preserve**. Each section of the preserve has hiking trails and picnic areas, and all are hugely popular with residents and visitors alike.

From Interstate 10, take the exit for AZ 51, the Piestewa Freeway, and head north. After 7 miles, you'll come up alongside **Piestewa Peak**, the second-highest summit in the city and a striking feature of the Phoenix skyline. The freeway skirts the base of the peak in a graceful curve just before traversing a low pass known as Dreamy Draw, so called for the "dreamy" state of the men who once mined mercury in this area, back in a bygone era before we knew that prolonged exposure to the toxic metal causes brain damage. The area surrounding the pass is also part of the preserve and it's lovely, particularly in spring, when yellow blossoms

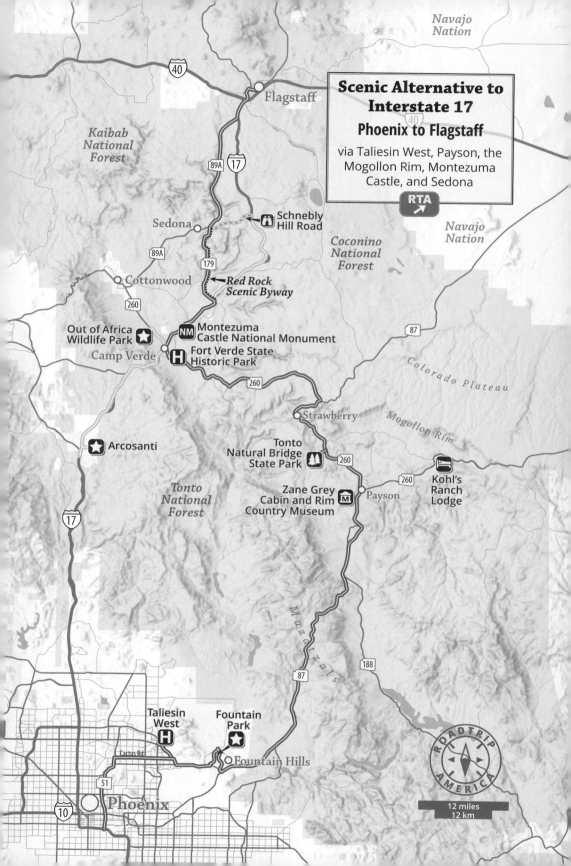

Navajo
Nation

40

Flagstaff

Kaibab
National
Forest

89A **17**

**Scenic Alternative to
Interstate 17**
Phoenix to Flagstaff
via Taliesin West, Payson, the
Mogollon Rim, Montezuma
Castle, and Sedona

RTA

40

Sedona

Schnebly
Hill Road

Navajo
Nation

89A

179

Coconino
National
Forest

Cottonwood

← Red Rock
Scenic Byway

260

Out of Africa
Wildlife Park

NM Montezuma
Castle National Monument

Camp Verde

H Fort Verde State
Historic Park

Colorado Plateau

87

260

Strawberry

Mogollon Rim

Arcosanti

Tonto
Natural Bridge
State Park

260

260

Kohl's
Ranch
Lodge

Tonto
National
Forest

Zane Grey
Cabin and Rim
Country Museum

M Payson

17

Taliesin
West

Fountain
Park

87

188

Mazatzals

Cactus Rd

H

51

Fountain Hills

ROADTRIP AMERICA

10 Phoenix

12 miles
12 km

cover the paloverde trees and desert wildflowers line the road. On the far side of the pass, you'll drop down into the northeastern suburbs, which stretch off into the distance nearly as far as the eye can see—an urban sprawl that, remarkably, dates only to the postwar boom of the 1950s. Stay on AZ 51 until you reach the Cactus Road exit, then follow Cactus east into Scottsdale. When you reach Frank Lloyd Wright Boulevard (the equivalent of 110th Street), go straight across the intersection onto Taliesin Drive and onto the grounds of **Taliesin West**.

This remarkable compound served as the winter home of the famous architect from 1937 to 1959; today, it's home to the Frank Lloyd Wright Foundation and the Frank Lloyd Wright School of Architecture. The long, low, interconnected structures that make up the compound flow with the contours of the land, and liberal use of native stone and natural light allows the complex to blend, visually, with the sur-

rounding desert terrain. Wright loved the desert and the rocky hills surrounding his estate. He found inspiration in that landscape, not just for this project but for many of his groundbreaking designs back East.

Wright called this place "the top of the world," and it's perhaps the most personal of all his creations. If you are

Taliesin West, Scottsdale, Arizona

interested in the golden age of 20th-century architecture, Taliesin West is definitely worth a look. Tours are offered throughout the year, beginning at 9 a.m. daily.

Leaving Taliesin West, head back to Frank Lloyd Wright Boulevard and follow that south for two blocks to Shea Boulevard; turn left (east), and drive another 6 miles to **Fountain Hills**. This area beyond Scottsdale is still lush desert, with healthy stands of saguaros, paloverdes, and mesquite trees. The town is surrounded by angular hills and backed by a dramatic range of desert mountains. The developers of this master-planned community believed it would take more than scenic views to lure home buyers to such a remote desert location, so they came up with a gimmick. They built a lake, surrounded it with green space, and put a giant fountain in the middle. A concrete sculpture in the shape of a water lily conceals an 18-inch water nozzle. Three 600-horsepower turbines drive the pumps, and 13 times every day that water lily erupts,

Fountain Lake, Fountain Hills, Arizona

sending a plume of water 330 feet straight up into the air, at a rate of 7,000 gallons per minute. On special occasions, they bump up the pressure, and the water rises to 560 feet, higher than the Washington Monument and visible for miles around. If you'd like to see the fountain up close, turn left off Shea onto Fountain Hills Boulevard. Follow that to El Lago Boulevard, which runs past **Fountain Park**. The fountain runs for 15 minutes at a time, at the top of every hour, from 9 a.m. to 9 p.m. daily.

> **North Scottsdale and Fountain Hills Highlights**
>
> **Taliesin West**
> 12621 N. Frank Lloyd Wright Blvd., Scottsdale, AZ 85259
> (480) 627-5340
> franklloydwright.org/taliesin-west
>
> **Fountain Park**
> 12925 N. Saguaro Blvd. Fountain Hills, AZ 85268
> (480) 816-5100

PAYSON AND THE RIM COUNTRY

Leaving Fountain Hills, head back to Shea Boulevard and turn east. After less than a mile, turn north on AZ 87, toward Payson. This is one of the principal highways leading out of the greater metropolitan area: the fastest, most direct route up into the cool pine forests, and a favorite of heat-exhausted desert dwellers. The road, vastly improved in recent years, is now a wide, divided highway with two lanes in each direction and it's a joy to drive. Shortly after leaving Fountain Hills, the road climbs rapidly into the mountains; the grade is relatively gentle, the curves are smooth and well banked, and there's very little truck traffic. You'll fairly sail along through some spectacular terrain. The rugged range of mountains you'll see on your left as you travel north are the **Mazatzals**, peaks rising to nearly 8,000 feet in the trackless Mazatzal Wilderness.

An hour's drive takes you to the small town of **Payson**, population 15,000, known as "the heart of Arizona" for its location near the geographic center of the state. Payson sits at almost 5,000 feet and is surrounded by pine forest—a welcome change from the desert around Phoenix, especially in summer.

Zane Gray Cabin, Payson, Arizona

Zane Grey, the celebrated author of *Riders of the Purple Sage* and dozens of other classic Western novels, had a cabin near Payson in the 1920s, when he was at the height of his fame. It was one of the writer's favorite spots, his personal connection to the wild backcountry of Arizona, a setting that he glorified in many of his books. The cabin was abandoned after his death in 1939 and nearly fell into ruin. It was very nicely restored in the late 1960s—only to be destroyed by a devastating wildfire in 1990. A replica of the original **Zane Grey Cabin** was built in 2003, not on the original site, but in a park next to the **Rim Country Museum** in Payson. The museum has a nice collection of 19th-century artifacts and photographs related to the history of the area; a tour of the reconstructed cabin is included in the price of admission.

Payson is situated at the foot of the **Mogollon Rim** (pronounced *MUGgy-own*). The Rim, as it's known locally, is a 200-mile-long escarpment that marks the southern edge of the Colorado Plateau, the uplifted foundation of Arizona's high country. Payson is not only the gateway to the forested mountains above the Rim, it is also a destination in its own right. Its cabins and campgrounds are jam-packed on summer weekends, and it is home to many country-style events, including the World's Oldest Continuous Rodeo, held every August since 1884, and the Arizona State Championship Old Time Fiddlers Contest, held every September. If you'd like to stay overnight in the Payson area, consider **Kohl's Ranch Lodge**, a woodsy resort property a few miles east of town off AZ 260.

Leave Payson on AZ 87/260, toward Camp Verde. After about 10 miles, you'll see the turnoff for **Tonto Natural Bridge State Park**. This is an exceedingly rare travertine arch, quite unlike the sandstone arches of Utah, and the largest of its kind in the world. Travertine is a thick crystalline limestone material composed of the precipitated minerals left behind when water flowing over rocks evaporates. This arch began as an accretion of minerals from natural springs in the canyon walls. Through a quirk of both geology and geometry, helped along by algae that provided a tiny latticework for crystallization, the mineral accretion grew, and grew, for many thousands of years, until it spanned the entire canyon, forming a travertine dam that's currently more than 400 feet long, 150 feet wide, and 180 feet high. The travertine is continually

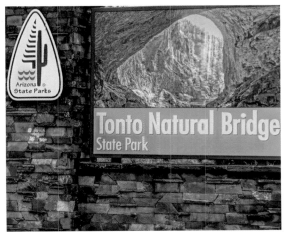

undercut by the flowing water of the creek, which has carved the dam into a natural arch that is truly something to see. You can get a good view of it from any of several overlooks near the parking area, and a fairly easy hike will take you to the best view of all: looking up from below.

Leaving the park, head back to the highway and continue on to the northwest. You'll pass through a pair of small towns, **Pine and Strawberry**—quaint little burgs that cater to hordes of vacationers in summer. There are cabins, bed-and-breakfasts, shops, and several nice places to grab a leisurely lunch while you're still among the cool pines. Strawberry boasts a historic **log cabin schoolhouse** that dates to 1877, the oldest school building still standing in the state.

Payson and The Rim Country Highlights

Zane Grey Cabin and Rim Country Museum
700 S. Green Valley Pkwy.,
Payson, AZ 85541
(928) 474-3483
rimcountrymuseum.org

Kohl's Ranch Lodge
202 S. Kohl's Ranch Lodge Road,
Payson, AZ 85541
(800) 438-2929
diamondresortsandhotels.com/
Resorts/Kohls-Ranch-Lodge

Tonto Natural Bridge State Park
North of Payson off AZ 87/260
(928) 476-4202
azstateparks.com/tonto

THE VERDE VALLEY

Leaving Strawberry, AZ 87/260 winds its way down out of the mountains, dropping steadily toward the Verde Valley. After 50 miles, you'll reach **Camp Verde**, where you'll cross the Verde River. Abundant water has created an oasis of sorts here, with groves of cottonwoods offering plentiful shade. Shortly after you enter the town, turn right onto Main Street and you'll come to the remains of Fort Verde. This once important military post was established in 1871 to protect settlers from Apache and Yavapai raiding parties. The area was remote at that time, and soldiers often had to march in from Fort Yuma, more than 250 miles away. When Geronimo and the last of his warriors surrendered to the Army in 1886, the Indian Wars effectively ended, and Fort Verde was decommissioned five years later. **Fort Verde Historic Park** features four historic structures: an

administration building, which is now a museum, and
three officers quarters, all filled with original furnishings
and military artifacts from the 1880s.

*Beaver Creek, near
Montezuma Castle
National Monument*

The museum has exhibits relating to
the history of the fort, the valley, and
the Indian Wars.

From Fort Verde, continue on Main
Street to Montezuma Castle Highway,
and follow the signs for about 5 miles
to **Montezuma Castle National
Monument**. The monument preserves an unusual cliff dwelling, a
20-room stone pueblo built into a
large natural alcove beneath a limestone overhang, well above the floor
of a narrow canyon. The canyon was

first occupied by people of the Hohokam culture who
came here from the Gila Valley, farther south, as early

as 300 BC. They lived in pit houses and used water from *Opposite: Montezuma Castle National Monument* the stream to irrigate their crops: maize, squash, beans, and cotton.

Around AD 1100, these people were joined by another group, people of the Sinagua culture who came south from the Flagstaff area. The Sinagua were pueblo dwellers, people who lived communally in interconnected apartment-style houses, and it was this group that built the elaborate structure that you can still see today. A dozen or so families called the "castle" home for nearly 150 years, but it was abandoned around 1400 when the Sinagua abruptly left the area, perhaps forced out by drought or by overcrowding. Left to the elements for 500 years and badly defaced by vandals, the pueblo fell into ruin before being declared a national monument in 1906. Since then, the structure has been significantly restored. Visitors are no longer permitted to climb into the ruin, but the view from below is impressive. Looking up, it's easy to imagine those peaceful people living their lives in this tranquil spot, growing their crops, hunting plentiful game, safe and secure in their big stone house with a view.

Leaving Camp Verde, consider taking a slight detour. Retrace your route back to AZ 260, and follow it west to Cherry Creek Road. From there, follow the signs to **Out of Africa Wildlife Park**, a small, privately operated and well put-together zoo where most of the animals roam free and visitors travel through the park in safari-type vehicles. It's an intimate experience, and memorable for the up-close-and-personal encounters with the wildlife. You might even be kissed by a giraffe.

Verde Valley Highlights

Fort Verde State Historic Park
125 E. Hollamon St., Camp Verde, AZ 86335
(928) 567-3275
azstateparks.com/fort-verde

Montezuma Castle National Monument
Montezuma Castle Road, Camp Verde, AZ 86335
(928) 567-3322
nps.gov/moca/

Out of Africa Wildlife Park
3505 W. AZ 260, Camp Verde, AZ 86322
(928) 567-2840
outofafricapark.com

Above and opposite: Arcosanti, Mayer, Arizona, below: Soleri Bells

Arcosanti

In 1970, the visionary Italian-born architect Paolo Soleri began work on a project named Arcosanti, an example of what Soleri called *arcology*, the embodiment of "elegant frugality" in an inspired combination of architecture and ecology. The basic premise: Minimize man's destructive impact on the environment by building small, self-sufficient, sustainable habitats, or villages, in maximum harmony with the land. Arcosanti was envisioned to house as many as 5,000 people, though it never reached that size. Today about 80 residents live and work communally at Arcosanti, where all structures are interconnected in an organic, unified design—a bit like Montezuma Castle. The community uses few resources, depends on renewable energy, and recycles almost everything that isn't consumed.

Arcosanti has always operated as a prototype: part architectural experiment, part social experiment, and part living laboratory. Workshops and classes have been held here for decades; the fees help to sustain the experiment. A foundry on the property produces unique cast-metal wind chimes called "Soleri Bells," a popular item that can be purchased in the gift shop. Tours are available, as are a limited number of guest rooms for overnight visitors.

Arcosanti is located 29 miles south of Camp Verde, off I-17 (13555 S. Cross L Road in Mayer, 928-632-7135, arcosanti.org). Visiting Arcosanti will add 58 miles and an hour of driving time to this route.

Sᴇᴅᴏɴᴀ ᴛᴏ Fʟᴀɢsᴛᴀғғ

From Camp Verde (or from Arcosanti), take I-17 north to Exit 298, and follow AZ 179 through the Village of Oak Creek into the town of Sedona. This exceptionally beautiful drive through the famous Red Rock country leads you past many well-known area attractions, including Bell Rock, said to be the center of a mysterious "energy vortex," and the Chapel of the Holy Cross, a Catholic church built into a red rock butte. If you're up for a little adventure, and you don't mind driving a rough road, there's an awesome alternative route into Sedona along **Schnebly Hill Road**. You'll need a four-wheel-drive vehicle, or at least a high-clearance SUV; if you're driving a rental, check the terms of your contract before setting out, because this route is not well maintained. To get to it, continue north on I-17 for 22 miles and take Exit 320, Schnebly Hill Road. The road is an unpaved, backcountry romp through some exceptional Red Rock country normally seen only by paying passengers on commercial Jeep tours. It's just 12 miles to downtown Sedona along this road, but you should take it slow, drive very carefully, and allow at least 90 minutes. Be sure to stop at Schnebly Hill Vista; the views are stupendous!

   Note. *If you wish to park along any of the roads in the Sedona area to explore on foot, you'll need to purchase a Red Rock Pass, available at the visitors centers in the Village of Oak Creek, and in Sedona.*

   Once you reach Sedona, you can take some time to explore it, or you can follow AZ 89A north through Oak Creek Canyon. Beyond that, you'll rejoin I-17, just south of Flagstaff. For a full description of the Sedona-to-Flagstaff run, along with recommendations for lodging, see **Scenic Side Trip 9**; for information about Flagstaff, see **Scenic Side Trip 13**.

Phoenix to Holbrook
via the Apache Trail and the Salt River Canyon

300 miles, **7** hours **45** minutes for drive time, more for optional routes, stops, and sightseeing

Over the river and through the woods to the Petrified Forest we go!

HERE IS ANOTHER ROUTE NORTH FROM PHOENIX, AN alternative to Interstate 17 that takes you to Holbrook, 100 miles east of Flagstaff. It's the opposite of a shortcut; in fact, it will add 60 miles and at least 3 hours to your journey. The trade-off? Some mind-blowing scenery: three lakes, two canyons, and some truly magnificent roads. ⏩

Be aware that the route includes the infamous Fish Creek Hill, part of the 20-mile section of AZ 88 between Tortilla Flat and Roosevelt Dam that has never been paved. It is quite rough and has hairpin turns that are not suitable for large RVs or vehicles pulling trailers. If you're in a rental car, check your contract before driving this route. The rest of you are in for a treat.

as it curves to the left and merges onto the busy Superstition Freeway. Drive east for 24 miles, through the sprawling eastern suburbs of Tempe and Mesa, to Apache Junction, where the freeway ends. Looming before you are the Superstitions, the easternmost of the mountains surrounding the Phoenix area. These craggy volcanic mountains and the surrounding foothills make up the

FROM PHOENIX TO GLOBE VIA THE APACHE TRAIL

From I-17—or anywhere else in Phoenix—make your way to Interstate 10, and head toward Tucson. A few miles south of the Phoenix city limits you'll reach the intersection with US 60; keep right and follow the ramp

Scenic Alternative to Interstate 17

Phoenix to Holbrook

via the Apache Trail and the Salt River Canyon

RTA

Navajo Nation

Painted Desert

89

Flagstaff

40

Winslow

Petrified Forest National Park NP

Wigwam Motel Holbrook

89A

Mormon Lake

Sedona

17

Coconino National Forest

87

Cottonwood

377

60

Camp Verde

260

Sitgreaves National Forest

260

Show Low

Payson

Tonto National Forest

288

60

17

87

Apache Trail Historic Road

Roosevelt Dam

Salt River Canyon

Salt River Canyon Viewpoint

Apache Lake

Theodore Roosevelt Lake

Fort Apache Indian Reservation

Canyon Lake

NM 188

Goldfield Ghost Town

88

Tonto National Monument

10 51

Tortilla Flat

60 Globe

Lost Dutchman State Park

Phoenix

Apache Junction

10

Tonto National Forest

87

Roosevelt Dam

Theodore Roosevelt Lake

8

Canyon Lake

Apache Lake

NM Tonto National Monument

Goldfield Ghost Town

88

Apache Trail Historic Road

Unpaved and rugged ~20 miles

10

Tortilla Flat

Lost Dutchman State Park

Superstition Wilderness Area

ROADTRIP AMERICA

60

25 miles
25 km

Tucson

Superstition Mountains, near Apache Junction, Arizona

Superstition Wilderness Area, 160,000 acres of unspoiled desert traversed by some of the most popular hiking trails in the state. The most popular activity besides hiking? Treasure hunting *(see sidebar)*!

In Apache Junction, exit US 60 at Idaho Road (AZ 88). Follow AZ 88 north for about 2.5 miles until it curves to the right, merging with the **Apache Trail Historic Road**, which will take you all the way to Roosevelt through some of the wildest countryside in Arizona.

The Lost Dutchman: Fact or Fantasy?

The Superstition Mountains are associated with one of the most abiding tales of the Old West: the legend of the Lost Dutchman Mine. There are several versions of that story, but the most often told is that of an old German prospector, Jacob Waltz, who had a secret gold mine, or a cache of gold bullion, hidden somewhere in the Superstitions. The treasure had something to do with a Spanish land grant. It was guarded by a band of hostile Apaches. There was a map scratched on stones in the desert, or maybe it was inscribed on crumbling parchment that was passed along by a mysterious stranger. In the favorite twist, the map was scrawled on the back of an envelope by Jacob Waltz himself, as he lay dying.

The story had legs, in the telling and the retelling, and even made the national newspapers in the Depression years, when a treasure seeker named Adolph Ruth was found shot through the head just off a trail in the remote wilderness. Who would do such a thing? And why? Speculation fueled more speculation, and the story has lived on, even to this day. It's been estimated that as many as 8,000 people hike back into that forbidding territory each year, in search of that legendary treasure.

On your way out of Apache Junction you'll pass **Goldfield Ghost Town**, a tourist-oriented mock-up of a Western town built on the site of what was once a working gold mine. Beyond Goldfield, you'll pass the entrance to **Lost Dutchman State Park**, which has a campground and some popular hiking trails in case you'd like to check out those golden legends for yourself.

After a couple of miles you'll reach Canyon Lake Vista, where you can pull over for a distant view of **Canyon Lake**, the first of the lakes you'll pass on this route. Those lakes are the reason this road exists. In the late 1800s, a group of visionaries came up with a grand plan: by damming the Salt River, they could provide a reliable water supply downstream in the Salt River Valley and turn the area around Phoenix into an agricultural paradise. And that's exactly what they did. Construction began on the Theodore Roosevelt Dam in 1905, and this road, the Apache Trail, was built to transport the men and material required to build it. The Roosevelt dam was followed by three others, creating a series of four lakes:

Apache Trail

Roosevelt Lake

Roosevelt, Apache, Canyon, and Saguaro (which is not visible from this route). For 50 years, the vast amount of water impounded by those lakes was used to irrigate cotton, citrus, and other crops that grow well in the arid climate. Ironically, that same water made it possible to replace the farmland with housing tracts in the boom that followed World War II, transforming the onetime agricultural paradise into the sixth-largest city in the United States.

Beyond the overlook, the Apache Trail starts doing its thing, twisting and turning like an unruly snake as it winds down the mountain to the shores of Canyon Lake. The highway is still paved here and all the way along the lakeshore as far as **Tortilla Flat**, where there's a campground and a popular restaurant and saloon. Four or five miles beyond Tortilla Flat, the pavement runs out, and the road narrows to a rocky dirt track barely wide enough for one car, much less two-way traffic. That's where the real fun begins. As you descend toward Fish Creek, keep an eye on the road ahead; if you spy a vehicle coming up from the other direction, start looking for a wide spot to

> **Mind Your Brakes**
> Steep downhill grades and tight turns are a dangerous combination, even for the most seasoned drivers. Resist the temptation to coast with your foot on the brake; instead, shift your transmission into a lower gear (even with an automatic) and let your engine slow you down to a safe speed. Otherwise, your brakes could overheat, and might not stop you properly when you need them most.

pull over—one of you will have to wait for the other. The mountains along this stretch are exceptionally rugged, and so is the road: very rocky, with lots of potholes. Take it slow, especially on the downgrades, and enjoy the spectacular views.

About 10 miles after leaving the pavement, you'll come to **Apache Lake**, a long, narrow reservoir that impounds more than 82 *billion* gallons of water behind **Horse Mesa Dam**. You can turn off and drive down to the marina if you want a closer look; otherwise, drive on, following the Salt River upstream to **Roosevelt Dam.** Completed in 1911, the dam was greatly enlarged and renovated between 1989 and 1996—so much so that it was taken off the National Register of Historic Places because it had lost its historic character. The original masonry structure, at one time the largest masonry dam in the world, was entirely encased in concrete. The new structure added 77 feet to the height of the dam and increased the capacity of **Roosevelt Lake** by 20 percent, making it the largest lake located entirely within the borders of Arizona. Pull over at Inspiration Point for a terrific view of the dam, the lake, and the graceful arch of the new suspension bridge that crosses the river here.

At the dam, pavement returns, and a short distance farther on, AZ 88 intersects AZ 188. If you turn left, the road crosses the bridge and continues on to Payson, but you should turn right and head toward Globe. After a little over a mile, you'll see signs for **Tonto National Monument**. This isn't a memorial to the Lone Ranger's

Opposite: Apache Lake from the Apache Trail

sidekick; it's a pair of cliff dwellings built by the Salado people, who occupied this area from about AD 1275 to AD 1450. The lower ruin is plainly visible from the parking area and is accessible by way of a half-mile-long trail; the trail isn't difficult, but it is a little steep, and you should allow a full hour for the round-trip. The upper ruin is larger, a 40-room structure that was opened to the public in 2016. To visit it, you'll have to join a Ranger-led tour, currently available on a limited basis in the cooler months; advance reservations are required.

The Salado people chose their site wisely. Sheltered from the weather and the blistering desert sun, these cliff dwellings were easily defended and provided access to Tonto Creek, a perennial stream that they used to irrigate their crops: cotton, corn, beans, and squash. Like all the cliff dwellings in the Southwest, these communal houses were abandoned by the 15th century, for reasons not yet fully known.

Tonto National Monument

Apache Trail Highlights

Goldfield Ghost Town
4650 N. Mammoth Mine Road, Apache Junction,
AZ 85119
(480) 983-0333
goldfieldghosttown.com

Lost Dutchman State Park
6109 N. Apache Trail, Apache Junction, AZ 85119
(480) 982-4485
azstateparks.com/lost-dutchman

Tortilla Flat
1 Main St., Tortilla Flat, AZ 85190
(480) 984-1776
tortillaflataz.com

Tonto National Monument
26260 N. AZ 188, Roosevelt, AZ 85545
(928) 467-2241
nps.gov/tont

GLOBE TO HOLBROOK VIA SALT RIVER CANYON

Leaving Tonto National Monument, return to AZ 188 and continue on to Globe, a mining town that was once one of the richest copper producers in the world. *(For more about Globe, including the Besh-Ba-Gowah Archaeological Park, another ruin of the Salado culture, see* **Scenic Side Trip 4**.*)* In Globe, you'll join US 60, which coincides with Ash Street, the main street through the center of town. At an intersection east of the town center, stay with US 60 as it splits off to the left toward Show Low.

This next section of road is a classic slice of Americana. Before the Interstates were built, long-distance travelers, tourists as well as truckers, used the U.S. Highway system. **Highway 60** was a particularly important road, stretching 2,760 miles from southwest Arizona all the way to the coast of Virginia. U.S. Highways were designed to a different standard than the Interstates. Instead of bulldozing their way through every obstacle to keep the course of the road straight and true, U.S. Highways tended to follow established routes, which went through towns rather than around them, and they followed the path of least resistance through difficult terrain.

In the case of US 60, that meant crossing the Salt River at its narrows, in the Salt River Canyon, a little more than 30 miles north of Globe. As you approach the crossing, the highway seems to drop over the edge of a cliff, making a rapid descent through a series of tight switchbacks. You cross the river on a short bridge, then zig and zag your way up the other side. The views are stupendous. Be sure to stop at the scenic overlook at mile 290, on the north side of the river, for an extraordinary perspective.

Like its famous cousin, the Grand Canyon, the **Salt River Canyon** was created by the abrasive action of silt-laden water flowing over rock, wearing it away over the course of hundreds of thousands of years. Such canyons are living laboratories for the earth sciences, places where geologists can examine the stratified layers of geological time: volcanoes ... ancient oceans ... mountains rising to the sky before wearing away to dust. It is astonishing to imagine and impressive to see, even through laymen's eyes. From the overlook, you'll see how the river has sliced it way through stair-stepped cliffs, exposing multicolored layers of sandstone seamed with darker bands of volcanic rock. Downriver, the river cuts deeper, through Precambrian granite and a thick layer of 1.6-billion-year-old metamorphic rock that's the color and rippled texture of chocolate ice cream. Like the Colorado, the Salt races through a stunning canyon of its own making, where white-water rapids provide thrills for river runners, particularly in the river's middle section, as it flows through the magnificently rugged Salt River Wilderness Area.

Back in the days when US 60 was still a major truck route, the Salt River Canyon was considered the most treacherous portion of that entire cross-country highway. Any trucker who lost his brakes on that wild downgrade was doomed. Before there were roads, this area was dangerous for another reason: renegade Apaches used the

Opposite: Salt River Canyon

US 60, Salt River Canyon

canyon as a sanctuary in the Indian Wars, staging raids and then retreating into this rugged terrain to hide. That strategy worked until 1872, when the U.S. Army, under General George Crook, rode through in force and flushed the Apaches out, forcing them to other strongholds, which they held until Geronimo's surrender in 1886.

Beyond the Salt River Canyon, US 60 climbs into the eastern Arizona pine forest. Scrubby junipers give way to scattered stands of Ponderosa pines that merge into wooded mountainsides. About 45 miles from the canyon viewpoint, you'll reach the town of **Show Low**, which, along with the adjacent towns of **Pinetop and Lakeside**, is the largest community in Arizona's White Mountains. It's a favorite summer recreation area and a year-round home to more than 100,000 people. The unusual name comes from Territorial days, when two neighboring ranchers solved a property dispute with a bet on a hand of cards: the player drawing the lowest card in a game called 7 Up would win. Corydon Cooley turned up the deuce of clubs, and his rival, Marion Clark, couldn't beat it, so Cooley stayed, and Clark pulled up stakes and moved on. A town grew up around Cooley's spread, and he named it Show Low, in honor of his winning hand.

From Show Low, take AZ 77 north about 47 miles to **Holbrook**. The chief attraction here is nearby Petrified Forest National Park. If you are arriving late in the day, head straight for the section of the park north of Interstate 40 known as the **Painted Desert.** The terrain here is badlands—low, rounded hills scattered across the landscape like the rumpled folds of an unmade bed. When the sunset plays over those hills, it sets the barren landscape aglow in muted shades of red, pink, gray, orange, and lavender that shift with the angle of the light. To get there, take I-40 from Holbrook about 26 miles east to Exit 311, where you will find the park entrance. The Painted Desert is just north of the visitors center.

Petrified Forest National Park covers a large area—230 square miles. The best way to see it is to follow the park road, which runs for 28 miles from the north visitors center, off I-40, to the south entrance, off US 180. You can drive the road in either direction. Stop at the Rainbow Forest Museum, a historic building with fascinating exhibits and access to several of the most interesting trails, including Giant Logs Trail and Long Logs Trail, which showcase famous specimens of petrified wood. The same geological process that preserved and petrified these trees, mostly conifers, also preserved the ecosystem in which they lived, producing a fossilized record of a broad range of plants, birds, reptiles, and other prehistoric creatures. The fossils are quite beautiful,

Salt River Canyon Highlights

Petrified Forest National Park
1 Park Road, Petrified Forest, AZ 86028
(928) 524-6228
nps.gov/pefo

Wigwam Motel
811 W. Hopi Drive, Holbrook, AZ 86025
(928) 524-3048

Petrified Forest National Park

Wigwam Motel, Holbrook

and the setting—the badlands of the Painted Desert—is out of this world.

If you elect to stay the night in Holbrook, consider the **Wigwam Motel**, a kitschy classic from the era of Route 66. The rooms are individual cabins built of concrete but shaped like teepees. Not the height of luxury, but definitely unique—and clean.

BEYOND HOLBROOK

From Holbrook, you can travel east or west on Interstate 40. If you're headed east and have plenty of time, **Scenic Side Trip 16** will take you to Gallup, New Mexico, by way of Canyon de Chelly, Monument Valley, and Shiprock. If you're headed west, take a look at **Scenic Side Trip 15; b**y reversing the itinerary, you will get to Flagstaff by way of the Hopi Mesas, Wupatki, and Walnut Canyon. This Four Corners region has some of the richest history and most interesting cultural traditions in the Southwest and is well worth an extended visit.

Part 3: Scenic Alternatives to Interstate 40

Interstate 40 is the third-longest expressway in the Interstate system, and the 475-mile stretch between Kingman, Arizona, and Albuquerque, New Mexico, is arguably the most scenic section. But driving through at 75 mph, you'll have to look quick if you want to see the sights from the highway. These eight Scenic Side Trips give you time and freedom to explore this region's spectacular high country—including the Grand Canyon, Monument Valley, and Canyon de Chelly—and to cruise along a stretch of Historic Route 66 that has remained frozen in time. Along the way you can travel through the heart of the Navajo Nation, visit Indian pueblos, get close-up views of volcanoes, see prehistoric cities, and explore hidden gems like the Bisti Badlands; there's even a road that leads all the way down to the Colorado River, at the very *bottom* of the Grand Canyon.

Most of the territory traversed in this section is high country, but summers can still be hot, so always carry plenty of water. The region is subject to "monsoon" storms in summer, especially in July and August; these are particularly dangerous on the Colorado Plateau because of the possibility of flash floods in dry washes and along normally sedate streams and rivers. When there is lightning close by, and you're on high ground, wait out the storm in your vehicle, at the side of the road, with your hands in your lap (not touching anything metal). In the winter, there can be snow across most of this region, causing the usual disruptions, especially on smaller highways and reservation roads that are less frequently maintained. Some roads, such as AZ 67 to the North Rim of the Grand Canyon, are closed for the entire winter season, from mid-October to May.

There are many seasonal roadside delights along these routes. You'll see wildflowers in the darndest places during the spring and summer; fall brings fabulous color to the aspens and sycamores in the high country, and to the cottonwoods that line the rivers and streams. Note that most popular attractions, like the South Rim of the Grand Canyon and Zion National Park, are very crowded from June through August, when schools are out; if that's a concern, try to visit outside that peak season.

The line of travel for most routes in this section is west to east. If you are traveling in the other direction, simply reverse the itinerary.

Kingman to Flagstaff

via Historic Route 66 and the Bottom of the Grand Canyon

160 miles, **3** hours **15** minutes for drive time, more for optional routes, stops, and sightseeing

Get your kicks on Indian Route 6. Be sure to watch out for the rapids!

AS INTERSTATE 40 PASSES THROUGH NORTHERN ARIZONA, IT follows the path of Route 66, that most historic of all American highways. There's a lot of interest in that history, and many travelers are disappointed to learn that the history is just about all that's left. Route 66 was officially decommissioned as a U.S. Highway more than 30 years ago, after it had been rendered obsolete by the Interstate Highway system. If you're among the many would-be road warriors who feel cheated by that, there's some good news: it's still possible to get a taste of what it used to be like. ▶▶

U.S. Highways were deliberately routed through the middle of nearly every town in their path. The Interstates are just as deliberately routed to bypass most towns, so in places like Williams, Flagstaff, and Holbrook, short segments of the original road were cut off and left behind when I-40 was built. Those orphaned bits have been designated as historic, many old buildings have been refurbished, and some of that charming Route 66 ambience has been restored to entice tourists passing by on their way to the Grand Canyon. If all you'd like to do is snap a selfie by a Route 66 road sign, or pick up a Route 66 bumper sticker, they've got you covered in any of those towns.

If what you'd most like to do is *drive* on old Route 66, Arizona has that covered as well. One of the longest continuous sections of Route 66 still in existence runs from Kingman to Ash Fork by way of Peach Springs and Seligman. This segment is a bit more than 100 miles of the original road, still maintained but never modernized, a scenic stretch that's like a journey through time, back to the era of the "Mother Road" as described in John Steinbeck's classic novel *The Grapes of Wrath.*

Opposite: Diamond Creek Road, Peach Springs. See page 180

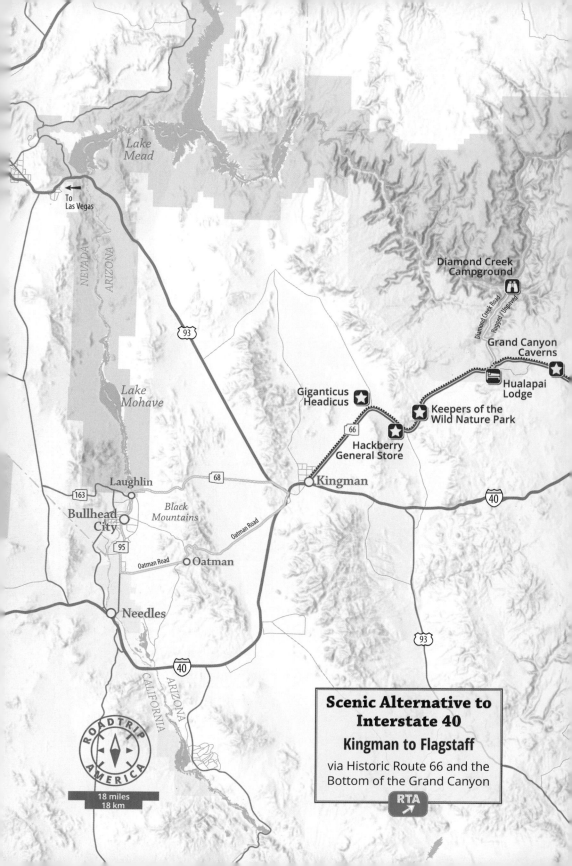

Lake Mead

To Las Vegas

NEVADA
ARIZONA

93

Lake Mohave

Diamond Creek Campground

Grand Canyon Caverns

Hualapai Lodge

Giganticus Headicus

Keepers of the Wild Nature Park

66

Hackberry General Store

Kingman

40

Laughlin

68

163

Black Mountains

Bullhead City

95

Oatman Road

Oatman Road

Oatman

Needles

40

ARIZONA
CALIFORNIA

93

Scenic Alternative to Interstate 40
Kingman to Flagstaff
via Historic Route 66 and the Bottom of the Grand Canyon

RTA

ROADTRIP AMERICA

18 miles
18 km

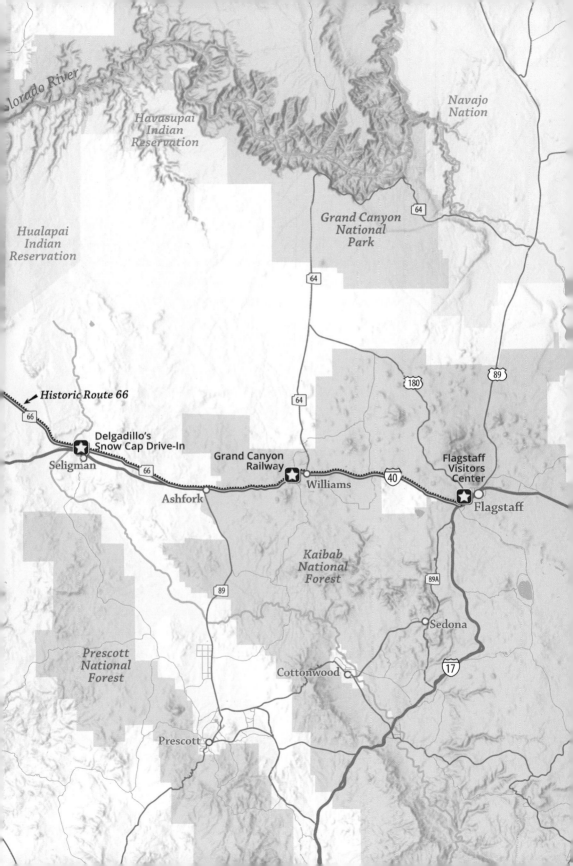

Route 66 is the centerpiece of this Scenic Side Trip, which differs from the others in this book in the sense that it has three distinct parts to it. Old Route 66 by itself is barely out of your way; it will add less than 20 miles and little more than an hour of driving to the Interstate trip between Kingman and Flagstaff. If you begin with the optional Oatman Highway loop, you will add another 90 miles and a bit more than 2 hours to the trip. Then there's Diamond Creek Road, a primitive road that takes you on a second optional detour, down to the Colorado River *inside* the Grand Canyon. That's another 38 miles, and another 2 hours of travel time. Let's do the math. If you drive all three sections of this route, you'll add 143 miles, 5 hours, a boatload of nostalgia, and a world-class adventure to your trip from Kingman to Flagstaff.

From Interstate 40 in Kingman, take Exit 53, Andy Devine Avenue, which soon becomes AZ 66, also known as Historic Route 66. If you have arrived late in the day and want to begin the drive in the morning, you'll find hotel rooms in good supply and reasonably priced. If you're not in a hurry, the following optional detour is a very cool way to begin the trip.

OATMAN HIGHWAY LOOP: AN OPTIONAL DETOUR

The original Route 66 had gentle grades for most of its length, making it all the more popular with motorists, especially truckers. There were a few exceptions to that rule, and perhaps the most notorious was a stretch through Arizona's Black Mountains between Kingman and the little mining town of Oatman. With the steepest hills and tightest hairpin curves on the Mother Road, the drive was sufficiently terrifying that local entrepreneurs made a good business hiring themselves out as "pilots" who would do the driving for you through the most treacherous section.

Today that stretch is known simply as the Oatman Road. The whole thing was paved as far back as the 1930s, so it hasn't really been terrifying for 80 years, but it still has enough twists and turns to make it great fun to drive, and Oatman itself is well worth a visit. The old mining town retains its 19th-century ambience, along with a herd of wild burros, descended from animals owned by gold seekers back in the day. Today, those burros famously roam the streets of Oatman, panhandling carrots from the tourists.

From Kingman, head west on Historic Route 66 for 5 miles, to Mohave County Road 10, the Oatman Highway. You'll reach Oatman after 22 miles, the last 5 of which include those hair-raising hairpins. From Main Street in Oatman, follow the Oatman-Topock Highway south, keep right to stay on the Oatman Road, then drive west for 5 miles to Boundary Cone Road (County Road 153); bear right, and follow CR 153 west for 11 miles to AZ 95. Take AZ 95 north through Fort Mohave, along the Colorado River to Bullhead City, where it turns into AZ 68. That state road will lead you east to US 93, which will take you back to Kingman. The loop takes you within a stone's throw of Laughlin, Nevada, where you will find Las Vegas-style casinos and resort hotels. It's just across the river from Bullhead City.

KINGMAN TO PEACH SPRINGS

Leaving Kingman, drive east on Historic Route 66 (Andy Devine Avenue). You'll run into your first roadside attraction in Antares, about 20 miles beyond Kingman: **Giganticus Headicus**, which is just what it sounds like—a gigantic head, 14 feet tall, dark green in color, made mostly of cement, and vaguely reminiscent of those mysterious Easter Island sculptures. This roadside attraction isn't actually old; it was created by a local artist

Giganticus Headicus, Route 66 near Kingman

Route 66 and the Birth of the Roadside Attraction

Route 66 is the only road that's ever had its own television series (featuring two guys and a Corvette, back in the 1960s). Then there was that popular song "(Get Your Kicks on) Route 66," which has been covered by everyone from Bing Crosby to the Rolling Stones, not to mention countless references in movies, books, and every travel magazine that's ever been published. In fact, Route 66 is probably the best-known automobile road in the world. It was one of the first numbered U.S. Highways created, in 1926, and the first transcontinental route to be paved along its entire length, in 1938. The original alignment ran for 2,448 miles, from Chicago all the way to Los Angeles, passing through portions of eight states.

The real heyday of Route 66 was during the years following World War II, from the late 1940s through the 1960s, when the baby boom generation was growing up and families were hitting the road like never before. Route 66 and the highways that came after it created both the inspiration and the opportunity for a new pastime that quickly became a time-honored tradition: the family road trip!

Entrepreneurs were quick to recognize the opportunities represented by all those travelers passing through, so new businesses sprang up all along the route: service stations, restaurants called "drive-ins" that catered to people in cars, and "motor courts," lodgings where travelers could park right by the door of their room.

And then there were the roadside attractions: natural wonders of every description from canyons to craters, as well as quirky man-made stuff, like giant dinosaur statues, the world's largest catsup bottle, and motels built to look like Indian teepees. The goal? Entice travelers to stop and then sell them something. Those roadside attractions, many of which are still operating, are the living legacy of Route 66, and a business model emulated worldwide.

in 2005 as part of some larger plan that is apparently still in the works. Headicus stands in front of a gift shop alongside what was once a Route 66 trailer park, along with a few other bizarre sculptures.

Six more miles down the road you'll come to the **Hackberry General Store**, a ramshackle establishment that's older than your grandfather, festooned with antique signs, antique gas pumps, rusted-out hulks of antique vehicles, and all sorts of fascinating memorabilia. It's a good place to stop for a cold drink, to buy some postcards, and to get into the Route 66 spirit.

Beyond Hackberry, the terrain becomes much more interesting. The road glides through an area of rocky, scrub-covered hills, offering sweeping views of the high desert to the south. Not far from the general store is the small community of Valentine, home to a private wildlife sanctuary called **Keepers of the Wild Nature Park**, where abused and neglected animals are cared for and offered a second chance. Tours are available,

Hackberry General Store, Route 66, Hackberry, Arizona

Kingman to Peach Springs Highlights

Hackberry General Store
11255 E. AZ 66, Hackberry, AZ 86411
(928) 769-2605

Keepers of the Wild Nature Park
13441 E. AZ 66, Valentine, Arizona 86437
(928) 769-1800
keepersofthewild.org

offering an up close look at lions, tigers, rare birds, monkeys, a grizzly bear, and other animals. Eighteen miles beyond Valentine, you'll come to Peach Springs, a town on the Hualapai Indian Reservation that was the inspiration for Radiator Springs, the fictional setting of Pixar's animated feature *Cars.*

Peach Springs started out as a water stop for the steam locomotives on the Atlantic and Pacific Railroad, which later became the Atchison, Topeka and Santa Fe. In the 1910s, the National Old Trails Road was built, following the course of the Santa Fe line through the area, and in the 1920s, that section of road became part of the original Route 66. The highway brought unprecedented prosperity to the town, but that disappeared, quite literally overnight, when I-40 was built 25 miles to the south, in the late 1970s. The land in this area has been home to the Hualapai, the People of the Tall Pines, for well over a thousand years. When the rest of the world abandoned Peach Springs, the tribe quietly reclaimed it, and the town became its administrative center.

DIAMOND CREEK ROAD INTO THE GRAND CANYON: AN OPTIONAL DETOUR

This section of the route is not for everyone. Diamond Creek is an unpaved primitive road. It's not steep, but parts of it are rough and rocky, and it gets a bit splashy at the bottom, where it runs along the creek bed. It is also prone to washouts during summer storms. Most rental car contracts prohibit travel on roads like this one, but if your personal vehicle is a van, truck, or SUV—anything with good clearance—you're in for a treat. This road takes you all the way down to the Colorado River at the bottom of the Grand Canyon, the only road of any kind that can make that claim. It can be driven in a conventional sedan if you're sufficiently determined and very careful; don't try it in

Diamond Peak from Diamond Creek Road, Peach Springs.

a low-slung sports car, a compact, or a large RV.

If you decide to go for it, stop at the **Hualapai Lodge** in Peach Springs, where you can get information and a day-use permit from the tribe to travel the road ($28 per person per day in 2017); if you live in Arizona, ask about the discount for state residents.

The road starts across the highway from the Hualapai Lodge, on the street next to the market. Head north through a residential area until you come to a gate with a cattle guard and a sign that spells out the rules of this road, officially known as **Indian Route 6**. This is where the pavement ends. If you haven't paid the applicable fees, go no farther; tribal police patrol the road routinely, and the fine for trespassing is much more than the price of the permit.

After 6 easy miles you'll start down Peach Springs Canyon. The grade is relatively gentle, but the terrain changes rapidly, sandstone walls rising up steeply on either side of you as you descend 3,400 feet to the creek, at the base of a pyramid-shaped mountain called Diamond Peak, which dominates the view much of the way down. The road, very rocky at this point, follows the bed of Diamond Creek for the last mile or so. The creek runs year round, and shallow water flows across the road in half a dozen places. If it has rained recently, the water will be deeper. At the end of the

road you'll find a small parking lot with picnic ramadas, some portable toilets, and a campground. From here it is an easy 50-yard walk to the Colorado River, where, depending on the time of day and the season of the year, there's a good chance you'll see one or more river rafting parties loading, unloading, or simply taking a break on the narrow beach.

Over the course of centuries, flash floods down the side creeks of the Colorado have deposited debris in the main channel of the river, and as the debris piles up, the

River runners, Diamond Creek Road, Peach Springs, Arizona

Colorado River, Diamond Creek, Grand Canyon

flow is restricted and turbulent rapids are created. That's what happened here. At the point where Diamond Creek meets the river, the Colorado is abruptly whipped into froth by Diamond Creek Rapid, one of nearly 100 named rapids in the Grand Canyon. From here you have a rare opportunity for a close-up view of the world of the river runners, the brave souls who challenge these rapids, some of the most thrilling, most outrageously scenic white water in the world. Feel free to take a hike along the riverbank, but don't even think about going in for a swim; it's cold, it's deep, and the current would snatch you up like a rag doll.

This part of the Grand Canyon, more than a hundred miles downstream from Grand Canyon Village, is known as the Lower Granite Gorge. Though it's less deep and less colorful than the picture-postcard views in the national park, this is a very special place. It's the *bottom* of the Grand Canyon, and you didn't even have to break a sweat to get here. Take your time down by the river. Attune all your senses to the power of the mighty Colorado. The steady rumble of the river is amplified by the canyon walls, with the sharper pitch of the boiling rapid adding counterpoint. This is more than a sound; it's an elemental force: concentrated, primal, a relentless flow of energy that you can literally feel in your bones. If it moves you, check out **Colorado River and Trail Expeditions** for information on Grand Canyon rafting trips, one of the world's grandest adventures.

Return to Peach Springs the same way you drove in. If you don't plan to stay in the campground overnight, bear in mind that the day-use permits are valid only until 5 p.m.

Diamond Creek Road Highlights

Hualapai Lodge
900 AZ 66, Peach Springs, AZ 86434
(928) 769-2636
goroute66.us

Colorado River and Trail Expeditions
crateinc.com

PEACH SPRINGS TO WILLIAMS

Leaving Peach Springs on Route 66, continue east across the high desert of the Colorado Plateau for about 11 miles to **Grand Canyon Caverns**, a roadside attraction since the 1930s with many kitschy accoutrements: a motel and restaurant, an RV park, metal dinosaurs, old cars and trucks, and other Route 66 memorabilia. But the real

attraction is 200 to 300 feet underground: the largest dry caverns in the United States. Like Carlsbad Caverns, these are limestone caves, but there's been no seeping water here in several million years, so they are frozen in time. There are tours available; access is provided by an elevator that drops you 21 stories straight down into the cave.

Miniature golf, Grand Canyon Caverns, Route 66, Arizona

Twenty-five miles beyond the caverns you'll come to **Seligman**, the town that's done more than any other to pull Route 66 back from the brink of irrelevance. Angel Delgadillo's barbershop in Seligman was the birthplace

Snow Cap Drive-In, Route 66, Seligman, Arizona

of the Route 66 Association, an alliance of regional organizations dedicated to the preservation of Route 66 and its history. **Delgadillo's Snow Cap Drive-In** is the ultimate homage to the 1950s, and downtown Seligman is the ultimate restoration of the spirit of the Mother Road.

On the highway approaching and leaving Seligman, you'll see another classic reminder of that bygone era: **Burma-Shave signs**! From the 1920s to the mid-1960s, thousands of those signs lined America's highways. The gimmick was simple: a series of five or six signs were installed along the roadside, spaced about 100 yards apart. Each sign had a piece of a rhyming verse, ending with a punch line, and a final sign: "Burma-Shave." These signs were entertaining and wildly popular, breaking up the monotony of lengthy road trips and making that

shaving cream a household name, long before the days
of mass-market advertising. A fun example:

WITHIN THIS VALE

OF TOIL

AND SIN

YOUR HEAD GROWS BALD

BUT NOT YOUR CHIN—USE

The original signs have been gone for more than 50
years, but you'll see a dozen different sets of reproduc-
tions near Seligman.

Leaving Seligman, look
sharp for the right turn
you'll need to take to
follow the last section
of the original Route
66, which runs roughly
parallel to the Interstate
here for about 17 more
miles. Five miles before
Ash Fork, the Mother Road disappears with a merge onto
I-40, which will take you the rest of the way to Flagstaff,
about 40 miles away. **Ash Fork**, "The Flagstone Capital
of the World," has some historic Route 66 buildings and
businesses, as does Williams, 15 miles farther down the
road. In Williams, you'll also find the **Grand Canyon
Railway**, which offers daily round-trip excursions to
Grand Canyon National Park—an enjoyable journey that
eliminates the considerable hassle of finding a parking
space in Grand Canyon Village.

*Burma-Shave signs,
Route 66 near
Seligman*

As you approach Flagstaff, take Exit 191 off I-40,
which will lead you straight to Flagstaff's historic

Grand Canyon Railroad, Williams, Arizona

downtown. **Flagstaff** has been a railroad town since the 1880s; there's still passenger service on Amtrak and a steady flow of freight trains passing through, day and night. The Flagstaff Visitors Bureau is located in the old train station downtown, right on Historic Route 66. It's a great source of information about the area. For more about things to do and places to stay in and around Flagstaff, see **Scenic Side Trip 13**.

BEYOND FLAGSTAFF

Where are you going next? This book offers five different side trips that connect in Flagstaff, heading north, south, and east: **Scenic Side Trips 9**, **10**, **13**, **14**, and **15**. Check them out for the best of what northern Arizona has to offer.

Peach Springs to Williams Highlights

Grand Canyon Caverns
Mile marker 115, AZ 66, Peach Springs, AZ 86434
(928) 422-4565
gccaverns.com

Delgadillo's Snow Cap Drive-In
301 AZ 66, Seligman, AZ 86337
(928) 422-3291

Grand Canyon Railway
233 N. Grand Canyon Blvd., Williams, AZ 86046
(928) 635-4010
thetrain.com

Flagstaff Visitors Center
1 Historic Route 66, Flagstaff, AZ 86001
(928) 213-2951
flagstaffarizona.org

St. George, Utah, to Flagstaff, Arizona,

via Zion National Park, North Rim of the Grand Canyon, and Page

409 miles, **10** hours **15** minutes for drive time, more for optional routes, stops, and sightseeing

From Angel's Landing to Angel's Window, the view is beyond breathtaking—it's heavenly!

THIS SIDE TRIP RUNS FROM ST. GEORGE, UTAH, TO FLAGSTAFF, Arizona, beginning on Interstate 15 and ending on Interstate 40. It's not a shortcut, and it's not a detour; think of it more as a bridge between those two highways, a connecting route that crosses some of the most extraordinary terrain in the Southwest. For travelers headed into Arizona by way of southern Utah, this route is the perfect segue, offering three of the most spectacular canyons on the planet, all in the course of a day's drive. If you're not in too much of a hurry, this trip really should be savored. Stretch it out, if you can, by making at least one overnight stop along the way.   ➡➡

ST. GEORGE TO ZION NATIONAL PARK

Leaving St. George, drive north on Interstate 15. Get off at Exit 16, and follow UT 9 toward Hurricane. After about 10 miles, the road curves north, climbing up and over a low ridge of mountains before dropping down the other side, into the valley of the Virgin River. Follow the highway as it runs east into **Zion National Park**, 20 miles farther along. At the park entrance, you must pay the entrance fee, even if all you intend to do is drive through.

As you approach the park entrance, traffic will slow to a crawl, if not a dead stop. Zion is the fifth most visited national park in the U.S., drawing more visitors than Yellowstone and almost as many as Yosemite; if you visit during the high season, from April through September, there *will* be crowds. Take a good look around as you're waiting in line. There's nothing subtle about Zion National Park: soaring cliffs; waterfalls that spring from clefts in the mountainsides; slot canyons that twist through a wonderland

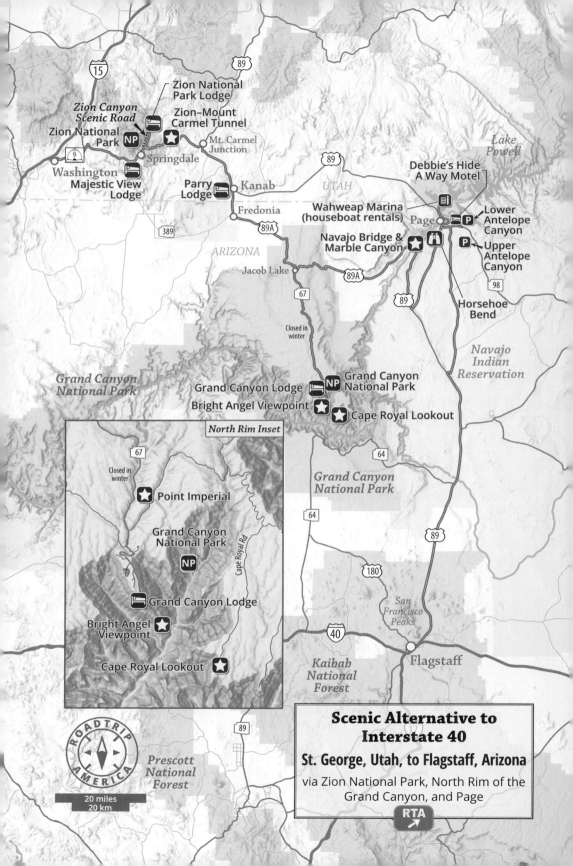

Scenic Alternative to Interstate 40

St. George, Utah, to Flagstaff, Arizona

via Zion National Park, North Rim of the Grand Canyon, and Page

National Park Passes

The fees to enter Zion and Grand Canyon National Parks are at the top end of the scale. Each park charges $30 per car for a 7-day pass; $60 for both parks. For $20 more ($80 total) you can purchase an **America the Beautiful Pass** when you enter Zion; it covers every national park and monument in the U.S. and it's valid for a full year. U.S. citizens 62 and older can get a **Senior Pass** for a onetime fee of $80, and it is valid for the rest of your life. There is also an annual Senior Pass which costs $20 per year. (These rates are accurate as of 2017 and are expected to rise.)

of multicolored stone. Zion has all that and more, and there are views, even from the road, that will take your breath away.

There is a canyon here, carved through the many-layered strata of the Colorado Plateau by the Virgin River, a major tributary of the Colorado. **Zion Canyon** is much smaller than its Grand Canyon cousin—half its depth, just 15 miles long, and so narrow in some places that sunlight never strikes the canyon floor—but it is astonishingly beautiful, a rhapsody in rock, with more "Oh, wow!" viewpoints than most people encounter in a lifetime. It is also a remarkable habitat. The park lies at the convergence of three distinct geographic regions: the Colorado Plateau, the Mojave Desert, and the Great Basin. The altitude change between the lowest point in the park and the highest is more than 5,000 feet, creating a range of ecological zones—deserts, grasslands, forests, even an alpine region—and an extraordinary range of local habitats that support hundreds of species of plants and animals, including 289 species of birds.

Like the Grand Canyon, Zion is a victim of its own popularity. By 1997, traffic had become so heavy that the Park Service banned private vehicles on the 6-mile-long Zion Canyon Scenic Road during the high season. Today shuttle buses ferry visitors to the many trailheads and scenic viewpoints along that route from March through September, and also on some weekends in the off-season; at other times the canyon road is open to private vehicles.

If you are driving a large van, truck, or RV, park workers will measure your vehicle at the entrance station; any vehicle over 11 feet 4 inches high or 7 feet 10 inches wide (including any mirrors, awnings, or jacks) will require a tunnel permit (currently $15) in order to pass through the park on UT 9 *(see below)*.

Many wonders of this park—places like The Narrows, **Angel's Landing**, and The Subway—can't be seen from the road; you'll need to get out and do some hiking, and for that, you should allow a full day. If you don't have that much time, don't worry. Simply driving through the park on UT 9, here called the Zion–Mount Carmel Highway, is a thrilling experience. This 25-mile stretch of road traverses the park from west to east and is open to private vehicles all year round (aside from temporary closures caused by rockslides or heavy snow). The panoramas along this road are stunning. Watch for the **Zion–Mount Carmel Tunnel** about 5 miles in. Bored through solid rock for more than a mile, it has a unique feature. The tunnel builders carved large openings into the sandstone cliff as access points for their equipment. When they were done, they shaped those openings into huge, arched gallery windows looking out over the valley below, providing amazing views and welcome fresh air for the benefit of motorists passing through.

Note. *Oversized vehicles may transit the tunnel only during daylight hours; check ahead for exact times, which vary seasonally. During those hours, all vehicles must follow an alternating one-way traffic pattern controlled by Rangers stationed at either end of the tunnel; in the peak season,*

Zion National Park Highlights

Zion National Park
163 Zion–Mount Carmel Highway,
Springdale, UT 84767
(435) 772-3256
nps.gov/zion

Zion National Park Lodge
1 Zion Canyon Scenic Drive,
Springdale, UT 84767
(435) 772-7700
zionlodge.com

Majestic View Lodge
2400 Zion-Mount Carmel Highway,
Springdale, UT 84767
(435) 772-0665
majesticviewlodge.com

Opposite: Virgin River, Zion National Park, Utah

Zion National Park, Utah

expect delays of as much as half an hour.

The historic **Zion National Park Lodge** is a wonderful place to stay inside the park, and there are several campgrounds. Reservations are a must, and should be made far in advance. The town of Springdale, near the west entrance to the park, also has lodging; the **Majestic View Lodge**, right on the main highway, is a good choice.

ZION TO GRAND CANYON NORTH RIM

Leaving Zion on UT 9, drive 13 miles to Mount Carmel Junction and the intersection with US 89. Bear right and follow that highway south to **Kanab**. If you couldn't find lodging close to Zion, try looking here; historic **Parry Lodge** on Center Street is a good choice. Beyond Kanab, US 89A splits from US 89 and heads south across the Arizona state line, on through the tiny town of Fredonia, and then up a series of switchbacks into mountains and pine forest, where the air is cool, even in summer, at an altitude of 8,000 feet. Thirty miles beyond Fredonia, you'll reach Jacob Lake and the intersection with AZ 67, the Grand Canyon Highway, which will take you 45 miles south to the **North Rim of the Grand Canyon** in Grand Canyon National Park.

It's a long detour, but you've got to go—even if you've been to the South Rim once or many times. It's the same canyon, yes, but the North Rim is off the beaten track and gets only 10 percent of the crowds, so the experience is more intimate. Seen from this side, the canyon seems to have a different texture and character; the buttressed towers of stone seem closer to you, the drop from the rim more precipitous. It's a beautiful drive in from Jacob Lake though conifers and stands of aspens that turn dazzling gold in autumn. Allow at least 2.5 hours for a quick round-trip excursion, which gives you enough time to stand a while at the rim, struck dumb by the view. **Bright Angel viewpoint,** a short walk from the park lodge, offers a breathtaking vista of multicolored buttes and spires rippling away into the distance. **Point Imperial,** 11 miles away, is well worth the extra half-hour drive out and back, offering a completely different perspective. If you have lots of time, drive to **Cape Royal overlook** (46 miles round-trip from the visitors center) for a 270-degree panorama, the most sweeping view of the canyon available from any point on

Aspens, AZ Route 67, approaching North Rim, Grand Canyon National Park

Grand Canyon from Point Imperial, North Rim, Grand Canyon National Park

Zion to Grand Canyon Highlights

Parry Lodge
89 E. Center St., Kanab, UT 84741
(435) 644-2601
parrylodge.com

Grand Canyon National Park North Rim
204 AZ 67, North Rim, AZ 86052
(928) 638-7888
nps.gov/grca

Grand Canyon Lodge
6225 AZ 67, North Rim, AZ 86052
928-638-2611
grandcanyonforever.com

either rim; the overlook is so remote, you might even have it all to yourself. From the right vantage point, **Angel's Window**, a large natural opening in the limestone cliff beneath the overlook, frames a perfect postcard view of the river running through the canyon, 6 miles away and 5,000 feet below.

There's a terrific campground at the North Rim, and the **Grand Canyon Lodge**, a hotel built in the late 1920s, is a great place to stay. In fact, it's the *only* place to stay, so reservations are a must.

Note. *All facilities at the North Rim close from mid-October to mid-May, whether the road is open or not. For more about the Grand Canyon, see* **Scenic Side Trip 14**.

GRAND CANYON NORTH RIM TO PAGE

Leaving Grand Canyon National Park, drive back out the same way you came in, on AZ 67. When you reach US 89A, turn right, and continue through the forested mountains until the road drops back down into open country, zigging and zagging through tight hairpin curves. Here the highway runs along the bottom step of the Grand Staircase, a series of escarpments, immense cliff-like ridges that drop in altitude, forming a series of steps as you travel south from Utah's Bryce Canyon to the Grand Canyon. Each step represents a different era in Earth's geological history. On your left as you travel from Jacob Lake toward Page, you'll pass by the **Vermilion Cliffs**, one of the most well-defined of these escarpments. This beautiful formation, made up of banded layers of vermilion-hued sandstone that go on for miles, is part of the vast **Grand Staircase–Escalante National Monument**, which protects 1.8 million acres of wilderness in southern Utah,

Opposite: Vermilion Cliffs, US 89A

the largest national monument in the U.S.

Forty miles from Jacob Lake you'll reach **Lee's Ferry**, where you'll cross over the Colorado River on the Navajo Bridge. This is the only spot along this part of the Colorado where the river can be easily approached from both sides, and it has been an important crossing point since the mid-19th century; regular ferryboat service was established in 1873. Today, there are two bridges. The newer one carries vehicular traffic, while the old bridge is reserved for pedestrians and provides a fabulous view of the river flowing between the sheer rock walls of Marble Canyon. There's a campground at Lee's Ferry, right by the river, and the beach is the launching point for many Grand Canyon river trips.

After crossing the bridge, drive 14 miles on US 89A to the junction with US 89 at Bitter Springs, and follow that another 26 miles to **Page**, a town of about 8,000 permanent residents, which was founded in 1957 to provide housing for the thousands of workers brought in to build Glen Canyon Dam. Construction began in 1956, when President Dwight Eisenhower pushed a button on his desk in the Oval Office, triggering the first dynamite blast at the work site, 2,000 miles away. The federally funded project took 10 years to complete. Once Glen Canyon filled with water, Page became the preferred access point for newly created Lake Powell, even though most of the lake is in Utah.

Lake Powell is quite a sight to behold. The water is the bluest blue imaginable; it is surrounded by sheer sandstone cliffs; and rising from the surface like strange islands are the multicolored buttes and pillars and ridges of the drowned canyon. **Glen Canyon National Recreation Area** gets as many as 3 million visitors a year, and the favorite activity is "house-boating." The

Opposite: Colorado River from Navajo Bridge, Lee's Ferry, Arizona

Opposite: Twisting passageways, Lower Antelope Canyon, Navajo Reservation

lake has almost 2,000 miles of shoreline and 96 major side canyons. You can explore with a houseboat for weeks at a time, spending every night in a different secluded cove, fishing off your back porch, lounging in deck chairs, or playing on Jet Skis while cruising the ever-changing shoreline. Rivalling the lake in popularity is **Antelope Canyon**, a place that few people outside the area had even heard of until the mid-1980s. Located on the Navajo Reservation just east of Page, this extraordinary slot canyon opened to public tours in 1997, when two sections of the canyon, Upper Antelope Canyon and Lower Antelope Canyon, were set aside as tribal parks *(see sidebar)*.

Another favorite spot, also extremely popular with photographers, is **Horseshoe Bend**. Technically, this natural wonder is an "entrenched meander" of the Colorado River, which snakes between steep cliffs in a spectacular 270-degree bend. Located just below Glen

Houseboats at Wahweap Marina, Lake Powell, Page, Arizona

Above: Tour group exiting Lower Antelope Canyon; Opposite: Sunbeams, Lower Antelope Canyon

Antelope Canyon

Even if you've never heard of Antelope Canyon, you've probably seen pictures of it. Twisting passageways through psychedelic spirals of reddish-orange sandstone, aglow with ethereal beams of light? That's Antelope Canyon, one of the most photographed locations in the Southwest. Slot canyons like Antelope are formed over the course of many thousands of years. Summer monsoons dump rain on the watershed faster than the ground can absorb it, causing flash floods down the side canyons. Year after year, huge volumes of rainwater sluice through channels and cracks in the soft sandstone; the abrasive, silt-laden torrent carves narrow, twisting channels into the cross-bedded layers of rock, sculpting it into swirling formations that look like petrified waves.

Upper Antelope Canyon is the more popular of the two sections because it's a bigger, wider space and it's entirely at ground level, so there's no climbing or clambering required. Tours leave from downtown Page, or from the small parking lot off AZ 98 just south of town, and include transportation to the canyon entrance, 2 miles or so off the highway. Upper Antelope is small, only 100 yards long, and because there are several tour companies, it can get very crowded. Most visitors don't mind; the sandstone formations here are jaw-dropping!

The parking area for **Lower Antelope Canyon** is right by the entrance, so no transportation is needed, but a visit to this section requires a steep climb down metal ladders bolted to the rock. The Lower Canyon is a half mile long, but very narrow, so visitors walk in single file. Because it's less accessible, Lower Antelope is less visited, and noticeably less crowded.

Tours of the two sections are run by different companies. They're ticketed separately, and each lasts about an hour. Ask about the photography tours, which give you more time in the canyons for a somewhat higher price.

Canyon Dam, Horseshoe Bend can be seen by hiking 1.5 miles round-trip from a parking lot off US 89 between mileposts 544 and 545, just south of Page. The overlook, nearly always crowded, provides a panoramic view from above. You'll need a wide-angle lens to capture the whole

Horseshoe Bend, Page, Arizona

thing with a single picture.

A great place to stay while in Page is on "The Street of Little Motels," located in the historic quarter of town, just off Lake Powell Boulevard. Turn east on either Elm Street or Navajo Drive, and drive two short blocks to

Grand Canyon to Page Highlights

Wahweap Marina (houseboat rentals)
100 Lake Shore Drive, Page AZ 86040
(928) 645-2433
lakepowell.com

Navajo Tours (Upper Antelope Canyon)
Off Indian Route 222, south of AZ 98, Page, AZ,
86040
(928) 698-3384
navajotours.com

Dixie Ellis' Lower Antelope Canyon Tours
Off Indian Route 222, north of AZ 98, Page, AZ,
86040
(928) 640-1761
antelopelowercanyon.com

Debbie's Hide A Way Motel
119 8th Ave., Page, AZ 86040
(928) 645-1224
debbieshideaway.com

Eighth Avenue. Between Elm and Navajo, Eighth Avenue is lined with vintage cinder-block apartments that were once home to the dam builders and their families. Now they've been converted into fully furnished apartment motels, with units offered at about the same price as a standard motel room—a great deal for families. Try **Debbie's Hide A Way**—not elegant, but clean, and very homey.

ON TO FLAGSTAFF

Leaving Page, take US 89 south, through Bitter Springs and Cameron, to Flagstaff. This scenic drive, which skirts the eastern side of Arizona's tallest mountains, the San Francisco Peaks, is about 135 miles, and will take about 2.5 hours. For more about US 89 between Flagstaff and Cameron, see **Scenic Side Trip 15**. For more about things to see and do in and around Flagstaff, including options for lodging, see **Scenic Side Trip 14**.

Flagstaff and the Grand Canyon Loop

257 miles, **7** hours **45** minutes for drive time, more for optional routes, stops, and sightseeing

A Grand Canyon sunrise and an alpine sunset, all in a fine day's drive

THIS LOOP TRIP, WHICH BEGINS AND ENDS IN FLAGSTAFF, GIVES you the grandest canyon in the world and the tallest—and prettiest—mountains in Arizona, both in the same beautiful day. It's an amazingly easy drive that you won't soon forget. ▶▶

FLAGSTAFF TO THE GRAND CANYON
Leaving Flagstaff, follow the I-40 Business Route (Historic Route 66) east from downtown until US 89 splits off to the left, just before the Flagstaff Mall. Stay on US 89 as it curves north out of town. Just off the highway on your left, Humphreys and Agassiz, the two highest of the San Francisco Peaks, rise to more than 12,000 feet, making a serious play for your attention. There will be snow on those mountains from late fall well into spring. That's quite a sight, in the early morning light.

Fifty-two miles north of Flagstaff,

shortly after you cross the unmarked boundary of the Navajo Nation, you'll reach a traffic circle, the intersection of US 89 with AZ 64. Stay on US 89 as it exits the circle, and keep going north another mile or so to **Cameron Trading Post.** You'll find it on the left, just before the bridge

Wupatki National Monument, Arizona

Sunset Crater and Wupatki National Monuments

From Flagstaff, it's less than 80 miles to the Grand Canyon, and most travelers, especially first-timers, are anxious to get there. If you don't mind slowing your roll, there are two national monuments along the way: **Sunset Crater Volcano** and **Wupatki**. These two parks are part of **Scenic Side Trip 15**, but if you're not planning to drive that route, consider including them with this one. Sunset Crater and its associated lava flow are the remains of a volcano that erupted only 900 years ago. Wupatki, "The Tall House," is a remarkable 800-year-old pueblo ruin. You can see them both by taking a slight detour off US 89, a 34-mile loop that's an exceptionally beautiful drive. *For more information and directions, see* **Scenic Side Trip 15** starting on page 221

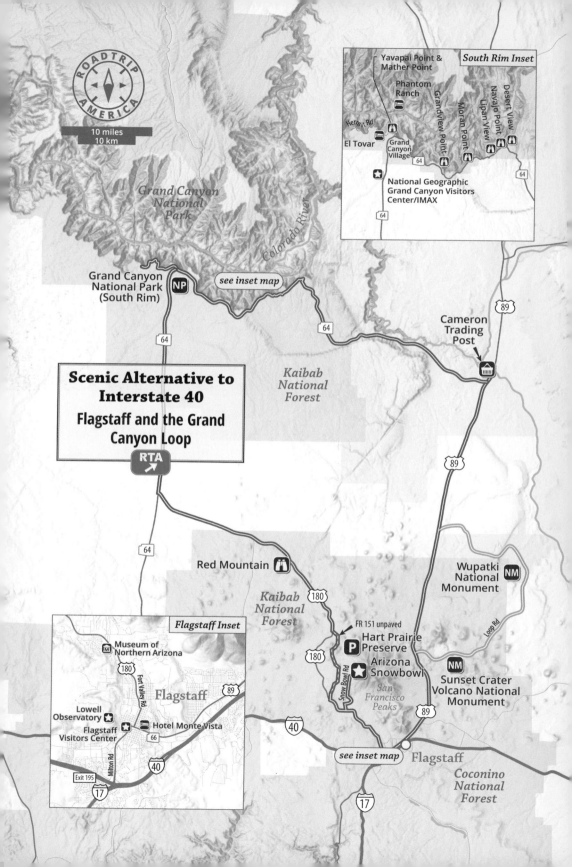

ROADTRIP AMERICA

10 miles
10 km

Grand Canyon National Park

Colorado River

South Rim Inset

Yavapai Point & Mather Point

Phantom Ranch

Hermit Rd

El Tovar

Grand Canyon Village

Grandview Point

Moran Point

Lipan Point

Navajo Point

Desert View

64

64

National Geographic Grand Canyon Visitors Center/IMAX

64

Grand Canyon National Park (South Rim)

NP

see inset map

64

64

Cameron Trading Post

89

Scenic Alternative to Interstate 40

Flagstaff and the Grand Canyon Loop

RTA

Kaibab National Forest

89

64

Red Mountain

180

Kaibab National Forest

FR 151 unpaved

Hart Prairie Preserve

P

Arizona Snowbowl

180

Snow Bowl Rd

San Francisco Peaks

89

Wupatki National Monument

NM

Loop Rd

Sunset Crater Volcano National Monument

NM

Flagstaff Inset

Museum of Northern Arizona

M

180

Fort Valley Rd

Flagstaff

89

Lowell Observatory

Flagstaff Visitors Center

Hotel Monte Vista

66

Milton Rd

40

Exit 195

17

40

see inset map

Flagstaff

Coconino National Forest

17

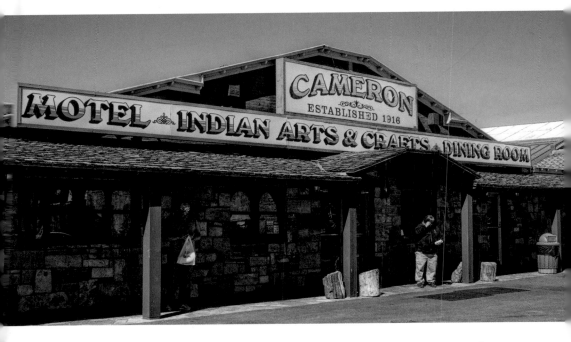

that spans the Little Colorado River. The first bridge on this spot, built in 1911, made it easy to cross a river that had long been a major obstacle to travel. The resulting traffic brought big changes to this once sleepy corner of the reservation, not the least of which was a new trading post, established where it could serve Native American communities on both sides of the river.

Cameron Trading Post, Cameron, Arizona

Trading posts were an important part of reservation life in the early 1900s. Isolated communities were completely off the grid, and the people relied on a barter economy, swapping their livestock, raw wool, woven blankets, and a variety of handmade crafts for dry goods and other supplies available at the post. The trader would resell the livestock and wool to other traders, and sell the blankets and crafts to tourists. By the 1920s, private automobiles were commonplace in the West, and adventurous travelers attracted by the nearby Grand Canyon began to explore farther afield, putting places like Cameron on the map.

The trading post still sells Native American arts and crafts, but today the emphasis is more on art than craft. There are floor-to-ceiling display cases loaded with Kachina dolls, pottery, weavings, and fine silver and turquoise jewelry—beautiful pieces made by Navajo, Hopi, and Zuni artisans. These days, such items are usually sold on consignment, not bartered for beans, and the quality of the high-end merchandise is off the charts. Imagine shopping in a museum, where most of the exhibits are for sale. The trading post also offers a good selection of less expensive souvenirs, and operates a restaurant and a motel on the property—something to keep in mind if lodging in Grand Canyon National Park is unavailable or out of your price range.

Flagstaff to The Grand Canyon Highlights

Sunset Crater Volcano National Monument
6082 Sunset Crater Road, Flagstaff, AZ 86004
(928) 526-0502
nps.gov/sucr

Wupatki National Monument
25137 N. Sunset Crater–Wupatki Loop Road, Flagstaff, AZ 86004
(928) 679-2365
nps.gov/wupa

Cameron Trading Post
466 US 89, Cameron, AZ 86020
(928) 679-2231
camerontradingpost.com

GRAND CANYON SOUTH RIM

Leaving the trading post, drive south on US 89 back to the traffic circle, and take the first exit, west on AZ 64. This section of highway, built in 1935, follows the course of the Little Colorado River as it makes its way toward that big canyon, a few short miles downstream. The point where the Little Colorado joins the big one is called The Confluence, and it marks the beginning of the Grand Canyon proper: 1,900 square miles of wilderness that was set aside in 1919 as **Grand Canyon National Park**. The Little Colorado has carved a canyon of its own here called the Little Colorado River Gorge; you'll see it off to your right, a preview of the wonders to come. As the road climbs into a low range of hills, the gorge veers off to the north, twisting its way across the plateau like a snake, a deep gash in the landscape as much as a quarter mile wide. At the top of a gentle grade, the road levels out,

and you'll come up on the east entrance to the national park, where you'll need to pay the entrance fee or show your pass (see sidebar, National Park Passes, page 191).

Little Colorado River Gorge, from US 64

The fun starts almost immediately. For the next 22 miles, AZ 64 hugs the South Rim of the Grand Canyon, and the first major viewpoint, **Desert View**, is just around the next curve. Here, you'll find a large parking lot, a visitors center, and the iconic 70-foot-tall **Desert View Watchtower**, which has stood sentinel on the rim here since 1932. Beyond the tower, there's a void.

You know what's out there.

Park your vehicle, walk to the edge, and take a good, long look. This isn't just a big hole in the ground; this is the *Grand Canyon,* and there is no other place like it, not even close. Nothing prepares you for your first live glimpse of the Grand Canyon— not photos, not films. It's so *big,* and so *wide,* and so *deep;* it simply isn't possible to wrap your mind around the scale of it.

Desert Watchtower, Grand Canyon National Park, South Rim

From Desert View, look to the northeast, where the canyon is widest, and you can clearly see the muddy river at the bottom. Scan the panorama. As the river comes toward you and then curves to the west, the canyon cuts deeper; it becomes a gorge within a gorge, lined with multicolored cliffs and angular buttes. A stone labyrinth fills the horizon as far as the eye can see; horizontal layers of burnt umber, mauve, and ochre traced with touches of ash, streaks of bone, and smears of peach, all edged with deep purple shadows.

Leaving Desert View, turn right (west) back onto AZ 64, and drive on toward Grand Canyon Village. There are

Grand Canyon Sunrise

If you want to see the sun rise over the Grand Canyon—an incomparable experience—your best bet is to stay overnight in Grand Canyon Village and walk, drive, or shuttle to the nearest overlook when the magic hour grows near. Mather Point and Yaki Point are considered best for the purpose, and the shuttle to those viewpoints starts running at 4:30 a.m., well before first light. If you're driving in from Flagstaff, you'll need to set out earlier than that. It's only 80 miles to the closest overlook, but you should allow 2 full hours for the drive.

more overlooks along the way, some with parking areas and others that require parallel parking along the side of the road. **Navajo Point** and **Lipan Point** are close to Desert View and offer a similar perspective. Farther west, you'll come to **Moran Point** and **Grandview Point**. From these, you'll have a good view of **Vishnu Temple** and **Wotan's Throne**, monumental rock formations within the canyon, instantly recognizable from classic photographs of this unique landscape.

Farther on you'll reach **Grand Canyon Village**. This is tourist central, the location of the biggest parking lot,

Colorado River in the Grand Canyon

the main visitors center, six hotels, the largest campground, a variety of restaurants, gift shops, trailheads, shuttle buses, a train station, a mule barn, and a post office. This is also where you'll find most of the people. In 2016, the Grand Canyon received more than 6 million visitors, making it the second most visited national park in the United States, after Great Smoky Mountains National Park in Tennessee. Divide 6 million by the number of days in the year, and you'll understand why it's so difficult to find a space in that parking lot.

Mather Point and **Yavapai Point** both offer fantastic canyon views, and both are near the Village, but because they're close to the main entrance, they're both very crowded, and parking can be a problem. For a less frustrating Grand Canyon experience, stay on the hunt until you bag a parking space, anywhere you can, then hop on one of the free shuttles. Your best bet is the Hermit Road shuttle, also known as the Red Route, which takes visitors to **Hopi Point** and **The Abyss**, along with six other jaw-dropping viewpoints along **Hermit Road**. Private vehicles are allowed on that road in the winter (December through February), but the rest of the year, the 8-mile loop along the rim is restricted to the shuttles. Be grateful for that. Without the shuttles, summer traffic on the South Rim drive would be pure gridlock.

If you'd like to stay the night within the park, try **El Tovar,** an elegant hotel built in 1905, situated right on the canyon rim. **Grand Canyon Lodges**, the primary park concessionaire, manages El Tovar and six of the other hotels inside the park through a centralized reservation system. Their most unusual property is **Phantom Ranch,** which was built in 1922 at the *bottom* of the Grand Canyon. The accommodations are rustic, but the location? Oh, my! To get to it, you'll have to hike—or ride a mule—9.3 miles down from the South Rim, and after your stay, it's 9.3 miles back up! A seventh hotel, Yavapai Lodge, as well as Trailer Village RV Park, are managed by the **Delaware North Company**.

Note. *All Grand Canyon lodges, including Phantom Ranch, are often booked solid as much as a year in advance, so plan well ahead. Accommodations are also available in Tusayan, just south of the national park on AZ 64.*

Follow AZ 64 south, out of the park. You'll pass through Tusayan, where **National Geographic's Grand Canyon Imax Theater** offers frequent showings of a spectacular documentary. Some claim it's better than the real thing. Not in my book, but it is pretty cool, and the film takes maximum advantage of the big-screen IMAX format, giving you a flyover experience without the price of a helicopter ride, as well as a taste of rafting the rapids, without getting wet.

THE SAN FRANCISCO PEAKS

Leaving Tusayan, drive about 25 miles to the intersection with US 180. Turn left, toward Flagstaff, and drive east/ southeast for about 18 miles to milepost 247. When you spot a dirt road and a cattle guard on the right side of the road, pull over and look due south. Rising 1,000 feet above the surrounding terrain is **Red Mountain**, an extinct volcano. Even from the highway, you can see that

South Rim Highlights

Grand Canyon National Park (South Rim)
(928) 638-7888
nps.gov/grca

National Geographic Grand Canyon Visitors Center/imax
450 AZ 64, Grand Canyon, AZ, 86023
(928) 638-2468
explorethecanyon.com

El Tovar
Village Loop Drive, Grand Canyon Village
(928) 638-2631
grandcanyonlodges.com/lodging/el-tovar

Grand Canyon Lodges and Reservations (including Phantom Ranch)
10 Albright St., Grand Canyon, AZ 86023
(838) 297-2757, 928-638-2631
grandcanyonlodges.com

Delaware North Company (Yavapai Lodge and Trailer Village)
11 Yavapai Lodge Road, Grand Canyon, AZ 86023
(877) 404-4511
visitgrandcanyon.com

Above: Inside the exploded crater, Red Mountain Volcano, Arizona

Opposite: Aspens in the fall, Hart Prairie Road near Flagstaff

the cinder cone has collapsed on the north side, forming a U-shaped amphitheater where the internal structure of the volcano is exposed. If you'd like a closer look, follow the dirt road to a small parking area; from there, you'll have a pleasant hike to an eerie, secluded space inside the ruptured caldera, filled with bizarre rock formations—a 3-mile round-trip that's well worth the effort.

From Red Mountain, continue south on US 180 for 11.8 miles, then keep your eye out on the left for Fire Road 151, an unpaved road that intersects US 180 at an angle just after you come around a curve. Follow FR 151 through a beautiful pine and aspen forest for about 5 miles, until you come to the **Hart Prairie Preserve.** This 245-acre protected area, home to the world's largest stand of rare Bebb willows, is administered by the Nature Conservancy. Guided nature walks are offered on summer Sundays and by appointment. The surrounding area, at an elevation of 8,500 feet, is exceptionally beautiful, especially in autumn when the aspens turn gold on the mountainsides.

Stay on FR 151, now called Hart Prairie Road, as it runs through forest and meadows for another 5 miles, until it rejoins US 180. Turn left onto the highway, and drive another 3 miles to Snowbowl Road. This fabulous road, paved all the way, takes you 7 miles up the mountain to **Arizona Snowbowl**, Flagstaff's ski area, at 9,200 feet. From there, moderately strenuous hiking trails take you all the way to the summit, or—easier—park your car by the lodge and hop on the ski lift, which operates year round. The lift will carry you a half mile higher, to 11,500 feet, where

San Francisco Peaks Highlights

Hart Prairie Preserve
(928) 779-6129

Arizona Snowbowl
9300 N. Snowbowl Road, Flagstaff, AZ 86001
(928) 779-1951
snowbowl.ski

Ski Lift, Snowbowl, San Francisco Peaks, near Flagstaff

you'll have a view all the way to the Grand Canyon, 70 miles away. On the mountain, you'll see snow in the winter, autumn leaves in the fall, and vast fields of wildflowers from spring all the way into August. If you haven't lingered overly long at the Grand Canyon, or at any of the other stops along the way, the sun will be low in the sky right about now, setting that landscape aglow.

FLAGSTAFF

Head back down the mountain to US 180 and turn left toward Flagstaff. After about 4 miles, you'll come to the **Museum of Northern Arizona**, a wonderful museum with exhibits drawn from a collection of more than 5 million artifacts, specimens, and fine art pieces related to the natural and cultural heritage of the Colorado Plateau. If it's already closed when you drive by, consider coming back in the morning.

Flagstaff is Arizona's playground, with winter sports in the snow season and cool temperatures in the summer (30 degrees cooler than Phoenix). It's long been a haven for hikers, bikers, campers, glampers, and vacationing families. It's also the home of **Northern Arizona University**, the smallest of the three state-operated universities but by far the most popular with young people who love the outdoors.

Just up the hill from campus you'll find the **Lowell Observatory.** Established in 1894, it is one of the oldest astronomical observatories in the United States. It was here, using a 13-inch telescope, that astronomer Clyde Tombaugh discovered the dwarf planet Pluto, back in 1930. Another vintage telescope is still in use today for stargazing in Flagstaff's clear night skies. The observatory offers tours and programs for visitors, and there's a fabulous view of Flagstaff from the road to the top. That view alone is worth the drive up.

Downtown Flagstaff has many historic homes, churches, and other buildings, most dating to the early 1900s, when Flagstaff was an outpost and railroad town with a growing lumber industry. The old Santa Fe Railroad Station does double duty as the Flagstaff Visitors Center; they have maps and other information for a variety of self-guided tours of the area. If you like the ambience of the old downtown, consider a night at the **Hotel Monte Vista.** Built in 1927, the hotel has hosted many celebrities, including John Wayne, Clark Gable, and Humphrey Bogart. In fact, a scene from one of Bogie's best-loved movies, *Casablanca*, was filmed in one of the rooms of this hotel. The building is showing its age and lacks some modern amenities, but it's clean and well run, and a fun place to stay.

Flagstaff Highlights

Museum of Northern Arizona
3101 N. Fort Valley Road, Flagstaff, AZ 86001
(928) 774-5213
musnaz.org

Lowell Observatory
1400 W. Mars Hill Road, Flagstaff, AZ 86001
(928) 774-3358
lowell.edu

Flagstaff Visitors Center
1 E. Historic Route 66, Flagstaff, AZ 86001
(928) 213-2951
flagstaffarizona.org

Hotel Monte Vista
100 N. San Francisco St., Flagstaff, AZ 86001
(928) 779-6971
hotelmontevista.com

BEYOND FLAGSTAFF

If you're headed south toward Phoenix and don't want to take Interstate 17, you can reverse the itinerary of either **Scenic Side Trip 9** or **Scenic Side Trip 10**; both routes include Sedona and the Red Rock country. Headed west? Try reversing **Scenic Side Trip 12**, which will take you along the best of Route 66 and down an amazing road to the Colorado River *inside* the Grand Canyon. Reversing **Scenic Side Trip 13** will take you to the North Rim of the Grand Canyon and on to Zion National Park, in Utah. Headed east? **Scenic Side Trip 15** will take you to Holbrook by way of the Hopi Mesas.

Flagstaff to Holbrook
via the Hopi Mesas

282 miles, **7** hours for drive time, more for optional routes, stops, and sightseeing

Don't worry, be Hopi!

IF YOU'RE TRAVELING EAST ON INTERSTATE 40, THE STRETCH between Flagstaff and Holbrook is only 90 miles, with a usual drive time of less than 90 minutes. This side trip is an out-of-your-way detour that will triple that mileage and requires at least 5 extra hours. What you'll get in exchange is a glimpse of a different world: an ancient world, a society that values humility more than celebrity, generosity more than wealth, and respect for the Earth as the ultimate source of power.   ➡

The Hopi Reservation, *Hopitutskwa*, or Hopiland, is bordered on all sides by the much larger Navajo Nation. Culturally and geographically isolated, Hopitutskwa truly is a different world—a world within a world within a world—comprising 2,500 square miles of high desert 60 miles southeast of the Grand Canyon. The reservation is centered on three mesas, flat-topped ridges that rise above the Colorado Plateau: **First Mesa**, **Second Mesa**, and **Third Mesa**. These narrow uplands are the ancestral home of the *Hopituh Shi-nu-mu*, one of the least assimilated of all the Native American tribes: a gentle, reclusive people whose roots in this arid region go back more than 2,000 years.

FLAGSTAFF AREA NATIONAL MONUMENTS

Leaving Flagstaff, take Interstate 40 to Exit 204, at the easternmost edge of town, and follow the signs to **Walnut Canyon National Monument**. There are two attractions here: a

beautiful canyon with unusually diverse plant life and, wedged into natural alcoves high on the canyon walls, the remains of Sinagua cliff dwellings dating to AD 1150. The most popular activity here is

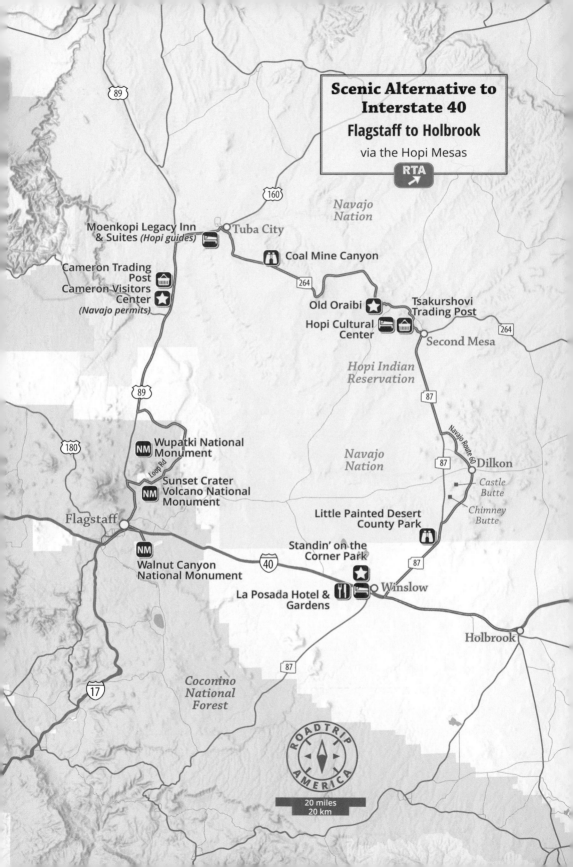

Scenic Alternative to Interstate 40
Flagstaff to Holbrook
via the Hopi Mesas

RTA

Navajo Nation

89

160

Moenkopi Legacy Inn & Suites *(Hopi guides)*
Tuba City

Coal Mine Canyon

Cameron Trading Post
Cameron Visitors Center
(Navajo permits)

264

Old Oraibi

Tsakurshovi Trading Post

Hopi Cultural Center

Second Mesa

264

Hopi Indian Reservation

89

87

Wupatki National Monument

Loop Rd

Sunset Crater Volcano National Monument

Navajo Nation

87

Navajo Route 60

Dilkon

Castle Butte

Chimney Butte

87

Little Painted Desert County Park

Flagstaff

180

Walnut Canyon National Monument

40

Standin' on the Corner Park

87

La Posada Hotel & Gardens

Winslow

Holbrook

17

Coconino National Forest

87

ROADTRIP AMERICA

20 miles
20 km

a mile-long hike from the visitors center down into the canyon, and back up again. The trail descends through several distinct vegetation zones and passes near the remnants of more than two dozen prehistoric Sinagua apartment-like structures, all with beautiful views. A second trail leads to

Walnut Canyon National Monument, Arizona

overlooks along the canyon rim and to a picnic area that's popular with locals.

Leaving Walnut Canyon, head east on Walnut Canyon Road, which crosses over the Interstate before swinging to the left and merging with Historic Route 66. Follow the old highway back toward town until it intersects US 89. Turn right and head north on US 89; after about 12 miles you'll see a sign for **Sunset Crater Volcano** and **Wupatki National Monuments.** Turn right and stay on that paved park road as it leads you on a curvy 35-mile loop, a beautiful cruise through both of these national monuments, before returning you to US 89, 15 miles north of where you left it. A single admission fee covers both parks.

First up is **Sunset Crater Volcano.** Stop in at the visitors center, 2 miles east of the entrance, and take a few minutes to watch the short documentary film, which shows, quite graphically, what happened here. The eruption that created Sunset Crater occurred just 900 years ago, forcing the people who lived nearby to abandon the land they had occupied for hundreds of years. The volcano is off-limits to hikers because the

Lava field, Sunset Crater National Monument, Arizona

Wupatki National Monument, Arizona

cinder crust is very fragile, but a mile hike along Lava Flow Trail takes you through the lava beds at the base of the mountain, and another hike, the Lenox Crater Trail, takes you to a smaller cinder cone where you can explore more freely. If hiking up and down hills at this breathless 7,000-foot altitude isn't your cup of tea, you can get a good look at the lava beds—a surreal landscape of jagged black rock—right alongside the park road, no hiking required.

Nineteen miles farther along that road are the remains of **Wupatki**, an imposing multistory structure that literally rose from the ashes of the volcano. The ash from the eruptions improved the soil of the area to such an extent that when native people returned to farming here, their efforts produced unprecedented yields of corn, beans, and squash; the bounty sparked a florescence of their culture that lasted

100 years. It was during that period that this remarkable pueblo was built.

Wupatki, which means "Tall House" in the Hopi language, rises unexpectedly from a flat area surrounded by low hills, and yet, in an odd way, it seems to belong in that spot. The communal house, which had as many as 100 rooms, was built of red sandstone slabs, limestone blocks, and chunks of basalt, all cemented together with a clay-based mortar. The complex incorporates a natural outcropping of the same red sandstone, and the weathered walls curve and flow around natural boulders, creating an organic architecture—the blocks, the stone, the eroded soil—all of it the same sunbaked shade of red. The tall house is literally part of the landscape where it has stood, largely intact, for more than 800 years.

There are a number of other ruins in the park, as well as several blowholes, openings in the sandstone from which the earth "breathes" in response to changes in temperature and barometric pressure. Sometimes a blowhole inhales, creating suction, and sometimes it exhales, blowing cool air at a velocity that can approach 30 mph.

National Monuments Highlights

Walnut Canyon National Monument
3 Walnut Canyon Road, Flagstaff, AZ 86004
(928) 526-3367
nps.gov/waca

Sunset Crater Volcano National Monument
6082 Sunset Crater Road, Flagstaff, AZ 86004
(928) 526-0502
nps.gov/sucr

Wupatki National Monument
25137 N. Sunset Crater–Wupatki Loop Road, Flagstaff, AZ 86004
(928) 679-2365
nps.gov/wupa

COAL MINE CANYON

Leaving Wupatki, drive 13 miles west on the park road back to US 89, and follow that highway north 20 miles to the visitors center in Cameron, on the Navajo Reservation. Here you can purchase Navajo backcountry permits, which are required if you wish to visit the spectacular and all but unknown geological marvel called **Coal Mine Canyon**, about 39 miles away.

To get to the canyon, continue north on US 89. Just before the bridge over the Little Colorado River, you'll

Windmill marking the road to Coal Mine Canyon, near Tuba City, AZ

Coal Mine Canyon, near Tuba City, AZ

come upon the **Cameron Trading Post,** which is well worth a stop (*see* **Scenic Side Trip 14**). About 14 miles farther on, bear right at the intersection with US 160, toward Tuba City, and continue for 10 miles to the intersection with AZ 264. Turn right, and follow AZ 264 east toward Keams Canyon and Hotevilla. After about 15 miles, between mileposts 336 and 337, you'll see a dirt track and a gate with a cattle guard on the north side of the highway. There's a two-story house in the distance, set well back from the road, but the important landmark is the windmill; it's the only windmill for miles around, and the top of it is just visible above a sandy hill. To reach the Coal Mine Canyon overlook, follow the dirt track, keeping to the right of the windmill. Drive slowly; the road is very bumpy, and you don't want to spook the cows. When you see the concrete picnic tables, you'll know you've arrived.

The view from this spot is startling when you come upon it all at once: a narrow gorge, some 4 miles long, walled in by brightly colored cliffs and bristling with fantastic rock formations: spires, fins, and hoodoos that rival those in Utah's Bryce Canyon. The layers of colored rock are so sharply defined they're like stripes on a flag: reddish-orange, white, tan, and gray. Equally astonishing? You're likely to have the place entirely to yourself. There are few visitors because there are no facilities here—no water, no toilets, not so much as a road sign—and the jurisdiction is a bit of a muddle. The picnic spot and the area along the canyon rim are on the Navajo Reservation. Everything below the rim—the canyon itself and all the primitive trails running through it—is on the Hopi Reservation. Your Navajo backcountry permit authorizes overnight camping, as well as travel to the overlook, but you have to provide your own ... everything.

To hike inside the canyon, you'll have to hire a Hopi guide; arrangements can be made through the **Moenkopi Legacy Inn** near Tuba City.

> ### Coal Mine Canyon Highlights
>
> **Cameron Visitors Center (Navajo permits)**
> Junction of US 89 and AZ 64,
> Cameron, AZ 86020
> (928) 679-2303
> navajonationparks.org/permits
>
> **Moenkopi Legacy Inn & Suites (Hopi guides)**
> 1 Legacy Lane, Tuba City, AZ 86045
> (928) 283-4500
> experiencehopi.com/hotel

HOPI RESERVATION

Leaving Coal Mine Canyon, retrace your route to AZ 264, and turn left. This is where you'll leave the Navajo Nation and enter Hopiland. AZ 264 is the main road through the reservation, connecting all the major towns and all three mesas. Coming from this direction, the first mesa you'll encounter is actually **Third Mesa**, which you'll see rising up from the plateau, dead ahead, as you travel east.

The highway climbs a fairly gentle slope to Hotevilla, a highly traditional Hopi community with a defiant history, and, just beyond it, the tiny hamlet of Old Oraibi, the oldest continuously occupied Native American community in North America. At one time the center of Hopi culture, Old Oraibi is now home to a dwindling population of about 75 people, living much as their ancestors did in ramshackle stone and adobe houses perched on the edge of the cliff. From a distance, parts of the village look ancient, despite some modern touches, like TV antennas and satellite dishes, solar panels, propane tanks, and pickup trucks; other parts mostly look poor—but by whose standard?

You might be tempted to turn off the road here for a better look, but before you do, be aware that many residential areas on the reservation are off-limits to visitors. Pay close attention to any signs you see posted, and don't carry a camera, as photography is strictly prohibited in the villages *(see sidebar)*.

Beyond Old Oraibi, AZ 264 crosses the flat region at the top of Third Mesa before descending the cliff through a series of graceful curves. Near the bottom, you'll pass Kykotsmovi, off the highway toward the south. This relatively new Hopi community, founded in 1906, is sometimes known as New Oraibi, or simply "K Town"; it is the administrative center for the tribe.

Beyond Kykotsmovi, you'll see **Second Mesa** rising up on your right. The area between the mesas is flat, but there's higher ground visible in every direction. Soon, the road starts climbing again, and after a few miles, you'll reach the top and another flat stretch, at the outskirts of the thinly populated town of Second Mesa. You'll see a relatively modern complex of pueblo-style buildings on your left; that's the **Hopi Cultural Center**, which boasts a small motel, a restaurant, and a gift shop.

Near there, at milepost 381, you'll come to **Tsak-urshovi Trading Post**, a small tan building with blue trim, just off the highway on the east side. The trading post, run by Joe and Janice Day, is the best place on the reservation to find Hopi arts and crafts, everything from traditional Kachina dolls to beautifully woven baskets

Old Oraibi, Second Mesa, Hopi Reservation, AZ

Hopi Etiquette

A visit to the Hopi Reservation is like a visit to a foreign country. People speak a different language, and there is a different code of conduct. Privacy and respect reign supreme here. What that means for visitors can be summed up in two requests: Keep your distance, and no pictures, please. Visitors should never enter a dwelling if they haven't been invited, not unless there's a sign offering items for sale. And please, no photos, not even with a cell phone, no matter how innocent your intent; most especially, no "candid" portraits of people, their houses, their kids, or their pets. When in the villages, or watching a ceremony, there are additional restrictions: no video or audio recording, no sketching or painting, no jotting down notes. That might sound extreme, but consider it an opportunity. When in Hopi, do as the Hopis do: Open your eyes, and look at what you're seeing. Pay attention, and listen to what you're hearing. You don't need a computer chip to record your experience. You have plenty of memory, right between your ears.

Hopi religious ceremonies are fascinating, but they are serious, highly traditional affairs. If you're so fortunate as to witness one of these colorful celebrations, stay outside the crowd, and don't interfere in any way with the dancers or other participants.

Hopi is the name of a people, it's the name of a language, and it's the name given to the heartland of a culture that is older than ours. Hopi is a reverent way of living upon the earth, a state of mind, and a state of grace. Be mindful of these truths as you make your way through this very different world.

Hopi Reservation Highlights

Hopi Cultural Center
AZ 264, Second Mesa, AZ 86043
(928) 734-2401
hopiculturalcenter.com

Tsakurshovi Trading Post
Milepost 381, AZ 264, Second Mesa, AZ 86043
(928) 734-2478

and fine silver and turquoise jewelry. The selection is amazing, and it's the only place in the entire world where you can buy a "Don't Worry, Be Hopi" T-shirt—a Joe Day exclusive. The best way to experience Hopi is with a local guide, and the folks at Tsakurshovi can help you arrange it; they're also an excellent source of advice and information about the many things that make this corner of the world unique.

TO WINSLOW AND HOLBROOK

Leaving Tsakurshovi, follow AZ 264 south as it winds down the face of the cliff toward the bottom of the mesa. If you look closely, you can spy the Second Mesa villages of

Sipaulovi and Mishongnovi, perched on hilltops to your left, blending so well into the landscape they're almost camouflaged from view. At the bottom of the grade, you'll come to the intersection with AZ 87. Follow that highway south for 22 miles to Indian Route 60, which makes a very pleasant 25-mile loop through Teesto and Dilkon before leading you back to AZ 87 a bit farther south. This minor

Tsakurshovi, "Unofficial Hopi Welcome Center"

detour takes you right past **Castle Butte**, **Chimney Butte**, and several other monolithic rock formations of note.

Once you're back on AZ 87, drive south toward I-40; after about 6 miles, you'll see a sign and a turnoff for **Little Painted Desert County Park**. This park, which is really more of a rest area, offers some grand views of a section of multicolored badlands: rumpled terrain in unlikely shades of red, orange, lavender, and gray that shift and blend with the angle of the sun, particularly when the sun is low in the sky. This is a piece of the same

Painted Desert that connects to Petrified Forest National Park, farther south and east of here. It's a perfect place to pull over while you plot your next move, and the wonderful view is free of charge.

Chimney Butte, Navajo Reservation north of Winslow

If it's late in the day, you have two options. You can press on to Holbrook, the end of this route, about 50 miles away; that will take you about an hour, mostly all on the Interstate. Or you can pull up for the night in **Winslow**, just 18 miles away. Winslow's **La Posada Hotel** is one of the nicest in this part of the state. Built in 1929, La Posada, "The Resting Place," was one of the renowned Fred Harvey Railroad Hotels and is considered the masterpiece of architect Mary Jane Colter. Recently restored, the hotel is a destination in itself, and the restaurant is excellent. Winslow has a historic downtown area where boosters have rekindled the spirit of old Route 66. One especially popular attraction is **Standin' on the Corner Park**, at Second Street and Kinsley Avenue, an homage to a snippet of lyrics in the classic rock song "Take It Easy," written in 1972 by Jackson Browne

Winslow and Holbrook Highlights

La Posada Hotel & Gardens
303 E. 2nd St.,
Winslow, AZ 86047
(928) 289-4366
laposada.org

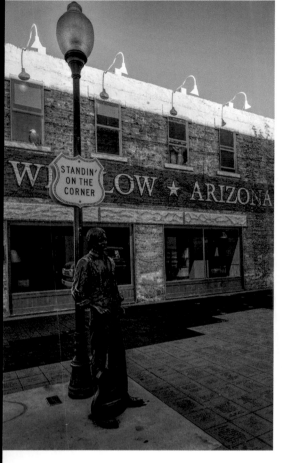

Standin' on the Corner in Winslow, Arizona

and his friend Glenn Frey, lead singer of what was then a brand-new band called the Eagles.

> *Well, I'm a-standin' on a corner*
> *In Winslow, Arizona*
> *And such a fine sight to see—*
> *It's a girl, my Lord, in a flatbed Ford,*
> *Slowin' down to take a look at me ...*

The park features a bronze statue of a long-haired dude with a guitar who is, well, *standing on the corner*. Behind him, a trompe-l'œil mural, painted on a brick wall, recreates a row of street-level shop windows that seemingly reflect the image of a girl driving by in—you guessed it—a flatbed Ford. In 2016, a second statue was unveiled at the park representing Frey, who passed away that year; he's sort of standing off to one side, giving us all a little wave, and a wisp of a smile.

Jump on I-40 for the last stretch of this route, which will land you in Holbrook, another 30 miles east. *For more about Holbrook, see* **Scenic Side Trip 11**.

BEYOND HOLBROOK

If you're headed to Phoenix, you can reverse the itinerary of **Scenic Side Trip 11** and travel by way of the Salt River Canyon and the Apache Trail. If you're continuing east, **Scenic Side Trip 16** will take you to Gallup by way of Canyon de Chelly and Monument Valley.

Holbrook, Arizona, to Gallup, New Mexico,

through the Heart of the Navajo Nation

441 miles, **9** hours **15** minutes
for drive time, more for optional
routes, stops, and sightseeing

Chasing John Wayne over Buffalo Pass, Gallup-ing all the way!

THE DRIVE FROM HOLBROOK TO GALLUP ON INTERSTATE 40 IS less than 100 miles and takes only about 90 minutes. If you're in any kind of hurry, that's the only option that makes any sense, but if you have a day or two to spare, and you're itching for an adventure, look no further. ➡➡

This route runs through the heart of the Navajo Nation, *Dinétah*, the homeland of the *Diné*, which means "The People" in the Navajo language. At 27,425 square miles, it's the largest Native American reservation in the U.S., occupying the greater portion of the vast Colorado Plateau. You can drive this side trip in a single day, but that wouldn't leave you much time to enjoy it. If it's at all possible, plan to make at least one overnight stop.

CANYON DE CHELLY

Leaving Holbrook, drive east on Interstate 40 to Exit 292 (10 miles), then head toward Keams Canyon on AZ 77. As you travel north, the desolate plateau changes in aspect. Squat sandstone buttes appear, like low isolated hills, some flat on the top, others more rounded, weathered by the millennia. Seventeen miles north of the Interstate, you'll cross a line on the map and enter the Navajo Nation. There's no border fence, no customs post, but make no mistake: this really is a different country, where people speak a different language, follow different rules, and have a different way of life. You are a guest here. Be mindful of that as you make your way through the starkly beautiful landscape.

Thirty-four miles beyond the Interstate, you'll see signs for Ganado and Chinle; bear right at the junction onto Navajo Route 15, and head northeast. This is very pretty countryside, if somewhat austere, a little greener and hillier than the landscape you've come through so far, the red earth and red rocks contrasting sharply against an intensely blue

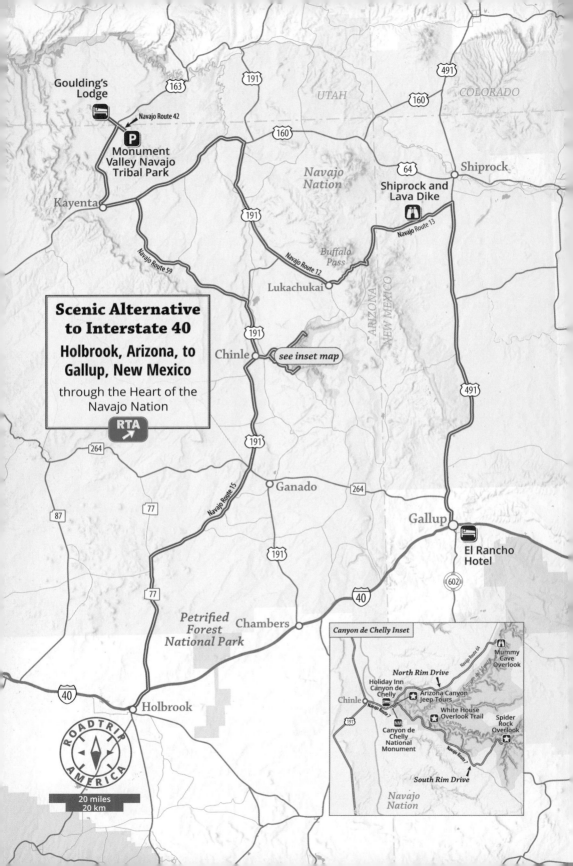

sky. In summer, masses of billowy white clouds line up along the horizon like an armada of sailing ships. Be wary if those clouds turn dark or spit lightning, especially in the monsoon season, from July to mid-September, when the weather gods can blow up a squall on a moment's notice, sending rain gushing down so fast and furious that you can lose sight of the blacktop.

After about 35 miles, Route 15 ends at a traffic circle connecting with AZ 264 and US 191. Take the second exit onto US 191 north, and follow that highway 30 miles to Chinle, the gateway to Canyon de Chelly (pro-nounced *d-SHAY*). When you reach the intersection with Navajo Route 7 (at the traffic light), turn right and drive about 3 miles, through the Navajo town of Chinle, all the way to the far end, where you'll find the visitors center for **Canyon de Chelly National Monument**. There is no entrance fee, but you'll want to stop anyway, to pick up a map and review your options.

If you're looking for a quick overview, take **South Rim Drive**, which runs 15 miles east from the visitors center; seven overlooks give you views of different sections of the canyon. The most spectacular formation comes at the end: **Spider Rock**, a 750-foot-tall sandstone pillar split into two spires, one higher than the other, like a pair of giant fingers pointing to the sky. The 30-mile round-trip requires about 2 hours. If you have another 2 hours to spare, you can hike down into the canyon on **White House Trail**,

South Rim Drive, Canyon de Chelly National Monument, Arizona

Opposite: Spider Rock, Canyon de Chelly National Monument, Arizona

Pictographs, Canyon de Chelly National Monument, Arizona

A Canvas Like No Other

With more than 800,000 visitors each year, Canyon de Chelly is one of the most popular national monuments in the U.S. That's remarkable, considering its remote location, but actually this verdant canyon with its sheer cliffs and astonishing rock formations has attracted visitors of one kind or another for more than 5,000 years, and the reasons for that are many.

Thousands of years before the modern era, nomadic hunters tracked game through these canyons and sheltered beneath rocky overhangs. Later, Anasazi farmers made permanent settlements, raising crops in the fertile soil and living in stone cliff dwellings that are still standing today. The Hopi followed the Anasazi, and the Navajo followed the Hopi. Each group left its mark on this special place, using the stone of the sheer canyon walls as its canvas.

Canyon de Chelly comprises the greatest concentration of diverse archaeological remains of any location in the Southwest. The rock art is particularly noteworthy. The images range from primitive to complex, and there are thousands of them: hunters and their quarry, a Spanish priest on horseback, a solar eclipse, a stick figure with a spear that hurls lightning bolts, and much, much more.

The only way to truly experience Canyon de Chelly, and its remarkable ruins and rock art, is to come down off the rim and explore the canyon floor, and for that, you must have a guide. There are a limited number of Ranger-led hikes that you can join for free, but most visitors go with one of the Navajo-owned companies that escort tourists into the canyons for a fee—on foot, on horseback, or, most commonly, in a four-wheel-drive vehicle. Most guided tours last 3 to 4 hours, though longer tours can be arranged (including overnight hikes). The best part of these tours is the running commentary of the extremely knowledgeable Navajo guides.

Opposite: White House Ruin, Canyon de Chelly National Monument, Arizona

a 2.5-mile round-trip from White House Overlook. This is the only area inside Canyon de Chelly where visitors are allowed to hike without an authorized guide. It's a pleasant stroll down to the bottom, some 600 feet below the rim. It's a little tougher coming back up as the elevation here is close to 6,000 feet. There is no shade, so you'd best carry water.

The payoff at the end of the trail is **White House Ruin**, a beautifully preserved Anasazi cliff dwelling built into a natural alcove in the face of a sheer sandstone cliff, about 20 feet above the floor of the canyon. The primary ruin is a multiroom communal dwelling that dates back almost 1,000 years. It occupied a good location—safe from flooding, easy to defend—but it was abandoned, like most of the cliff dwellings in the area, around AD 1275, after a long drought. The reddish-tan face of the cliff above and to the right of the ruin is striped with a dark, natural discoloration known as "desert varnish," like broad streaks of paint on a massive earth-toned canvas. The ruin, the setting, the view of the canyon from below—it's really quite something to see.

Mummy Cave Ruin, Canyon de Chelly National Monument, Arizona

On your way back to the visitors center, you have another option. By turning right (east) on Navajo Route 64, you can take **North Rim Drive** to three overlooks that offer splendid views into a second canyon: Canyon del Muerto, the Canyon of the Dead. From the last of those viewpoints, Mummy Cave Overlook, you'll have a good look at **Mummy Cave Ruin**, the largest of the Anasazi cliff dwellings

here, magnificently set 300 feet above the canyon floor. Allow at least 90 minutes for the 28-mile round-trip from the visitors center to Mummy Cave Overlook and back.

If you stay in Chinle overnight, you'll have time to take a guided tour inside the canyon (*see sidebar*). **Arizona Canyon Jeep Tours** is one of the better tour companies, and the **Holiday Inn Canyon de Chelly**, located at the east end of Chinle, is a good choice for lodging.

MONUMENT VALLEY

Leaving Chinle, head north on US 191 for 14 miles, toward Many Farms. At the intersection with Navajo Route 59, turn left and follow that highway northwest for 44 miles, until it ends at an intersection with US 160. Turn left again, and drive 8 miles to US 163, which will lead you through Kayenta to the border with Utah, 20 miles farther north. Each of those turns, each of those highways, takes you a little deeper into the middle of nowhere. What's the attraction?

Look east, where blocky sandstone rock formations line up along the horizon. Even if you've never been here before, the scene will look familiar. **Monument Valley** is the quintessential Southwestern landscape. It's not that big, perhaps 5 square miles, and yet somehow this swath of landscape has come to define the world's image of the entire Colorado Plateau.

One man can take most of the credit for that. In 1939, Hollywood director John Ford brought a film crew to Monument Valley and used the little-known location as the setting for *Stagecoach*, a Western starring his good friend John Wayne. The movie launched Wayne's career as an A-list actor and brought Monument Valley to the attention of the rest of the world. Ford returned

Canyon De Chelly Highlights

Canyon de Chelly National Monument
Indian Route 7, Chinle, AZ 86503
(928) 674-5500
nps.gov/cach

Arizona Canyon Jeep Tours
Indian Route 7, Chinle, AZ 86503
(928) 781-2113
arizonacanyonjeeptours.com

Holiday Inn Canyon de Chelly
Indian Route 7, Chinle, AZ 86503
(928) 674-5000
www.ihg.com

Opposite: Road in Monument Valley, Navajo Reservation, Arizona

Driving in Monument Valley, Navajo Tribal Park

to the valley again and again, creating 10 wildly popular films featuring the dramatic landscape as backdrop to his dramatic action scenes. It didn't matter if the story was set in Arizona, Texas, or New Mexico—they all featured the same rectilinear sandstone buttes, shot from every conceivable angle. Is it any wonder that the moviegoing public came to believe that all of the American West looked like that?

Today, Monument Valley is a Navajo tribal park that is popular with tourists from all over the world. Just after you cross over the state line into Utah, turn right on Monument Valley Road, and follow that 3 miles southeast to the park entrance. Just beyond the fee station and visitors center is the start of an unpaved **17-mile scenic loop** through the park. (If you are driving a rental vehicle, check your contract for unpaved-road exclusions before starting out.) For the first mile, the road descends into the valley along a series of switchbacks; the surface is quite rough, and it can be very dusty, but as long as you drive slowly, the road is suitable for passenger cars. That first mile is the worst. From that point on, you can cruise at your leisure through the heart of Monument Valley and get a close-up view of many of the most famous formations. Over millions of years, these "monuments" have been carved by the elements into fantastic shapes with fanciful names like East and West Mitten (each with a skyward-pointing

Monument Valley Highlights

Monument Valley Navajo Tribal Park
US 163, Oljato–Monument Valley, UT 84536
(435) 727-5874
navajonationparks.org

Navajo Spirit Tours
US 163, Oljato–Monument Valley, UT 84536
(435) 444-9595
navajospirittours.com

Goulding's Lodge
1000 Main St., Oljato–Monument Valley, UT 84536
(435) 727-3231
gouldings.com

thumb), Elephant Butte, King on His Throne, and the Totem Pole. Allow a couple of hours for a self-guided tour. Late afternoon is the best time for photos.

The Mittens and Merrick Butte, Monument Valley, Navajo Tribal Park

If you'd rather not drive the park road in your vehicle, or if you'd like to see sections of the larger 91,000-acre preserve that are off-limits to private vehicles, you can join a guided tour. These tours, most of which use open pickup trucks modified to carry passengers in the back, take in places like Mystery Valley and Hunts Mesa, which can only be visited with an authorized Navajo guide (on open-truck tours, a scarf or bandana makes a good dust mask). Sunrise and sunset tours operate outside normal park hours, providing photo opportunities you can't get from your own vehicle. Information about tours is available at the visitors center; one highly rated operator is **Navajo Spirit Tours**. A great place for an overnight stay

Opposite: Yei Bi Chei and the Totem Pole, Monument Valley

is **Goulding's Lodge,** just west of US 163 on Monument Valley Road. The modern motel is attached to the original **Goulding's Trading Post**. Built in 1923, the trading post was like a second home to John Ford, John Wayne, and their movie crews back in the day; a small museum tells the story.

Navajo Route 13

Leaving Monument Valley, reverse course on US 163 and drive south, through Kayenta, to US 160. Turn left and follow that highway east for 41 miles, to the intersection with US 191. Turn south, and drive 33 miles to Round Rock and merge onto Navajo Route 12, which you'll follow southeast for 14 miles to the intersection with **Navajo Route 13**, a fabulous paved road that will take you up and over the Lukachukai Mountains, into New Mexico.

Drive east on Route 13. After you pass the small town of **Lukachukai,** the road starts to climb through a section of red rock hills and cliffs reminiscent of the Red Rocks of Sedona. It is lovely country, and quiet. There are no towns in the Lukachukais, just some summer camps for shepherds and an oil and gas field (not visible from the road) that requires occasional maintenance. The sporadic traffic comes mostly from locals taking the scenic shortcut to Shiprock, and you just might have the road to yourself.

The mountains here are big enough to create weather. Rain that falls on the 8,000 to 10,000-foot peaks of the Lukachukais and the adjacent Chuska Range provides more than half of the surface water in the Navajo Nation, including the floods that periodically roar through Chinle Wash in Canyon de Chelly, part of the ongoing geological process that created the canyon in the first place. The rainfall makes the higher elevations green, in dramatic contrast to the surrounding countryside. Beyond the

red rocks, the road climbs into piñon and juniper forest, and then keeps climbing into thick stands of Ponderosa pines.

You'll cross over the mountains at **Buffalo Pass**, well above 8,000 feet, where it's cool in the summer and often snowy in winter; ask locally about road conditions before attempting a winter crossing. In fact, take it easy through here in all seasons; the road is in good condition, but there are potholes, and it's a bit narrow in places. Beyond the pass, there are broad views to the east, and you'll see the distinctive profile of the monument called Shiprock—looking rather like a ship under sail, plowing through the valley—far below. The road descends through a series of switchbacks, dropping quickly out of the forested area; once you reach the bottom, it veers north to Red Valley before angling northeast.

About 14 miles beyond Red Valley, keep your eye out along the left-hand side of the road for an unusual earthen dike crowned by a wall of jagged rock that rises 20 feet or more straight up out of the ground. Just beyond the dike, you'll see a weathered dirt road that runs parallel to it all the way to Shiprock; the massive formation rises almost 1,600 feet above the surrounding terrain, 3 miles due north. Pull over alongside the road here, and stop.

Some 27 million years ago, the formation we now call **Shiprock** lay deep within the throat of a volcano that exploded, opening cracks in the earth that radiated from

the crater like the spokes of a wheel. Magma filled the cracks, cooled, and solidified into rock. Over the eons, the bulk of the extinct volcano eroded away, along with most of the surrounding plateau, exposing that plug of harder rock from its core and the hardened magma that had filled those cracks. The latter created unusual formations known as "lava dikes," and the biggest of those is right here, cut through by Navajo Route 13. The view from this spot, with Shiprock rising up before you to the right, and the lava dike rising up on the left, is otherworldly. If you're here at sunset, grab your camera. Many a prizewinning photo has been taken from this exact vantage point.

Navajo Route 13, east of Canyon de Chelly

Shiprock itself is off-limits, for a variety of reasons,

and so is the lava dike, so don't try to get any closer to either formation (much less climb them). It's all posted private property, and it is a place of great religious significance to the Navajo people.

After another 7 miles, Navajo Route 13 terminates at US 491. From that point, it's a straight shot 86 miles south to Gallup and Interstate 40, the end of this route. The historic **El Rancho Hotel** in Gallup is a great place to stay.

Beyond Gallup

From Gallup, you can continue east on Interstate 40. If you have plenty of time, consider **Scenic Side Trip 18,** which will take you to Albuquerque along some beautiful back roads, or **Scenic Side Trip 17**, which can be combined with **Scenic Side Trip 19** to connect you with Interstate 25 at Socorro.

Navajo Route 13 Highlights
El Rancho Hotel
1000 E. Highway 66, Gallup, NM 87301
(505) 863-9311
route66hotels.org

Shiprock at Sunset, from Navajo Route 13

Gallup to Grants

via Farmington and Chaco Canyon

313 miles, **7** hours **45** minutes for drive time, more for optional routes, stops, and sightseeing

Bisti in the morning, Aztec in the evening, Chaco at supper time ...

FOR TRAVELERS HEADED EAST ON INTERSTATE 40, THE STRETCH from Gallup to Grants is only an hour's drive. If you're in a hurry to get to Albuquerque, that's the only way to go, but if you have a day or two to spare and you're looking for an adventure, here's a route that offers some of the most fascinating prehistoric ruins in North America, along with some of the strangest terrain on the planet. ➤➤

It's not for everyone. This side trip will add 250 miles and nearly 7 hours of driving to your journey, and there are several sections of unpaved road that can become impassable in rainy weather; add water, and the clay-based soil in this region turns to gumbo. The risk of washout is usually small, but in the summer "monsoon" season, from mid-June to mid-September, serious storms can blow up quite suddenly. Before you set out, check road conditions near Chaco by calling the National Park Service (505-786-7014); conditions near Bisti will be similar. For a detailed weather forecast, as well as a history of recent storms, check www.weather.gov (enter Farmington NM as your location); if you see heavy rain coming or going, save this adventure for another time. As always, if you are in a rental vehicle, check your contract before driving unpaved roads.

GALLUP AND ENVIRONS

If you arrive in Gallup at least 4 hours before sunset, you have two options. First, you can top up your tank, grab a quick bite to eat, and head straight out to the Bisti Badlands; you'll arrive in the golden light of afternoon—a photographer's dream. You can then stop for the night in Farmington and finish the route the following day, all at a very casual pace.

Your second option is to stick around, explore **Gallup**, and start the route in the morning. Gallup has long

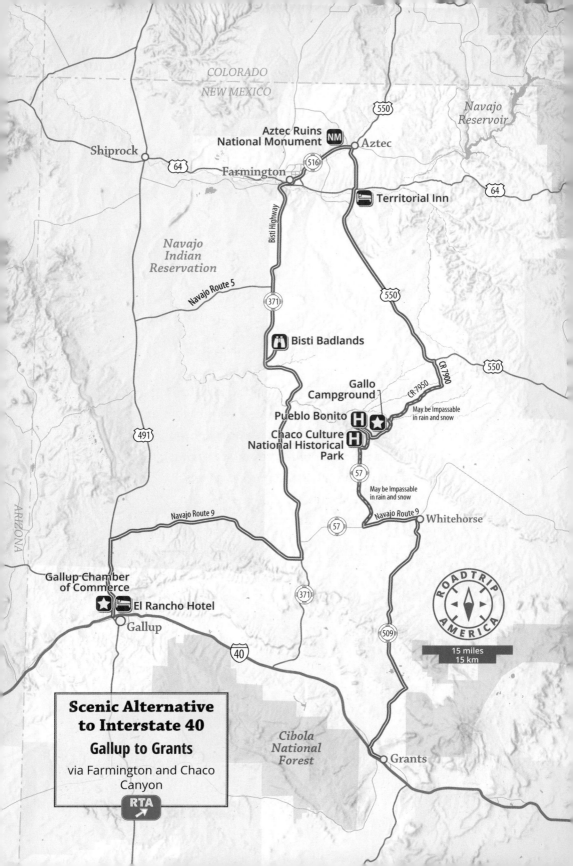

COLORADO

NEW MEXICO

Navajo Reservoir

550

Shiprock

Aztec Ruins National Monument NM Aztec

64

516

Farmington

64

Territorial Inn

Navajo Indian Reservation

Bisti Highway

Navajo Route 5

371

550

Bisti Badlands

CR 7900

550

CR 7950

Gallo Campground

May be Impassable in rain and snow

491

Pueblo Bonito H ★

Chaco Culture National Historical Park H

57

May be Impassable in rain and snow

Navajo Route 9

57

Navajo Route 9 Whitehorse

ARIZONA

371

ROADTRIP AMERICA

Gallup Chamber of Commerce ★

El Rancho Hotel ⬛

Gallup

509

15 miles
15 km

40

Scenic Alternative to Interstate 40
Gallup to Grants
via Farmington and Chaco Canyon

RTA ➚

Cibola National Forest

Grants

been a trading center for goods produced on the nearby reservations. Even today, the city boasts more than 100 trading posts, galleries, and specialty shops selling Native American arts and crafts: baskets, pottery, Navajo weavings, Hopi Kachina dolls, and silver and turquoise jewelry made by Navajo, Hopi, and Zuni silversmiths—all handcrafted items that provide an important source of income to the reservations. Most of the shops are strung along Historic Route 66, and many of them date from that era. Gallup's historic downtown district is quite walkable. Vibrant murals adorn many of the buildings, and Indian dances are performed every evening in the summer—a colorful pageant that always draws a crowd. Stop by the Chamber of Commerce visitors center for a small but interesting exhibit on Navajo "code talkers" in World War II.

El Rancho Hotel on Historic Route 66 is a good choice for lodging. The historic property proudly displays a long list of celebrity guests, most from the days when Hollywood Westerns were shot on location in the Gallup area. (*For more about Gallup, see* **Scenic Side Trip 18**.)

Gallup Highlights

Gallup Chamber of Commerce
106 W. Historic Route 66, Gallup, NM 87301
(505) 722-2228

El Rancho Hotel
1000 E. Highway 66, Gallup, NM 87301
(505) 853-9311
route66hotels.org

Gallup to Farmington Via the Bisti Badlands

Leaving Gallup, take the US 491 exit off Interstate 40 and drive north for 20 miles, through Yah-Ta-Hey, to Navajo Route 9. Travel east on Route 9 for 40 miles to Crownpoint and the intersection with NM 371. This is flat, open range, a bit desolate even by reservation standards. You'll see scattered homesteads, most consisting of one or more prefabricated houses or doublewide mobile homes surrounded by a scattering of vehicles that might or might not be operable. Many of these homesteads have outbuildings that appear round from a distance but on closer inspection prove to be eight-sided, the prescribed octagonal shape of traditional Navajo dwellings called **hogans**. Many Navajos, particularly in the older generation, prefer living in a hand-built hogan to living in a prefab box, even if the box has all the modern amenities and the hogan has no plumbing. Unemployment is high on the reservation, and opportunities are few, so the people who have their own spreads are better off than most.

When you reach NM 371, turn left (north) toward Farmington, and make note of your odometer reading. After about 30 miles the mostly flat terrain gets a bit hilly. Just after cresting the last of those hills, exactly 44.9 miles from Navajo Route 9, look sharp on your right for a wooden Bureau of Land Management sign marking the **Bisti/De-Na-Zin Wilderness** area. Photographers, nature lovers, and travelers who appreciate curiosities will be delighted by what they'll find here in what is popularly known as the Bisti Badlands. Turn right onto the dirt road, County Road 7297, and drive about 2 miles northeast to a T-intersection at County Road 7290. Turn left, and drive north another mile to the parking area, on your right. There are usually a few other vehicles here, but it's not uncommon to have the place to yourself.

Laid out before you is a broad wash running through an area that was once the bed of an ancient sea. Primordial geological dramas took place here, creating an otherworldly landscape just out of sight over the horizon. The ancient waters receded, leaving a swampy river delta that was later choked off by thick layers of volcanic ash. A desert arose, and over millions of years, immense shifting dunes compacted into a thick mantle of sandstone. Tectonic plates shifted, and the entire Colorado Plateau was forced upward, a micromillimeter at a time, bending and fracturing the multicolored layers of rock. Over millions of years, wind and water sculpted some of the world's most extravagant rock formations: hoodoos, arches, balanced rocks, and boulders shaped like everything from birds to beehives, including giant mushrooms, a barking seal, and the head of a wolf, tilted skyward, howling at the moon.

Sunrise at the Bisti Badlands, New Mexico

"The head of a wolf, tilted skyward, howling at the moon," Bisti Badlands, New Mexico

The heaviest concentration of these formations requires a bit of hiking on some barely-there trails that begin at the parking area. If you've had some experience with wilderness hiking and are confident that you can find your way back to your vehicle after tromping around in confusing terrain, you can strike out to the north from the well-marked gap in the fence where the not-trails begin. Take plenty of water, and allow at least a couple of hours to explore.

If you're not comfortable hiking into a trackless wilderness, keep driving north on CR 7290, about a half mile past the official parking lot. After the dirt road cuts through a section of heavily eroded rocky hills, you'll see a flat area to your left marked by tire tracks from vehicles that have pulled over and turned around. Park wherever you'd like, make a mental note of your position relative to the tallest visible landmark, and then set out on foot. Even a short hike through this rocky jumble, in any direction, will take you through the Looking Glass into the world of the Mad Hatter. The labyrinth of sandy pathways winds among striped pillars and platforms crowned with fantastic shapes: rats and bats and cats with hats, along with many others that are just plain ... *strange*.

Leaving Bisti, head back to NM 371 the same way you came in, and turn right (north). It's about 36 miles to Farmington. Located at the intersection of three rivers—the San Juan, the Animas, and La Plata—**Farmington** was a major crossroads even before there were roads here. It is the largest town in the area and your best bet for lodging if you're ready for an overnight break. One good choice is the **Best Western Territorial Inn**, in Bloomfield, a suburb on the eastern edge of town.

Gallup to Farmington Highlights

Bisti/De-Na-Zin Wilderness
CR 7297, Bloomfield, NM 87413
(505) 564-7600

Best Western Territorial Inn
415 S. Bloomfield Blvd., Bloomfield, NM 87413
(505) 632-9100
bestwestern.com

Aztec Ruins to Grants Via Chaco Canyon

Leaving Farmington, head east on Main Street (NM 516). A few miles beyond downtown, Main Street becomes Aztec Boulevard, which reaches the small town of Aztec about 5 miles farther on. Just before the bridge over the Animas River, turn left onto Ruins Road and follow the signs to **Aztec Ruins National Monument.** Stop in at the visitors center to pay the entrance fee and borrow one of the laminated booklets for the self-guided walking tour. The easy half-mile stroll requires about an hour.

This complex of masonry ruins (which has no connection whatsoever to the Aztecs of Mexico) dates to AD 1100 and was built by the Anasazi, the same Ancestral Pueblo people who built the cliff dwellings in Canyon de Chelly and many other places in the Four Corners region. The Great House, which occupies most of the site, was a communal dwelling with more than 400 rooms. The walls

Aztec Ruins National Monument

Ancient doorways, Aztec Ruins National Monument

are timeworn now, but a walk through the old buildings, ducking to pass through the low doorways, provides a fascinating perspective on the ancient settlement. This place must have buzzed like a beehive with the voices of all those people living so close to one another, generation after generation.

The people here were farmers for the most part, but there were artists and craftspeople and architects among them, innovators with new ideas who were part of the florescence of the Puebloan culture that began in the Great Houses and Great Kivas of nearby Chaco Canyon and spread from there, along the trade routes, throughout the Southwest. The Anasazi had a sweet life here, during a golden age that lasted for 150 years.

All Puebloan villages had at least one kiva, a specially designed room used exclusively for religious purposes. Kivas in this area were usually round and dug in below ground; entry was through an opening in the roof, using ladders or stairs. Aztec Ruins had several kivas, including a Great Kiva that was dug only halfway below ground, with a low doorway in the outside wall. In 1934, this sacred space was painstakingly reconstructed, and the result is really something special. Steps lead down into a silent circular room, 40 feet in diameter, lit by soft beams of sunlight slanting down through small rectangular windows that ring the building at ground level. The Great Kiva has the air and solemnity of a cathedral; your natural inclination will be to speak in hushed tones—or not at all.

Leaving Aztec Ruins, reverse course on Ruins Road back to Aztec Boulevard; turn left to cross the river, then bear right onto Chaco Street. Follow Chaco for two blocks to Maine Avenue (US 550 South). Turn right, and stay on US 550 as it leads you out of town—Maine Avenue to

Broadway to Bloomfield Boulevard—then keep going south for 40 miles. About 3 miles past the small Navajo town of Nageezi, you'll see a National Park Service sign announcing **Chaco Culture National Historical Park**, off to the right down County Road 7900. The route is well marked. Follow the signs along this good, paved road for 5 miles to its intersection with CR 7950, and then turn right (west). Shortly beyond that intersection, the pavement runs out; 16 miles farther, at the park boundary, the pavement returns. The unpaved segment can be a bit rough, but as long as you travel at an appropriate speed, it's suitable for passenger cars.

The sprawling, 34,000-acre historical park, commonly known as Chaco Canyon, is the largest, densest, and most impressive concentration of Ancestral Puebloan ruins in the American Southwest. You'll need several hours to even begin to explore them, but you can see quite a

Sandstone butte off NM 371 north of Thoreau

lot in a relatively short time. Stop at the visitors center, 2.5 miles beyond the entrance, to pay the admission fee and pick up a park brochure and map. A one-way scenic park road leads you past most of the major structures.

If Aztec Ruins was an Anasazi town, Chaco Canyon was the big city, the center for commerce, administration, and ceremonial life of the Ancient Puebloan people here in the high desert. Built in stages from the mid-800s to the early 1100s, the Great Houses at Chaco were the largest buildings anywhere in North America until the 19th century. **Pueblo Bonito**, the largest of all, was four stories tall, comprising more than 600 rooms and 35 kivas, many of them quite large. Today, the kivas are empty, masonry-lined pits; try to imagine them as they once were: roofed over, with ladders climbing up to openings at the top, hundreds of people gathered for ceremonies that are now lost in the mists of time.

Pueblo Bonito Ruin, Chaco Canyon National Historical Park

Like all Anasazi sites, Chaco was abandoned by 1300,

following a period of extended drought. The remarkable culture that built this place rose, flourished, and faded away—all more than 250 years before the arrival of the first Europeans in this part of the New World. Chaco has been extensively studied, but the more we learn about the place, the less we really know (see sidebar).

There are hiking trails through the park, and more than a dozen sites of major archaeological significance outside the massive ruin of Pueblo Bonito. If you want to explore further, check out **Gallo Campground**, the only overnight accommodation in the park; it has 39 spaces, available by reservation (see below).

As you near the end of the scenic drive, follow the signs for NM 57, toward Crownpoint. This road will take you out the south entrance to the park; as before, the pavement will run out once you cross the park boundary. The

Aztec Ruins to Grants Highlights

Aztec Ruins National Monument
725 Ruins Road, Aztec, NM 87410
(505) 334-6174
nps.gov/azru

Chaco Culture National Historical Park
1808 CR 7950, Nageezi, NM 87037
(505) 786-7014
nps.gov/chcu

Gallo Campground
(877) 444-6777
recreation.gov

A Riddle, Wrapped in an Enigma

Mysteries abound in Chaco Canyon. Pueblo Bonito had 600 rooms, for example, yet it never housed more than a few dozen people. Who were they? Royalty? Priests? Prisoners? The construction of these massive buildings required wood from 200,000 trees, yet the closest forest was high in the Chuska Mountains, nearly 50 miles away. The Anasazi had no wheeled vehicles and no draft animals, so all that timber came in on the backs of workmen. What could have justified so much effort?

There's an intriguing clue in the orientation of the buildings—north to south, and east to west—and in the alignment of key architectural features during important celestial events, such as solstices and the closest approach of the moon. Clearly, the Anasazi were watching the sky, but to what purpose? And then there are the "Chaco Roads," wide boulevards that went on for miles, built perfectly straight and true, sometimes climbing cliffs with stairs, never deviating an inch from their course. The roads are clearly visible from the air, and they end ... nowhere, in particular. What were they used for?

The Anasazi created the most complex and technically advanced culture in ancient North America. Excavations have uncovered such exotic items as dried cacao pods, copper bells, and macaw bones, evidence of trade with the cultures of ancient Mexico. Was there trade in ideas as well? By 1200, Chaco's influence had spread throughout the Southwest, yet less than a century later, the Anasazi abandoned the canyon and disappeared. Traces of the culture remain in the traditions of native peoples living in the pueblos of modern New Mexico. As for the mysteries? Short of a major breakthrough, all we can do is wonder.

unpaved section of this road runs for about 19 miles, and though it's a state highway, it's infrequently maintained and conditions can vary from quite rough to nearly impassable (in bad weather). The road is suitable for passenger cars as long as you take it easy and watch for ruts and potholes; it's not recommended for RVs.

At the intersection with Navajo Route 9, you'll be back on pavement. Turn left, and follow Route 9 east for 10 miles to NM 509. Turn right (south), and follow NM 509 for 35 miles to the intersection with NM 605, which will take you the rest of the way, 17 more miles, to Interstate 40, Historic Route 66, and the end of this route in the small town of **Grants**. If you're ready to call it a day, you can find lodging at one of the national chain motels clustered along Santa Fe Avenue, near the I-40 interchange at the east end of town.

BEYOND GRANTS

From Grants, you can continue on to Albuquerque, a bit more than an hour east on Interstate 40. If you still have time to spare, consider **Scenic Side Trip 19**, which will take you from Grants to Socorro by way of El Malpais National Monument and Bosque del Apache National Wildlife Refuge. From Socorro, you can head south to Las Cruces on Interstate 25, or north to Albuquerque, either on I-25 or by way of the Salinas Missions; see **Scenic Side Trip 20**.

Gallup to Albuquerque

via Zuni, El Morro National Monument, Acoma, Laguna, and the Rio Grande

236 miles, **6** hours **15** minutes for drive time, more for optional routes, stops, and sightseeing

Passing by the pueblos on a path to the Rio Grande

THE DRIVE FROM GALLUP TO ALBUQUERQUE ON INTERSTATE 40 takes about 2 hours, but there isn't a lot to see along the way, not if you stay on the freeway. This scenic side trip offers an alternative: a southerly meander that takes you across the foothills of the Zuni Mountains, through two national monuments, and to three Native American pueblos before finishing with a lovely drive up the valley of the Rio Grande. The route will add 100 miles to your travels and take most of a day, bringing you into Albuquerque from the south, by way of Los Lunas. ➠

GALLUP TO ZUNI

The route begins in **Gallup**, sometimes called "The Indian Capital of the World," in part because it's surrounded on all sides by Native American trust land: the Navajo Nation to the north and west, Zuni to the southwest, Ramah to the south, and Acoma and Laguna Pueblos to the east. One third of Gallup's population has Native American roots, and the community celebrates that connection every night in summer, when dancers from several of those nearby native communities don full regalia and perform in the Courthouse Square. It's an enactment—a colorful pageant of Native American music and dance, staged for the benefit of tourists—but the moves and the costumes, as well as the songs and the drumming are the real thing, and it's fun to watch.

Traditional Native American arts and crafts are big business in Gallup, which has more trading posts, Indian-themed gift shops, and Southwestern art galleries than any other town in New Mexico. You can learn about native crafts at the **Gallup Cultural Center**, located on Historic Route 66 in the old Santa Fe Railroad Depot. The center has an art gallery and museum with exhibits related to Native American history and culture; profits from the gift shop and café

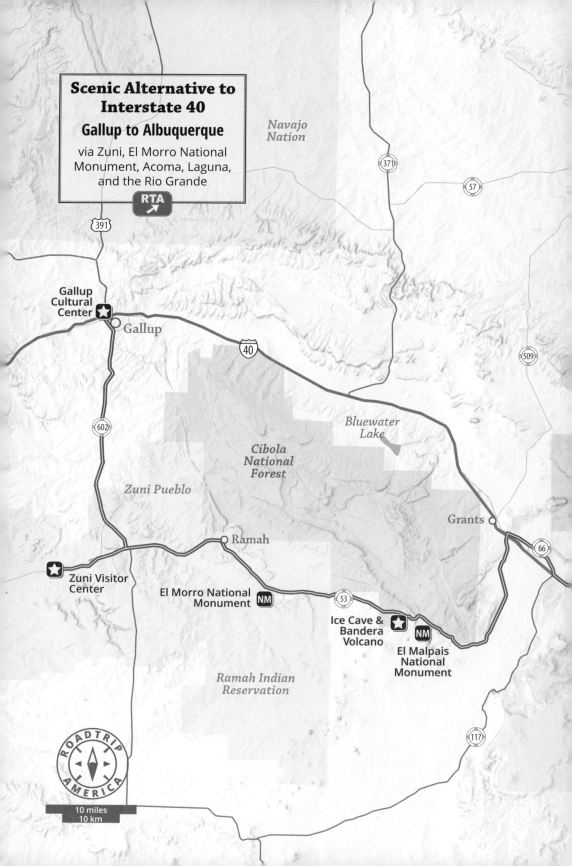

Scenic Alternative to Interstate 40

Gallup to Albuquerque

via Zuni, El Morro National Monument, Acoma, Laguna, and the Rio Grande

RTA

Navajo Nation

371

57

391

Gallup Cultural Center

Gallup

40

509

Bluewater Lake

Cibola National Forest

602

Zuni Pueblo

Grants

66

Ramah

Zuni Visitor Center

El Morro National Monument **NM**

53

Ice Cave & Bandera Volcano **NM**

El Malpais National Monument

Ramah Indian Reservation

117

ROADTRIP AMERICA

10 miles
10 km

Chaco Culture
National
Historical Park

Albuquerque Inset

40

Rio Grande Blvd

Mountain Rd

12th St

🅷 San Felipe de Neri Church

⭐ Old Town Plaza

Casas de Suenos
Historic Old Town Inn 🏨

Lomas Blvd

Central Ave

Central Ave

Tingley Drive

WEST
PARK

Rio Grande

Albuquerque

Lead Ave

8th St

Zia Indian
Reservation

550

Albuquerque

see inset map

40

40

66

Indian Route 38

🅷 Pueblo of
Laguna:
San Jose
Mission Church

23

Laguna
Pueblo

Isleta
Pueblo

314

Ⓜ
Sky City Cultural
Center and Haak'u
Museum (Acoma)

25

Acoma
Pueblo

6

Los Lunas

Gallup, New Mexico: city of murals

go to help nearby Native American communities. *(For more about Gallup, see* **Scenic Side Trip 17.***)*

If you arrive in Gallup late in the day, **El Rancho Hotel** on Historic Route 66 is a good choice for lodging. Built by the brother of Hollywood director D. W. Griffith, the hotel has a gallery of photos featuring celebrities who stayed here back in the days when the Gallup area was a popular location for shooting Hollywood Westerns.

Leaving Gallup, take Exit 20 off Interstate 40, and drive south on NM 602 through a region of rocky, scrub-covered hills. After about 25 miles, bear right on Indian Route 4, and take that road south 5 miles to NM 53. Turn right and follow signs to Zuni Pueblo, 6 miles farther west. The pueblo has been a home to people of the Zuni tribe for more than 800 years. By the 16th century, there were at least half a dozen separate pueblos thriving in this area, well-constructed villages built of adobe and thatch. When Chaco and Aztec and the other great

Anasazi sites were abandoned around AD 1200, many of the refugees joined with the people here, and this is where they've stayed.

The old pueblo of **Hawikku**, 12 miles southwest of Zuni Pueblo, was the first indigenous village in the American West to be visited by European explorers. The expedition of Friar Marcos de Niza passed this way in 1539, followed by Francisco Vásquez de Coronado, in 1540. Coronado was chasing the fabled Seven Cities of Gold. Imagine his disappointment when all he found at the end of his trail were six villages made mostly of mud!

Much of **Zuni Pueblo** is off-limits to nonresidents; staff at the visitors center can tell you where you may walk unaccompanied, or how to join a guided tour. The Middle Village walking tour, offered weekdays, is the most popular; it takes in the core of the historic old pueblo, which has buildings that date to the 1600s. In 2017, the mission church, famously decorated with colorful murals representing Zuni Kachinas, was closed to tours "for the foreseeable future" as work was underway to stabilize the 300-year-old structure, but other tours are available, including tours of local artists' workshops and outlying archaeological sites, including the ruins of Hawikku. Those tours require reservations, usually a week in advance.

Note. *Photography is strictly forbidden anywhere in Zuni unless you have purchased a photo permit. Ditto for audio and video recording—even note taking is discouraged. Native communities in these parts safeguard their privacy, and while they welcome tourists, they do have rules laying out expected behavior; see sidebar, Hopi Etiquette, page 229.*

Several shops and galleries in Zuni offer

Gallup and Zuni Highlights

Gallup Cultural Center
201 E. Highway 66, Gallup, NM 87301
(505) 863-4131

El Rancho Hotel
1000 E. Highway 66, Gallup, NM 87301
(505) 863-9311
route66hotels.org

Zuni Visitors Center
1239 NM 53, Zuni, New Mexico 87327
(505) 782-7238
zunitourism.com

silverwork, jewelry, and other crafts made by local artisans. If you have an interest in such items, shopping in Zuni Pueblo is like going straight to the source.

El Morro National Monument

Leaving Zuni, drive east on NM 53. On your left you'll see the foothills of the Zuni Mountains, a very old, 9,000-foot mountain range that spans the Continental Divide. After about 30 miles of hilly high desert sparsely covered in sagebrush, piñon, and juniper, you'll see a sandstone bluff on your right, off by itself. As you approach from the west it's not very impressive, but once the road swings around to the far side, you'll realize how big it is. This is El Morro, one of the most prominent landmarks for many miles around, and a place with a fascinating history. A sign on your left announces **El Morro National Monument**; the road to the parking area is on the right, directly opposite. There is no entrance fee for this park, but if you stop at the visitors center, you can borrow a

El Morro Highlights

El Morro National Monument
NM 53, Ramah, NM 87321
(505) 783-4226
nps.gov/elmo

El Morro National Monument

laminated booklet that describes points of interest on the self-guided trails.

The primary attraction here is a pool of water at the base of a cliff, created by runoff from higher ground. Why is that even interesting? Because the pool is perennial: a shady green oasis in every season. It is the only reliable water source for miles around, and that made the pool a favorite stopover for overland travelers dating back to prehistoric times. More interesting? The soft stone

of the adjacent cliff face served as a message board for passersby. Native Americans who settled here hundreds of years ago carved petroglyphs, depictions of animals and other symbols. The Spanish colonizers who passed by in the 17th and 18th centuries carved their names, along with the date, and *paso por aquí*, Spanish for "passed by here." During

Desert oasis and Inscription Rock, El Morro National Monument

the 19th century, American soldiers and settlers added their marks. The tradition continued until 1906, when the national monument was created and "Inscription Rock" was protected from any further carving.

A paved, half-mile-long path, **Inscription Rock Trail**, leads visitors to the pool and along the base of the cliff, offering a close-up view of 700 years of graffiti—a ledger carved in stone, with more than 2,000 entries. A second trail, a 2-mile round-trip, takes you all the way to the top of the bluff, where you'll find fabulous views and the ruins of **Atsinna Pueblo**, the communal home of as many as 1,500 people, that was built atop El Morro in the late

1200s and abandoned about 75 years later.

EL MORRO TO ACOMA AND LAGUNA PUEBLOS

Leaving El Morro, return to NM 53 and continue east. As the road gains elevation, the pine trees close ranks and declare a forest, providing a cool respite from the surrounding desert. About 16 miles beyond El Morro, you'll crest a barely perceptible pass at 7,882 feet and cross the Continental Divide. Continuing on NM 53, the road curves around the base of a hill, a steep-sided pine-clad hump that's actually a cinder cone, formed during the eruption of Bandera Volcano a bit more than 10,000 years ago.

This is a real-world land of fire and ice. At the base of what was once an explosive cauldron of super-heated molten rock, there's now an ice cave: a collapsed lava tube where, over the last thousand years or so, a 20-foot-thick plug of ancient ice has accumulated. The surrounding rock acts as insulation, and the odd shape of the opening acts as a stopper, trapping the cold air, effectively creating the world's largest thermos bottle. The temperature never rises above 31 degrees, so the ice, which is the color of semi-translucent jade, never melts.

This unlikely combination of geological features, the **Ice Cave and Bandera Volcano,** is a privately owned

roadside attraction, open for tours every day of the week from March through October; pay your admission fee at the trading post, which dates to the 1930s. One trail leads to the top of the crater, where you get a stunning view of the caldera, which has a huge breach in the rim and a solidified lava flow pouring down from it—a cataclysmic event, frozen in time. The second trail leads down to the ice cave, a bit anticlimactic after the volcano, but interesting nevertheless.

A couple of miles beyond the entrance to the ice cave, you'll enter **El Malpais National Monument.** Malpais, which is Spanish for "badlands," is a region of lava flows and associated otherworldly terrain that was created,

over the course of tens of thousands of years, by the concerted efforts of two dozen nearby volcanoes. The last eruption in the area was 2,000 to 3,000 years ago, but it all still seems quite fresh. You'll find a visitors center about a mile beyond the park boundary, right on NM 53; open Friday through Sunday. Beyond the visitors center, travel east and then north on NM 53 as it sweeps through the western section of the badlands. Most of the lava flows will be off to your right, but only a small portion of the jumbled terrain is visible from the road. Stay on NM 53 as it crosses I-40 on an overpass, near the outskirts of Grants. Beyond the interchange, bear right on Santa Fe Avenue, old Route 66, and stay on that road all the way through town. *(For more about El Malpais and Grants, see* **Scenic Side Trip 19.***)*

El Malpais National Monument

Route 66 runs roughly parallel to Interstate 40; you'll need to look sharp to stay on it as Santa Fe Avenue peels off to the right. A couple of miles past the edge of town, Route 66 swings south and runs alongside I-40, like a frontage road, at one point crossing under the highway, then running along the south side of it for a couple of miles. When you reach Pueblo Road, turn right; when you reach Indian Route 38, follow the signs toward Acoma.

Sky City, one of three villages that make up **Acoma Pueblo**, is the most visually striking of all New Mexico's Native American communities. A flat-topped mesa, the

Acoma Pueblo: Sky City

*Dwelling near
Acoma Pueblo*

centerpiece of an array of smaller sandstone formations, rises 365 feet above the surrounding plain. Atop that mesa is the pueblo, like a castle on a pedestal, or an aerie, protected on all sides by sheer cliffs. There's an overlook alongside Indian Route 38, just before it begins its descent toward the plain. From here, the pueblo is below you, off in the distance. This picturesque spot was the scene of a terrible massacre in 1599, when Spanish soldiers slaughtered 800 people, including 300 women and children, demolishing the pueblo and enslaving many of the survivors, all in retaliation for the deaths of 12 Spaniards in an altercation with Acoma warriors the month before. The pueblo was rebuilt, but a way of life—and an entire generation—was lost.

There are still about 300 buildings clustered atop the mesa, but there's no electricity or running water, and most of the families that own homes there use them only on weekends, or during holidays and festivals. These days, there are only 30 or so full-time residents in a village that was once home to 6,000 people. A road was built to the top of the mesa in the 1950s, carved into the side of the cliff, but there are prominent signs at the bottom prohibiting entry to nonresidents. If you'd like a closer look, you can join one of the guided walking tours that leave every hour from the **Sky City Cultural Center**, the modern building at the foot of the mesa. The center houses the **Haak'u Museum**, which features exhibits of Acoma art and cultural artifacts; traditional Acoma pottery is extraordinary and fetches a pretty price in the galleries of Santa Fe and Taos.

Indian Route 38 near Acoma Pueblo

Leaving the Cultural Center on Indian Route 38, turn left (east) on NM 23 (Kaatsiima Drive). Close to the village here, there are more sandstone bluffs and buttes, a beautiful scene of classic Southwestern terrain. Drive east and north on NM 23 for 13 miles, crossing over Interstate 40. Just north of the interchange, you'll

Bandera, Acoma, and Laguna Highlights

Ice Cave and Bandera Volcano
12000 Ice Caves Road (NM 53), Grants, NM 87020
(505) 783-4303
icecaves.com

El Malpais National Monument
11000 Ice Caves Road (NM 53), Grants, NM 87020
(505) 876-2783
nps.gov/elma

Sky City Cultural Center and Haak'u Museum (Acoma)
Haaku Road, Acoma Pueblo, NM 87034
(505) 552-7861
acomaskycity.org

reconnect with Route 66. Follow the old highway east for about 6 miles, to the **Pueblo of Laguna**. This pueblo was founded in 1699, after the Pueblo Revolt *(see sidebar, page 336)*. Back in the days when Route 66 was a major thoroughfare, Laguna was the only major pueblo easily visible from the highway, so it got lots of tourist traffic. The favorite attraction: **San Jose Mission Church**, a lovely white structure that dates to the pueblo's founding. The church crowns the highest point in the pueblo and is visible for miles in every direction. Tours of the

Laguna Pueblo

church are available, and vendors offer beautiful local crafts in the village. As in most pueblos, photography is prohibited here, unless you have special permission.

Rio Grande, Albuquerque, and Beyond

Leaving Laguna, stay on Route 66 for 7 miles; the old highway zigs and zags a bit, first merging with the I-40 frontage road, and then merging with I-40 east, at Mesita Road. Once you're on I-40, you'll have two options. You can call it a day and head straight for Albuquerque, which is only 45 miles away on the Interstate. Or, if you still

have some daylight, consider one more detour: a lovely drive along the **Rio Grande** that will take you 28 miles out of your way, and cost you about an hour if you take your time about it. To do that, get off Interstate 40 at Exit 126, and follow NM 6 south and east for 34 miles to **Los Lunas**. From there, turn north onto NM 314 for a lovely stretch of highway along the river: a corridor of irrigated fields and wetlands that stretches for 24 miles all the way into the southern suburbs of Albuquerque, New Mexico's largest city.

In **Albuquerque**, stay on NM 314 until it crosses the river on Bridge Boulevard, then take the first left onto Eighth Street. Drive north to the first major intersection, Tingley Drive, and follow the riverfront all the way to Central Avenue. Turn right on Central, and follow it into Old Town, the historic heart of the

Albuquerque Highlights

Casas de Suenos Historic Old Town Inn

310 Rio Grande Blvd. SW, Albuquerque, NM 87104

(505) 247-4560

casasdesuenos.com

city. Take a left on Rio Grande Boulevard. One block to your right, off Plaza Street, is the **Old Town Plaza**, a charming remnant of Spanish heritage in the city, and **San Felipe de Neri Church**, which fronts the plaza. Built in 1706, and rebuilt in 1793, it's one of the oldest surviving buildings from the early days of Albuquerque. Find your way back to Rio Grande Boulevard (beware the many one-way streets), and follow it north to Interstate 40, and the end of this route.

If you like small hotels, consider **Casas de Suenos** (Houses of Dreams), a historic inn right on Rio Grande Boulevard in Old Town. For more about Albuquerque and the surrounding area, see **Scenic Side Trip 20** and **Scenic Side Trip 21**. North from Albuquerque, **Scenic Side Trips 21-25** offer alternatives to Interstate 25, the well-traveled corridor through Santa Fe to the Colorado border. These side trips feature some amazing roads, scenery, and history—the best of northern New Mexico, the vibrant heart of the Land of Enchantment.

Along the Rio Grande, north of Las Lunas

Grants to Socorro

via El Malpais National Monument, the Very Large Array, and Bosque del Apache National Wildlife Refuge

251 miles, **5** hours **30** minutes for drive time, more for optional routes, stops, and sightseeing

Snowbirds flying out over the river of fire should stop for a slice of that chile pepper pie

THIS SIDE TRIP TAKES YOU FROM GRANTS, 80 MILES WEST OF Albuquerque on Interstate 40, to Socorro, 80 miles south of Albuquerque on Interstate 25, without passing through Albuquerque at all. It's a circuitous succession of roads that will add 116 miles to the most direct route between Grants and Socorro, and it will triple your driving time. What you'll get in exchange is scenic grandeur of the first order, wildlife in great numbers, and a close-up look at some massive, sci-fi technology. Best of all, if your timing is right, you'll get ... *pie!* ➡➡

GRANTS TO PIE TOWN

Grants is a town of about 10,000 residents that was founded in the 1880s as a stop on the Atlantic and Pacific Railroad. Its economic base has changed over the years. First it was timber, hauled out of the Zuni Mountains, then agriculture—carrots, to be precise, shipped all over the U.S. by the trainload—and finally, uranium. A Navajo shepherd with a Geiger counter discovered one of the richest deposits in the U.S., making Grants, for a time, the uranium capital of the world. The **New Mexico Mining Museum** has interesting exhibits on uranium mining, including a realistic mock-up of an underground mine, along with Native American artifacts dating back hundreds of years, and some fossils dating back millions.

Leaving Grants, take Exit 85 off Interstate 40. At the bottom of the off-ramp, turn right (south). Just ahead on your left you'll see a drive leading back to the **El Malpais National Monument Visitors Center**, off by itself in an open area. There is no entrance fee for this little-known national monument, but there's no real infrastructure, either, so it's a good idea to stop here for maps and information before you

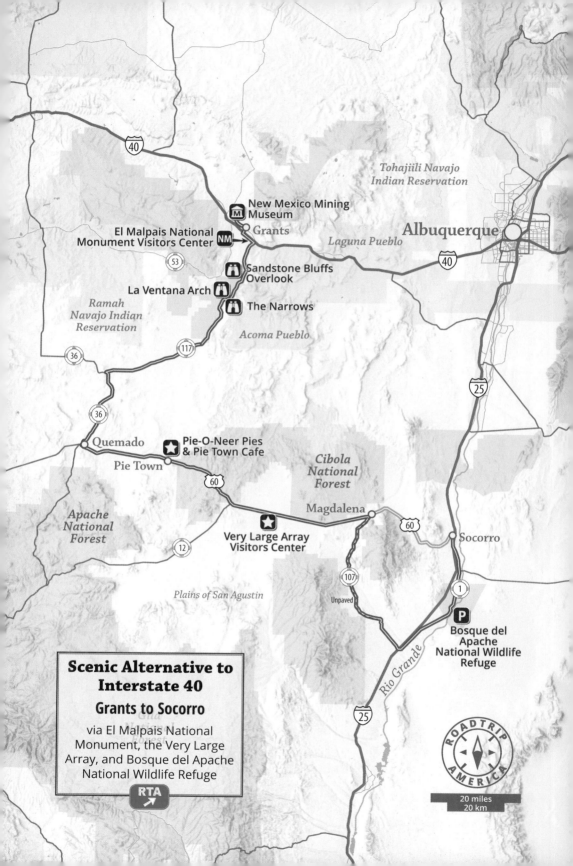

40

New Mexico Mining Museum

M

Grants

El Malpais National Monument Visitors Center

NM

53

Tohajiili Navajo Indian Reservation

Albuquerque

Laguna Pueblo

40

Sandstone Bluffs Overlook

La Ventana Arch

The Narrows

Ramah Navajo Indian Reservation

Acoma Pueblo

117

36

25

36

Quemado

Pie-O-Neer Pies & Pie Town Cafe

Pie Town

60

Cibola National Forest

Apache National Forest

Magdalena

60

Socorro

12

Very Large Array Visitors Center

Plains of San Agustin

107

Unpaved

1

P

Bosque del Apache National Wildlife Refuge

Rio Grande

25

Scenic Alternative to Interstate 40

Grants to Socorro

via El Malpais National Monument, the Very Large Array, and Bosque del Apache National Wildlife Refuge

RTA

ROADTRIP AMERICA

20 miles
20 km

set out for the monument, a good 10 miles from here, south and west of Grants. From the visitors center, head back to I-40 and drive east about 4 miles to Exit 89, NM 117, and turn south. After about 10 miles, you'll enter the parkland. El Malpais (Spanish for "badlands") presents a spectacularly wild landscape. The principal attractions are the lava flows, cinder cones, and lava tubes left behind thousands of years ago, when this area was a field of active volcanoes; at that time, rivers of fire streamed through these shallow valleys, burning everything in their path. Today, jagged black rock and weathered sandstone cliffs dominate the landscape, the black lava running right to the edge of the cliffs in a unique juxtaposition that creates a stunning tableau.

At milepost 11, stop at the small parking area on the right and check out Sandstone Bluffs Overlook; at mile 18, a small parking lot, this one on your left, offers a view of La Ventana Arch, an impressive natural sandstone

El Malpais National Monument

Grants to Pie Town Highlights

New Mexico Mining Museum
100 Iron Ave., Grants, NM 87020
(505) 287-4802

El Malpais National Monument Visitors Center
Exit 85, Interstate 40, Grants, NM
(505) 876-2783
nps.gov/elma

Pie-O-Neer Pies
US 60, Pie Town, NM 87827
(575) 772-2711
pieoneer.com

Pie Town Cafe
US 60, Pie Town, NM 87827
(575) 772-2700
pietown.com

Pie-o-Neer Café, Pietown, New Mexico

formation. This section of the highway is known as "The Narrows" because the road is squeezed between a 2-mile-long sandstone cliff and the lava fields. The quality of the light late in the day is magical.

Follow NM 117 for another 56 miles, until it intersects NM 36. Turn left and follow the signs toward Quemado, 22 miles farther south. When you reach US 60, turn left again (east). After about 22 miles on that old two-lane U.S. highway, you'll roll up on a tiny town with a memorable name. Back in the 1920s, when US 60 was first built, a man opened a filling station here. He liked to bake, so he started making dried-apple pies to sell to his customers. The pies were so popular that the one-time wide spot in the road developed a reputation, and when the community grew big enough to need a name, they called it **Pie Town**.

The quality of the pies has varied over the years, but in Pie Town today, there are at least three establishments that crank out good homemade pies at a prodigious pace: Pie Town Cafe, the Pie Source, and Pie-O-Neer Pies. The local favorite flavor is New Mexico Apple, with green chiles and piñon nuts—a combination that most definitely lingers on the palate. Red chiles, peaches, pecans, and other regional ingredients also make their way into pies here, but there are also many traditional fruit pies and cream pies on offer. There's just one problem: you have to properly time your arrival. If you pass though in winter or too late in the day—no pie for you! But come early, in spring or summer, and there will be a pie with your name on it (literally, if you call ahead).

VERY LARGE ARRAY AND BOSQUE DEL APACHE

Leaving Pie Town, continue east on US 60. You'll pass through a forested area as the road climbs up and over the Datil Mountains, then, as you come down the other side, an ancient lake bed will spread out before you to the north and east. This wide open grassland, called the Plains of San Agustin, is home to antelope and cattle and little else, though some people say a UFO crashed here in 1947, around the same time as the rather more famous purported crash of a UFO in Roswell, some 200 miles away (see **Scenic Side Trip 1**).

Radio telescope, Very Large Array, off US 60 east of Datil, New Mexico

Also occupying the plains is the extraordinary radio astronomy observatory called the **Very Large Array** or VLA. This isn't a telescope in the usual sense. It's an installation of 27 enormous dish antennas positioned along three 13-mile-long rail lines that meet in a Y-shape. Every three or four months, each

of the 82-foot-wide, 230-ton behemoths is moved to a different position along the rails, allowing astronomers to precisely focus the massive mechanism and point it toward different sectors of the sky. Radio telescopes like these don't render a conventional image; they pull in the faint radio waves emitted by distant stars, black holes, quasars, and clouds of gas that fill interstellar space. By analyzing these signals, scientists literally travel through time, "witnessing" celestial events that took place billions of years ago, opening a window on the evolution of celestial objects and the origins of the universe. That's heady stuff. Contrary to popular belief, the array isn't being used to search for signs of extraterrestrial intelligence. It's strictly a coincidence that it was built in the exact same spot where a UFO crashed. *Or maybe not ...*

It's tough to appreciate the size of the telescope's dishes until you get close to one of them, and you will, because US 60 passes right through the middle of the whole business. Staff at the visitors center, open daily, can set you up on a self-guided tour; guided tours are offered on the first Saturday of each month. Standing at the base of one of the huge dishes, looking up, you feel pretty small. From the cosmic perspective encompassed by this amazing technology, our entire *planet* is small: a mere speck of dust. Don't think about that too hard; it'll make your head hurt.

Leaving the Array, return to US 60 and drive east 24 miles to the once bustling cow town of Magdalena and the intersection with NM 107, where you'll turn right (south). This state highway starts out paved, but after about 4 miles, the pavement runs out; you'll be on graded gravel for almost 30 miles before the asphalt returns.

NM 107 is a lonely road, wild and empty. New Mexico has a lot of highways just like this one. They're maintained by the state, but there's not enough traffic to justify the expense of paving them. The lack of traffic is a boon for wildlife watchers. There's a good chance you'll see **pronghorn antelope** along this route: small bands in spring and summer, and herds of as many as 100 in the winter. These aren't true antelope—their closest living relative is actually the giraffe—but they move like antelope, and it's a joy to see these magnificent animals bounding across the wide-open landscape. Pronghorns are the fastest land mammals in North America, capable of running full tilt across the Plains of San Agustin at a sustained speed of 55 miles an hour.

About 8 miles after the pavement resumes, you'll intersect Interstate 25. You're just 34 miles from Socorro, and the end of the route, but there's one final detour to make. Cross the Interstate on the overpass, and when you come to NM 1 (also known as old U.S. Highway 85), turn left. The old highway runs along the east side of the Interstate like an access road until, after about 7 miles, it veers off to the northeast. Eleven miles beyond that slight curve, look for a small complex of buildings and a parking area on the west side of

Alternate Route

Many rental car contracts prohibit travel on unpaved roads like this section of NM 107; if that's your situation, you'll have to skip this segment. Instead, drive on to Socorro on US 60, and loop down to the Bosque del Apache from there.

NM 107, south of Magdalena, New Mexico, pronghorn antelope, seen from NM 107

the road: the visitors center for **Bosque del Apache National Wildlife Refuge.**

The Bosque is a 60,000-acre preserve, half of it protected wilderness, all managed by the U.S. Fish and Wildlife Service. The central feature is a 3,800-acre floodplain, which together with 9,100 acres of wetlands and a wild section of the Rio Grande create a ribbon of green through an otherwise arid landscape. Mild winters and reliable forage are powerful magnets for migratory birds; every year, from November through February, tens of thousands of sandhill cranes, snow geese, and other water-seeking species congregate on ponds in this area, waiting out the worst of the bitter winter in their spring and summer nesting grounds, a thousand miles or more to the north. This cycle has repeated annually for hundreds of thousands—perhaps millions—of years, part of the natural rhythm of life on earth. Here in the middle Rio Grande Valley, this living symphony, this cycle of the seasons, is concentrated and amplified in a

Fall colors, Bosque del Apache National Wildlife Refuge

way that is increasingly rare in our modern world, providing a right-in-your-face connection to a time, not so long ago, when an abundance of wildness was the rule, and not the exception.

From the visitors center on NM 1, the main entrance to Bosque is about 500 yards south (there is a fee to enter; National Park passes accepted). After crossing a short bridge over a canal,

Bosque del Apache National Wildlife Refuge

you'll enter the loop road. There are actually two one-way loops, both smooth-surfaced dirt roads that run through the best part of the preserve. The Marsh Loop runs south, and the Farm Loop runs north. Each is only about 7 miles long, but you should allow plenty of time for the drive, because you'll want to make lots of stops. Birds and other wildlife are everywhere—as many as 377 species have been spotted in the refuge—but it's the migratory flocks that make the biggest impression.

In winter, from mid-November through the end of February, the premier attraction is the daily "fly-out," an astonishing event involving thousands upon thousands of ducks and geese that spend winter nights on these ponds. A half hour or so before sunrise, those flocks awaken, and they all start honking and quacking. First a few, and then the rest—a cacophony of birdcalls louder than anything you've ever heard—and then, as if

VLA and Bosque Del Apache Highlights

Very Large Array Visitors Center
Old U.S. Highway 60, Magdalena, NM 87825
(575) 835-7410
public.nrao.edu/telescopes/vla

Bosque del Apache National Wildlife Refuge
1001 NM 1, San Antonio, NM 87832
(575) 835-1828
fws.gov/refuge/Bosque_del_Apache

on a prearranged signal, every one of those thousands of ducks and geese takes off out of the water in a whirring and flapping explosion of wings and feathers so powerful that it will squeeze the air from your lungs. Flock upon flock, from pond after pond, pass overhead in waves that blanket the sky, honking like mad as they all fly off to feeding grounds along the river, where they'll spend most of the day foraging. It's over in a matter of seconds, literally, but the experience will leave you buzzing for hours. The imperious sandhill cranes *(see sidebar)* also

Sandhill Cranes, Bosque del Apache National Wildlife Refuge

Sandhill Cranes

Cranes are big birds with long legs, long necks, and a wingspan that's the avian equivalent of a Boeing 747. Of the 15 species of cranes in the world, only two are found in North America: the whooping crane, famous for being rare and endangered, and the sandhill crane, the stars of the show at Bosque del Apache. You can't miss 'em: gray plumage, white feathers on the head and neck, and a characteristic red spot on the forehead and around the eyes. Birds in this Rocky Mountain population of Greater Sandhill Cranes stand 4 feet tall and have a wingspan of more than 6 feet. They nest in the vicinity of Yellowstone National Park, and every fall, 30,000 of them fly 1,000 miles south to spend the winter here in central New Mexico along the Rio Grande, arriving around mid-November and flying home again by March. When migrating, they can soar 500 miles in a 12-hour day, flying in a V formation at an altitude of 12,000 feet.

When you observe these birds at Bosque, you'll see the whole wild range of crane behavior, including their courtship displays, when they dance to attract a mate: bobbing and bowing, spreading their wings, squawking, and flipping things into the air. Sometimes that mood is so infectious you'll see a whole big group of cranes doing the do-si-do to a fiddler that only they can hear. Serious birders from all over the world come to this place. It's a grand and wonderful spectacle.

move across the Bosque to feed, but they don't all jump up at once. For them, it's a more leisurely process, taking off one and two at a time.

Sandhill Cranes, Bosque del Apache National Wildlife Refuge

   An hour before dawn is a tough wake-up call, but if you miss the fly-out, no worries: there's still plenty to see here. The cranes, in particular, are wonderful to watch. In fall, you'll catch the gorgeous display of cottonwoods turning gold along the river. In spring, the waterfowl will be gone—back to Idaho, Montana, and points farther north—but you'll see shorebirds and warblers and other species passing through on their own migrations, and the hills and fields will be alive with wildflowers. In summer there are hummingbirds, quail, roadrunners, and other native birds, and the blue skies will fill with dramatic monsoon storm clouds that produce phenomenal sunsets. In the fall, the cranes fly in from the north, and the cycle begins again.

Snow geese, Bosque del Apache National Wildlife Refuge

To Socorro and Beyond

Leaving Bosque del Apache, stay on NM 1 and drive 18 miles north to Socorro. If you're ready to call it a day, or if you'd like to stay close by so you can get up early and catch the fly-out at Bosque the next day, you'll find a good selection of hotels in Socorro, with most of the national chains represented.

After Socorro, you can go directly to Albuquerque, 96 miles north on Interstate 25, or you can consider **Scenic Side Trip 20**, which will show you more of Socorro and take you to Albuquerque by way of the Salt Mission Trail, a lovely detour that takes in three Spanish missions and some beautiful scenic roads along the way. Or, you can follow Interstate 25 south to Las Cruces, where you can connect with Interstate 10.

Part 4: Scenic Alternatives to Interstate 25

Interstate 25 is a major north/south highway that begins off Interstate 10 near Las Cruces, New Mexico, and runs for 1,068 miles, ending at an intersection with Interstate 90 60 miles short of Wyoming's border with Montana. Three hundred miles of this Interstate runs through Wyoming, and 300 more through Colorado. The rest is all in New Mexico, where I-25 crosses the state in a diagonal curve like a backwards, lazy S. The highway follows the Rio Grande from Las Cruces, past Albuquerque, and most of the way to Santa Fe before swooping south and east, skirting the southern end of the Sangre de Cristo Mountains, then running true to the course of the old Santa Fe Trail, all the way to Raton Pass, on the border of Colorado, at the bottom edge of the Rockies.

This is a fabulous landscape of purple mountains, high desert, and grassy plains traversing a fascinating region where the entire spectrum of history, both geological and human, becomes so real you can literally reach out and touch it. If you absolutely had to, you could cover that whole distance in about 6.5 hours. Follow the scenic side trips in this book, instead, and it will take you closer to 6.5 days—best call it a full week, because you'll need a little extra time to catch your breath. Here are six scenic side trips specifically designed to bypass Interstate 25 in New Mexico, ranging from 96 miles to 270 miles in length. Along the way you'll see some wondrous sights—from Spanish missions and ancient pueblos to the remains of a supervolcano and the birthplace of The Bomb. There are geological wonders of the first order, and some of the most beautiful roads in the Southwest.

Seasonal considerations are similar to those for the region that straddles Interstate 40: wildflowers in spring and summer, and in the fall, golden aspens in the high country and golden cottonwoods along the rivers and streams. The conditions that make for great skiing in the winter resorts around Santa Fe can make travel a bit treacherous. In winter, check road conditions in advance of any travel in the mountains, and review the general "Seasonal Considerations" on page xviii.

These routes are all sequenced for drivers headed north from Socorro. If you are traveling the other way, just reverse the itineraries.

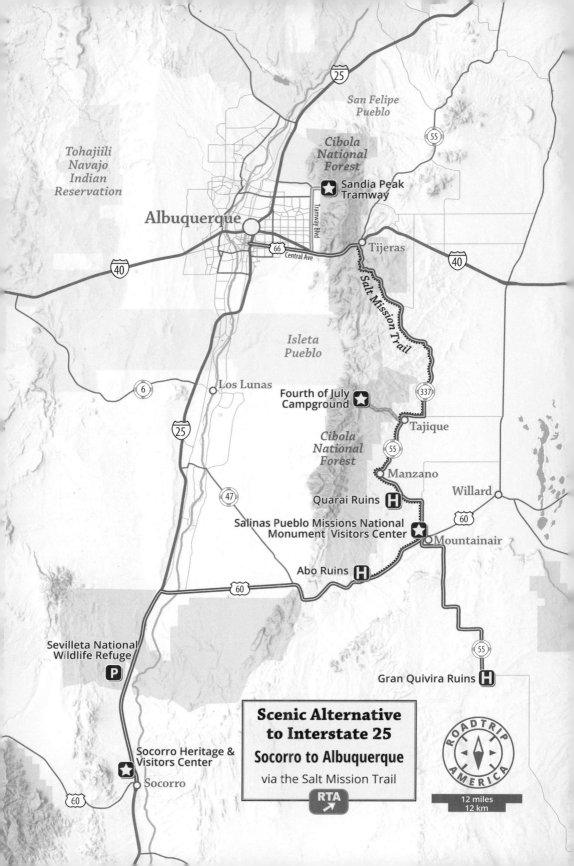

Tohajiili
Navajo
Indian
Reservation

Albuquerque

San Felipe
Pueblo

Cibola
National
Forest

★ Sandia Peak
   Tramway

Tramway Blvd

25

55

66 Central Ave

Tijeras

40

40

Isleta
Pueblo

Salt Mission Trail

Los Lunas

6

★ Fourth of July
   Campground

337

25

Tajique

47

Cibola
National
Forest

55

Manzano

Willard

Quarai Ruins H

Salinas Pueblo Missions National
Monument Visitors Center ★

Mountainair

60

Abo Ruins H

60

55

Sevilleta National
Wildlife Refuge
P

Gran Quivira Ruins H

**Scenic Alternative
to Interstate 25
Socorro to Albuquerque**
via the Salt Mission Trail

RTA ↗

ROADTRIP
AMERICA

12 miles
12 km

Socorro Heritage &
Visitors Center

★

Socorro

60

Socorro to Albuquerque

via the Salt Mission Trail

195 miles, **4** hours **30** minutes for drive time, more for optional routes, stops, and sightseeing

Mysterious Missions, Apaches, and the Cities that Died of Fear

FROM SOCORRO, INTERSTATE 25 TAKES YOU NORTH THROUGH the broad valley of the Rio Grande to Albuquerque, New Mexico's largest city. Desert mountains rim the horizon in both directions, and the river flows between them, a sinuous ribbon of water, trees, and irrigated fields tracing a swath of green through the arid landscape, sometimes near the highway, sometimes off in the distance. It's a pleasant enough drive that takes only about 90 minutes. ▶▶

The Salt Mission Trail Scenic Byway is a circuitous alternative. It takes you 100 miles out of your way, and it will cost you a good 3 extra hours, but if you're intrigued by the idea of seeing remote, empty ruins and driving beautiful mountain roads, this little-known scenic byway is a lovely way to go. The route takes in three long-abandoned Spanish missions before leading you up and over the Manzano Mountains and on into Albuquerque from the southeast.

SOCORRO TO MOUNTAINAIR

Socorro, which means "help" in Spanish, got its name from an act of kindness bestowed on a party of early Spanish settlers by Pueblo Indians in this part of the Rio Grande Valley. The colonists had just crossed the treacherous desert known as the Jornada del Muerto, "Journey of the Dead Man," just south of modern Socorro. They'd gone days without water and were desperately low on food when they encountered the Indians, who saved their lives with a gift of "much corn." To commemorate the event, the Spanish built a mission on the site, Nuestra Señora de Perpetuo Socorro (Our Lady of Perpetual Help), which was erected here between 1615 and 1626.

The original mission church was abandoned, along with the rest of the town, after the Pueblo Revolt of 1680 *(see sidebar, page 336)* but it

Rio Grande from US 60, North of Socorro

was rebuilt in 1816 and renamed San Miguel. You can still see the original *vigas*, wooden beams hewn from logs felled in distant mountain forests and hauled here on the backs of the Indian laborers. Near the church is the historic plaza, and in the surrounding side streets you'll see lovely old adobe homes from the resettlement period, in the early 19th century, alongside later, Territory-era adobe buildings, which commonly have big wooden porches. The discovery of a lode of silver ore in the late 19th century brought new wealth to the town, reflected in stately red brick mansions in Victorian and Queen Anne styles. A leisurely walking tour is the best way to appreciate Socorro's architecture; check in at the **Socorro Heritage & Visitors Center** for maps and brochures.

Leaving Socorro, head north on Interstate 25 for 20 miles, to Exit 169, where you'll find signs directing you to the visitors center for the **Sevilleta National Wildlife Refuge**, just west of the highway. Sevilleta is centered along the Rio Grande, but the river is only a small part of this refuge. Four different ecological zones intersect

Mural. Mountainair, New Mexico

here—prairie, desert, woodland, and steppe—and the diverse environments attract and foster a broad diversity of life: 250 species of birds, more than 1,200 species of plants, and 80 species of mammals, including prairie dogs, kangaroo rats, bears, and mountain lions. The protected area is vast, almost a quarter of a million acres, and the principle management objective is to maintain the refuge in its natural state. To that end, visitors are restricted to a small portion of it. More information, including maps of the hiking trails, can be obtained at the visitors center; admission is free.

From Sevilleta, drive another 6 miles north on I-25 to Exit 175, and follow US 60 as it curves away to the east. You'll see mountains in the distance, but once you've crossed the Rio Grande, the area north and south of the two-lane highway is flat scrubland studded with creosote, sagebrush, and scattered ramshackle homesteads: small parcels of land, occupied by woebegone double-wides, single-wides, junked cars, and dilapidated

Socorro to Mountainair Highlights

Socorro Heritage & Visitors Center
217 Fisher Ave., Socorro, NM 87801
(575) 835-8927
socorronm.org

Sevilleta National Wildlife Refuge
West of I-25, Exit 169, La Joya, NM 87028
(505) 864-4021
fws.gov/refuge/sevilleta

RVs that appear to have grown roots here. Many of the trailers appear long-abandoned, stripped to their frames by the elements. For 10 miles or so, the highway passes through this post-apocalyptic landscape, a boulevard of broke-down dreams.

SALINAS PUEBLO MISSIONS

After about 18 miles on US 60, just past the merge with NM 47, the highway curves south for a couple of miles as it climbs up and over Abo Pass at the southern end of the Manzano Mountains. The terrain becomes more rugged as you leave the broad Rio Grande Valley, and there are beautiful mountain views in every direction. Twelve miles beyond the pass, you'll see signs for **Abo Ruins**, the first of three archaeological complexes that make up **Salinas Pueblo Missions National Monument**. The three widely separated sites are all old Spanish missions, all built about the same time, each in a different setting, and each worth the drive.

The Abo Ruins lie half a mile north of US 60 along NM 513, a winding, tree-lined country lane. The complex includes the ruins of the mission church, the adjacent *convento* (living quarters for the friars), and the Indian pueblo, all built from the same flat red sandstone, laid horizontally, like bricks. At the visitors center, you can see a good scale model of what Abo looked like 350 years ago, when it was still a thriving community. Abo is a quick visit. The walking tour of the mission takes less than half an hour; allow a bit more time if you want to check out the ruins of the pueblo.

The Spanish first explored this area in 1581, arriving through the same mountain pass that's now traversed by US 60. The conquistadores were attracted by rumors of "Seven Cities of Gold" in the mountains of New Mexico. What they found instead were pueblos, native villages

Abo Mission Ruins, Salt Missions Scenic Byway

made of stone and adobe. The architecture was fairly sophisticated, but the people were farmers, and they had no gold. Their wealth was all in their land, so the Spanish took that—all of it—claiming it for the King of Spain. The Spanish soldiers had cavalry, cannons, and swords made of fine Toledo steel. The Pueblo Indians were peaceful people who didn't stand a chance against any of that, so the conquest of this particular corner of New Spain was all too easy.

By 1622, a Catholic mission had been established here at Abo, and Spanish missionaries set about the business of converting the indigenous people, first conscripting their labor to build the imposing church that now lies in ruins here. The plan worked well until the late 1660s, when an extended drought took the people of the valley to the brink of starvation. Marauding Apaches took advantage of their weakness, raiding every community east of the Manzanos, repeatedly and relentlessly. That

Kindly Pass the Salt

Salt is pretty important stuff. We crave it, instinctively, because our bodies need it to function. As civilization advanced, people found many uses for the mineral: flavoring food, curing meat, tanning hides, extracting silver from its ore. It's one of the world's most common chemical compounds. In our modern age, we seldom give it a thought, but in the old days, salt was often scarce, a valuable trading commodity, nearly on a par with gold. Think of camel caravans crossing the Sahara and traveling the Silk Road through Asia. Salt was always part of the cargo, transported from places where it was plentiful to places where it was not.

The ancient Americas were no different: salt was prized and it traveled widely. In New Mexico, the very best source of salt in the precontact era was an ancient lake bed, the Estancia Basin, east of the Manzano Mountains. Shallow salt lakes, called *salinas* in Spanish, formed seasonally here; when they dried up, they left deposits of natural salt crystals that were easy to harvest. When the Spanish arrived here in the 16th century, they found 10 pueblos in this area, all of them prosperous, and all heavily involved in a wide-ranging salt trade that had been going on for hundreds of years. Blocks of the stuff went from village to village; in exchange, the people in these pueblos received turquoise from the mines near Santa Fe, shells from distant shores, buffalo hides from the Great Plains, exotic feathers from the mountains of Mexico—all manner of wonderful things.

The Salinas Missions were named for these salt lakes, which still exist, not far from Quarai. They continued to produce salt in commercial quantities up until the 1930s.

proved to be the undoing of the Salinas missions. In 1673, there was an exodus from the area around Abo, the Native Americans resettling in the Rio Grande Valley, west of the Manzanos, and the Spanish retreating to Mexico. Left to the whims of the victorious Apaches, who controlled this territory for the next 200 years, the ghostly Salinas missions and abandoned Spanish settlements became known as "the cities that died of fear."

Leaving Abo, head back to US 60 and continue east about 10 miles to the small town of Mountainair. Here you'll find the main visitors center for all three units of Salinas Pueblo Missions National Monument. A video documentary tells the interesting history of the Salinas Valley, from the building of the pueblos to the modern era.

To reach Gran Quivira, the second and largest of the three archaeological sites, drive 26 miles south from Mountainair on NM 55. This country road zigs and zags through ranchland, first running due south, then east,

then south again, then east again—left, right, left. Just follow the signs and stay on NM 55 until you come up on a hill topped by crumbling ruins built of gray limestone, nothing at all like the red sandstone buildings you saw at Abo. Signs will lead you to the visitors center. From there, you'll have a bit of a hike up a moderately steep set of stairs to reach the ruins. The original Native American settlement here was huge—practically a city—comprising several pueblos, including a very unusual circular pueblo that has been fully excavated, along with the foundations of a massive structure than once contained 226 separate rooms.

Gran Quivira Ruins, Salt Missions Scenic Byway

The Spanish mission here, begun in 1627, was a satellite of the mission at Abo, so the church wasn't nearly as grand, and much less of it remains. The location, atop a hill with a commanding view of the surrounding area, had military advantages, but there weren't enough soldiers in all of New Mexico to hold off starvation and the Apaches. In 1668, 450 Indians in the pueblo died of hunger, and the Spanish were reduced to eating cowhides. Brutally attacked by Apaches, who were also starving, Gran Quivira was abandoned in 1672.

Leaving Gran Quivira, return to Mountainair on NM 55, then head north out of town for about 5 miles, staying left as the highway swings west toward Manzano. Three miles farther along, turn left on County Road B076, and follow it about a mile to **Quarai**, the last of the three missions and the best preserved of the lot. The old church stands sentinel on a slight rise. Built of red sandstone, like the ruins of Abo, its walls were as much as 6 feet thick at their base, and rose to a height of almost 40 feet; large portions of them are still standing. Many of the windows and doorways are still intact, too, as are rows of square holes that once held the timbers that supported the second floor and roof. Nearby, the ruins of the *convento* include a square kiva; why it is square, no one knows. As you stand in the center of this space and look up at those walls, try to imagine the back-breaking labor that went into the construction of this church, and the conflicted emotions of the once-free people forced into servitude by the Spanish friars.

Quarai was home to a group of Tewa-speaking people, cousins to the Tompiro speakers of Abo and Gran Quivira. Like its sister missions, Quarai stood for about 50 years, surrounded by verdant fields and pasture, until drought and Apaches arrived. The missionaries held out until 1678, and then retreated to Mexico; the Indians escaped to an area in what is now Texas. Today, these lonely, windswept ruins still evoke a powerful sentiment.

Opposite: Quarai Mission Ruins, Salt Missions Scenic Byway

Salinas Pueblo Missions Highlights

Salinas Pueblo Missions National Monument Visitors Center
102 S. Ripley St., Mountainair, NM 87036
(505) 847-2585
nps.gov/sapu

Abo Ruins
One-half mile north of US 60 on NM 513
(505) 847-2400

Gran Quivira Ruins
26 miles south of US 60 on NM 55
(505) 847-2770

Quarai Ruins
8 miles north of US 60 on NM 55, then 1 mile west
(505) 847-2290

SALT MISSION TRAIL TO ALBUQUERQUE

Leave Quarai as you came in, back to NM 55, and turn left. This highway is part of the **Salt Mission Trail Scenic Byway**, a lovely road that follows the Manzanos Range north to Albuquerque. You'll pass though the little town of Manzano, which means "apple" in Spanish, so called for the apple trees planted there by early settlers; some are still standing after nearly 200 years. Follow the scenic byway north on a winding route through the tiny towns of Torreon and Tajique until you reach the intersection with NM 337. Turn left onto that road, which continues through the foothills to Chilili. At that point, the road cuts northwest and climbs into low mountains, crossing

San Felipe de Neri Church, Old Town Albuquerque

An Autumn Detour

In the middle of the Manzanos, there's an autumn surprise. In the small town of Tajique, turn left (west) from NM 55 onto CR A013, the Torreon Tajique Loop. This graded dirt road takes you up into the cool pines of the Cibola National Forest. After about 7 miles, you'll reach the Fourth of July Campground. Stop! The surrounding hillsides are covered by the state's largest stand of red maples. Beautiful in any season, but around mid-October? Those hills are ablaze in a breathtaking display of fall color!

through an area dotted with small farms and cattle ranches; these roads can be icy in winter. Stay on NM 337 for about 20 miles, as far as Tijeras, which means "scissors" in Spanish, named for the pass that "cuts" between the Manzanos and the Sandias. Sandia is Spanish for "watermelon"; folks say the mountains are called this for the way the sunset often sets the peaks aglow with a pinkish hue. The Sandias are Albuquerque's signature mountain range, the backdrop to its modern skyline.

At Tijeras, NM 337 intersects Interstate 40, which you'll follow west for 5 miles to Exit 167. Follow the off-ramp to Central Avenue, also known as Route 66, which will take you all the way downtown. Or, if you'd like to get a better look at the Sandias, take a right on Tramway Boulevard about a block after you exit I-40. Follow Tramway north for about 10 miles to Tramway Road NE. Turn right, and after about a mile you'll reach the base of the **Sandia Peak Tramway**. The tramway gondolas will carry you all the way to the top of Sandia Peak, a 2.7-mile ride that takes about 15 minutes and tops out at an observation platform at 10,378 feet; bring a sweater, as the summit can be quite cool. From here you get a panoramic view of the city. The trams run until 9 p.m., making this an ideal

Albuquerque Highlights

Sandia Peak Tramway
30 Tramway Road NE, Albuquerque, NM 87122
(505) 856-7325
sandiapeak.com

Sunset, Old Town Albuquerque

Old Town Albuquerque

sunset activity and a great introduction to the city for first timers. For more about Albuquerque, including recommendations for lodging, see **Scenic Side Trip 18** and **Scenic Side Trip 21**.

Beyond Albuquerque

Where to from here? If you're headed north, keep turning the pages; there are five more scenic alternatives to Interstate 25 ahead. Headed west? Reverse the itinerary of any of the scenic alternatives to Interstate 40 in Part Three of this book, and you'll have some grand adventures!

Albuquerque Loop:

Petroglyphs, Tent Rocks, Turquoise Trail, and Sandia Peak

190 miles, **6** hours **15** minutes for drive time, more for optional routes, stops, and sightseeing

Rocking and rolling on The Turquoise Trail

THIS SCENIC SIDE TRIP MAKES A COMPLETE LOOP AROUND THE Sandias, Albuquerque's signature mountain range, performing a double bypass of Interstate 25—first to the west and then to the east—before cutting back through the mountains to return to the city. It's a great way to explore the area around New Mexico's biggest burg while taking in the whole spectrum of its history, from prehistoric times to the modern era. As a bonus, you get two very unusual national monuments, some of the world's finest turquoise, a hair-raising mountain ride, and a sunset view of the Rio Grande Valley that will darned near stop your heart. ➤➤

ALBUQUERQUE TO PETROGLYPH NATIONAL MONUMENT

From anywhere in Albuquerque, jump onto I-25, and take it to Interstate 40. From the interchange, take I-40 west, toward Gallup, but get off immediately, at Exit 158 (6th-12th St.), and follow the frontage road west to 12th Street. Turn right, and on your left you'll find the **Indian Pueblo Cultural Center**, a combination museum, gallery, and performance venue owned and operated by a consortium of 19 Pueblo Indian tribes. Here you can get an overview of the history and living traditions of New Mexico's Pueblo culture, told from the perspective of the native people themselves. The center houses an impressive collection of pottery, textiles, baskets, paintings, murals, handcrafted jewelry, and other artisan works. Native American dances are staged in the courtyard every weekend throughout the year; the restaurant offers dishes based on traditional recipes; the gift shop is exceptional; and the center hosts many special events.

Leaving the IPCC, follow 12th Street back to I-40, drive west 4.5 miles to Exit 154, Unser Boulevard, and take that 3.5 miles north to **Petroglyph National Monument**. This 7,200-acre site encompasses a field of small volcanoes and an escarpment of

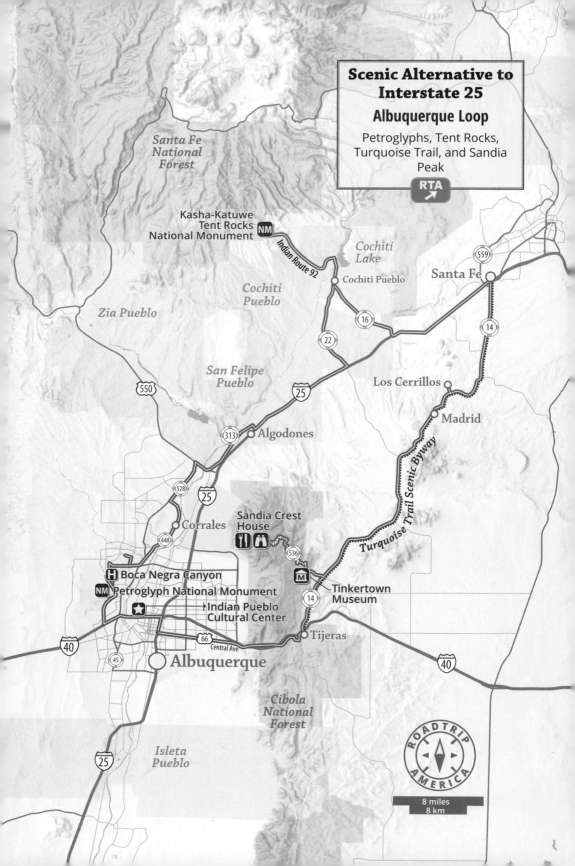

volcanic rock that snakes across the landscape for 17 zigzagging miles. The escarpment is the crumbling edge of a sheet of lava that spread across the floor the Rio Grande Valley 130,000 years ago. As the softer rock to the east eroded away, the harder rock remained, creating a wall studded with angular black boulders that forms a natural western border to this part of the city.

The rocks along the escarpment have a high concentration of iron and manganese, which has oxidized over the eons to form a dark coating on the surface of the stone known as "desert varnish." Long ago, people discovered that they could create permanent marks on these dark boulders by pecking away the coating, exposing the lighter-colored rock underneath. There are more than 25,000 of these petroglyphs within the national monument, one of the largest concentrations of rock art in the Southwest, and by far the most accessible. The oldest have been dated at about 3,000 years, marks left by prehistoric hunters passing through the area, but most of them are 400 to 700 years old, created by ancestors of today's Pueblo Indians, who consider such images sacred.

Petroglyph National Monument, Albuquerque, New Mexico

It is a motley and fascinating collection. Some are obvious depictions of birds and animals. Some look like masks or ceremonial figures. There are many handprints, and certain symbols and geometric designs, such as spirals and zigzags, are repeated in many different locations. Others appear to be unique creations, their meaning a mystery. Aliens? Flying saucers? The abominable snowman? A few glyphs, most notably Christian crosses, depictions of sheep, and symbols representing livestock brands, were added by Spanish sheep herders who settled this area in the 18th century.

There are four separate locations of interest to visitors; none of them is adjacent to the visitors center off Unser at Western Trail, but stop there anyway for maps and general information about the monument (there is no entrance fee). The location with the largest number of petroglyphs is **Rinconada Canyon**, just south of the visitors center; that section is undeveloped, and involves a 2-mile hike. The next biggest collection is in **Piedras Marcadas Canyon**, several miles north, with a 1.5-mile trail. **Volcanoes Day Use Area,** on the west side of the park, offers 3 miles of moderately strenuous trails that will take you around a trio of cinder cones and alongside ancient lava flows—very interesting, and with some great views.

If your time is limited, head to the fourth site, **Boca Negra Canyon**, the closest and most developed section of the park. To get there, drive 2.5 miles north on Unser Boulevard, and follow the signs to the parking lot on the right (there is a small parking fee, waived for holders of National Parks passes). The site has three popular trails of different lengths through the desert terrain; you can hike them all in about an hour and see a hundred or more petroglyphs—enough to at least get a sense of the place. It makes a good family outing. *Be sure to take water, especially in the summer.*

West Albuquerque Highlights

Indian Pueblo Cultural Center
2401 12th St. NW, Albuquerque, NM 87104
(505) 843-7270
indianpueblo.org

Petroglyph National Monument
6001 Unser Blvd. NW, Albuquerque, NM 87120
(505) 899-0205
nps.gov/petr

Albuquerque International Balloon Fiesta

Every year during the first week of October, Albuquerque plays host to the world's largest gathering of hot air balloons. It's a signature event that's grown exponentially in popularity, attracting a thousand balloonists and as many as a million spectators to Albuquerque during the 10 days of the fiesta. The sight of hundreds of huge, colorful balloons lifting off all at once, a "mass ascension" into the heavenly blue New Mexico sky, is almost a religious experience. The sight of those same balloons at night, aglow from the flames of their burners is otherworldly. Area hotels are booked solid far in advance, so plan ahead if you'd like to attend.

Hot air ballooning has been big in New Mexico for more than 100 years; the clear skies and vast open countryside around Albuquerque make it the perfect launch site. A balloon ride gives you an extraordinary perspective on the terrain and the roads below, like a "Satellite View" come to life. The flights are expensive—$150 to $200 per passenger—but for many, it's the high point of their trip. More than a dozen established operators offer balloon rides in the Albuquerque area, all year round, weather permitting; sunrise is a great time to go.

balloonfiesta.com

PETROGLYPHS TO TENT ROCKS NATIONAL MONUMENT

Leaving Petroglyph National Monument, drive north on Unser, then east on Paseo del Norte to NM 45 (Coors Boulevard), and follow that north. NM 45 becomes NM 448, and then Coors Boulevard turns into Corrales Road. A couple of miles farther on, you'll reach the **Village of Corrales**; right on the main drag you can see San Ysidro Church, a historic adobe structure that dates to 1868. These days, Corrales is a partially gentrified suburb, with nice shops and restaurants, but there are still vestiges of the little farming town that it used to be, until not so very long ago.

San Ysidro Church, Corrales, New Mexico

From Corrales, drive north on NM 448 (Corrales Road) to NM 528 (Pat D'Arco Highway). Turn right, and follow that for 5 miles to US 550; right again, and drive east, across the bridge over the Rio Grande, to NM 313, the Camino del Pueblo, where you'll turn left (north). After about 6 miles you'll enter the small farming town of **Algodones**; here NM 313 becomes the Camino Real, the "Royal Road," named for the route once followed by Spanish colonists traveling between Mexico and Santa Fe. Most of the houses in Algodones have barns, and tractors, and a field out back growing one thing or another; at this point, you're officially in rural New Mexico. To the west, beyond the river, it is all Indian land: Santa Ana, Jemez, and Zia Pueblos; a little farther along the road, San Felipe Pueblo stretches out to the east.

You've been running parallel to I-25 since crossing the river; past Algodones, jog right on NM 315, and then turn left to merge onto the freeway headed north (the Interstate is your only good option along this particular stretch). After 11.5 miles on the Interstate, take Exit 259, NM 22, toward Cochiti Lake and Santo Domingo Pueblo. Stay on that road through Peña Blanca to Cochiti Pueblo,

Tent Rocks Highlights

Kasha-Katuwe Tent Rocks National Monument
Near Cochiti Pueblo, NM 87072
(505) 331-6259

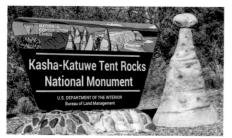

where signs will direct you to **Kasha-Katuwe Tent Rocks National Monument**, a few miles farther down the road, and around a couple of corners. The land is the property of Cochiti Pueblo, but the monument, created in 2001, is managed by the Bureau of

Land Management; there is a small entry fee.

This place is a fabulous, utterly unique geological curiosity. Three miles of well-maintained trails lead you through a narrow canyon and along a slope studded with cone-shaped "tent rocks": strange, nearly symmetrical hoodoos, some as high as 90 feet tall, most of them wearing a hard capstone at their peak. The "tents" are composed of ashy "tuff," a lightweight, porous rock that was laid down by explosive volcanic eruptions and pyroclastic flows 6-7 million years ago; relentless erosion carved the bizarre formations you see. Give yourself at least an hour to walk partway up Canyon Trail and back; go farther if you can spare the time, because the views from Lookout Point, at the top of the trail, are spectacular. *The last portion of this trail is very steep—not for the faint of heart!*

Opposite and above: Kasha-Katuwe Tent Rocks National Monument, New Mexico

THE TURQUOISE TRAIL: CERRILLOS AND MADRID

Leaving Tent Rocks, drive back the way you came in, on NM 22, but after about 5 miles, bear left onto NM 16, and follow that road back to I-25 north. Take the Interstate 11 miles to Exit 276. Turn right onto NM 599, and after half a mile turn right again on NM 14, the start of the 50-mile scenic byway known as **The Turquoise Trail.**

The trail gets its name from the rich turquoise mines near **Los Cerrillos,** the first town you'll come to. These mines have been worked since prehistoric times, and the beautiful blue-green stones produced there have been valuable trade items since the beginning of commerce in this part of the world. Turquoise from Los Cerrillos was prized by the Aztec emperors of Mexico and by native tribes throughout the Southwest. In later years, Cerrillos turquoise was favored by Spanish royalty, who received

Tree trunk sculpture outside Church of St. Joseph, Cerrillos, New Mexico

it along with the gold, emeralds, and other treasures that flowed into their coffers from their New World colonies. A high concentration of iron in the matrix affects the color of the semiprecious mineral, which ranges from a pale greenish blue to a richer, darker variation of that hue. There are shops in Los Cerrillos where you can purchase jewelry made with Cerrillos turquoise, which is still being mined by hand on small claims.

Turquoise Jewelry on the Turquoise Trail, Madrid, New Mexico

Turquoise Trail Highlights

Turquoise Trail
turquoisetrail.org

The road makes its way through a wide-open expanse of piñon and juniper scrubland sunbaked to shades of muted brown and stone-washed green; you'll see mountains at a bit of a distance. Continue south to **Madrid**, the next town on the trail, for an interesting study in the dramatic reinvention of a community. Madrid was a boomtown back in the 1830s, not from turquoise or a

gold strike, but from coal, which was needed for smelting ore and, later, for powering trains. Area mines produced as much as a quarter of a million tons per year; at that peak, Madrid had a larger population than Albuquerque. But demand for coal fell after World War II, and the once prosperous town went into a long decline. Somewhere around the mid-1970s, an assortment of artists and counterculture types, attracted by dirt-cheap real estate, started moving in and fixing the place up. Now Madrid has become a destination again, with one-of-a-kind shops, art galleries, restaurants, and beautiful turquoise jewelry. For those old enough to remember, it's like a throwback to the hippie days of the '60s and '70s. The area is especially popular on weekends in the summer and fall.

Above and opposite: Street Scene on the Turquoise Trail, Madrid, New Mexico

SANDIA CREST

The road continues south through the rumpled foothills

of the Placer and San Pedro Mountains for 11 miles to the small town of **Golden**, which actually did have a gold mine, back in the 1870s, but was never rich enough to go boom. Today, it's a not-quite ghost town, with a nicely restored adobe church atop a hill near the highway. Eleven miles farther along, you'll come into the eastern foothills of the Sandias at **San Antonito**, where you'll find the beginning of NM 536, the road to Sandia Crest.

Tinkertown Museum, Sandia Park, New Mexico

After the first mile you'll come to the **Tinkertown Museum**, a fabulously wacky miniature Western town created by a local couple who kept adding to it ... and adding to it ... until it became a museum filled to bursting with miniatures of every description, along with a bizarre assortment of Americana, much of it animated. The wall surrounding the property, which is just off the road, was constructed using 50,000 glass bottles. The founder passed away in 2002, but the family keeps up the tradition. Fun, funky, and often hilarious, Tinkertown is a local treasure well worth the stop; open April through October.

If you're seriously afraid of heights and steep, curvy mountain roads, you might want to skip this next part. Everyone else, hang on to your hats, because you're in for a wild ride!

Keep driving on NM 536, up, up, and up even more. The road turns back on itself again and again through a series of dizzying switchbacks. The vegetation is much denser on this side of the mountains, and it changes as the road rises, transitioning from those scrubby piñons to thick stands of pines, then to aspens and spruce. You'll pass the base of the popular Sandia Peak Ski Area at

8,600 feet, but the road keeps going up, finally reaching a true alpine zone near the top of the mountain, at 10,678 feet. There's a parking area at **Sandia Crest** with a forest of TV and radio towers at the north end, an observation area along the west side, and a restaurant and gift shop, the **Sandia Crest House**, at the south end. If you plan to park in the lot for more than a few minutes, you'll need to purchase a permit (available at the Sandia Crest House).

On a clear day, the valley of the Rio Grande is spread out before you, including Albuquerque and all of its suburbs. Squint your eyes just right and you can see all the way to Mount Taylor, which is halfway to Arizona. As the sun drops low in the sky toward evening, the river will gleam like a ribbon of silver; if there are clouds in

View of Albuquerque, looking west from the Sandia Crest

Sandia Crest Highlights

Tinkertown Museum
121 Sandia Crest Road, Sandia Park,
NM 87047
(505) 281-5233
tinkertown.com

Sandia Crest House
(505) 243-0605
sandiacresthouse.com

the west, as is common in summer, there's a good chance of a jaw-dropping sunset. Wait half an hour and the lights of the city will begin winking on across the valley floor, filling the void. Spectacular! The only problem with staying past sunset? You'll have to drive back down the mountain in the dark!

Leave the peak the same way you drove up. *Mind your brakes on the downgrade, and use lower gears!* At the bottom, turn right onto NM 14, toward the town of Tijeras. From there, you can either get on I-40 and head straight back to the city, or you can stay on NM 14, pass under the Interstate, and turn west onto NM 333, also known as Route 66. Follow the signs to stay on Route 66 through Tijeras, and keep with it as it runs alongside the freeway for a few miles—first south of it, then north of it, then south of it again—finally becoming Central Avenue. Follow Central all the way through Albuquerque to I-25, and you're back where you started.

BEYOND ALBUQUERQUE

Headed north? **Scenic Side Trip 22** will take you to Santa Fe by way of the Jemez Valley, Abiquiu, and Bandelier National Monument. Headed south? Reverse the itinerary of **Scenic Side Trip 20**, and travel to Socorro by way of the Salinas Missions. West? Reversing the itinerary of **Scenic Side Trip 18** will take you to Gallup by way of three Indian pueblos and two national monuments. For more about the city of Albuquerque, including lodging, see **Scenic Side Trip 18**.

Albuquerque to Santa Fe

via the Jemez Valley, Abiquiu, Bandelier, and Los Alamos

254 miles, **6** hours **45** minutes for drive time, more for optional routes, stops, and sightseeing

Running circles around the big boom, with Georgia on my mind

THE DRIVE FROM ALBUQUERQUE TO SANTA FE IS A STRAIGHT SHOT on Interstate 25, just a little over 50 miles, and it usually takes about an hour. For most of that distance, the route crosses a high desert plateau sparsely studded with piñon and juniper scrub, gradually gaining 1,900 feet in elevation before arriving in New Mexico's capital city. If you're in a hurry, it's a great way to go, but if you have some extra time, and you'd like a little more zing in your salsa, consider this scenic alternative: a route that circles a supervolcano, visits an ancient city carved in stone, tours the birthplace of the atomic bomb, and, as a bonus, travels some of the most beautiful mountain roads in New Mexico. The full trip will add 200 miles and about 6 hours to your journey; if a shorter excursion has more appeal, there's an optional shortcut ➡➡

ALBUQUERQUE TO JEMEZ

Take Interstate 25 north to Exit 234, Tramway Road/Roy Avenue (NM 556). At the bottom of the ramp, turn left (west) and follow Roy Avenue about 1.5 miles to Fourth Street, NM 313. Turn right, and drive north for about 8 miles through an increasingly rural area.

The road runs very near the Rio Grande here, alongside a stretch of irrigated fields separated by rows of trees: a cool, green landscape, especially west of the highway. Here the road is called Camino Real, after the "Royal Road" of the early Spanish colonists, who followed this same riverside route when traveling from Mexico to their colonial capital in Santa Fe. You'll pass through Sandia Pueblo, then the small town of **Bernalillo**, which bills itself as "the City of Coronado" after the Spanish conquistador, Francisco Vásquez de Coronado, who led the first European expedition into this area in 1540.

When you reach US 550, turn left, and drive about a mile west, over the Rio Grande, to Kuaua Road; turn right, and follow the signs to

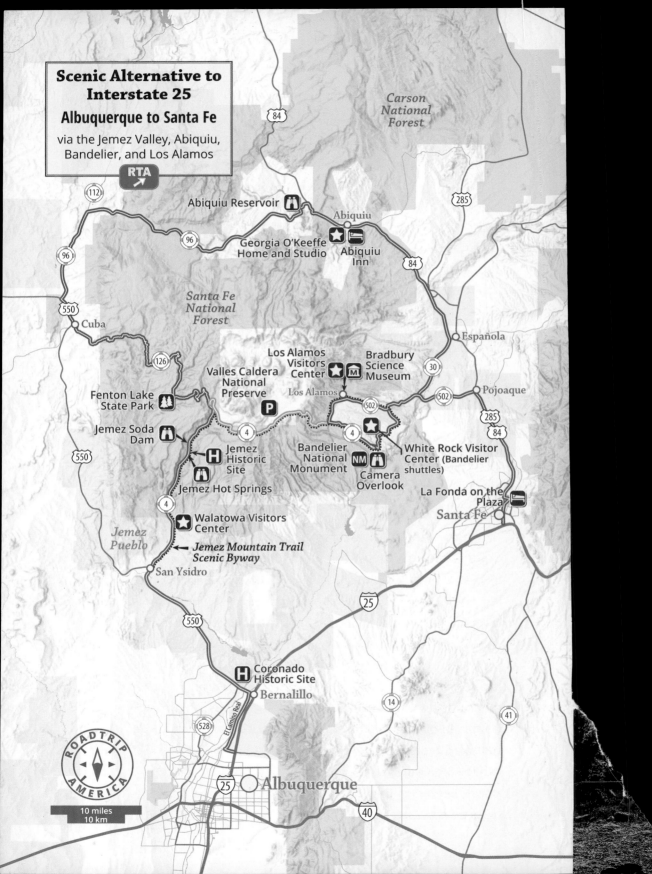

Scenic Alternative to Interstate 25

Albuquerque to Santa Fe

via the Jemez Valley, Abiquiu, Bandelier, and Los Alamos

RTA

Carson National Forest

84

285

Abiquiu Reservoir

96

Abiquiu

Georgia O'Keeffe Home and Studio

Abiquiu Inn

84

112

96

550

Cuba

Santa Fe National Forest

126

Española

Los Alamos Visitors Center

Bradbury Science Museum

30

Valles Caldera National Preserve

Los Alamos

Pojoaque

502

502

285

84

Fenton Lake State Park

4

Jemez Soda Dam

4

White Rock Visitor Center (Bandelier shuttles)

Jemez Historic Site

Bandelier National Monument

550

Jemez Hot Springs

Camera Overlook

La Fonda on the Plaza

4

Santa Fe

Walatowa Visitors Center

Jemez Pueblo

◄ *Jemez Mountain Trail Scenic Byway*

San Ysidro

550

25

Coronado Historic Site

Bernalillo

14

41

528

El Camino Real

ROADTRIP AMERICA

25   Albuquerque

40

10 miles
10 km

Fall color along the Rio Grande, Coronado Historic Site, New Mexico

Coronado Historic Site, a New Mexico state park. The location is exceptional, offering a splendid view of the river in a serene pastoral setting, with the ridge of the Sandia Mountains forming an impressive backdrop to the east.

The main attraction at this wonderful little park is the ruined **pueblo of Kuaua**, a "first contact" site. The people of this settlement were among the first to encounter Coronado's expeditionary force, a small army consisting of thousands of men and horses. The expedition camped near here through the harsh winter of 1540–1541, demanding food and clothing from the Indians. Conflict between the two groups culminated in an attack on one of the nearby pueblos, a series of one-sided battles that became known as the Tiguex War. By the time Coronado moved on, hundreds of Indians had been slaughtered, many of them burned alive. In the wake of those atrocities, the Indians abandoned their villages in the central Rio Grande Valley, some moving south, others north, into the nearby mountains. By the late 1500s, Kuaua and the other riverside pueblos stood empty, beginning their slow decline into the crumbling ruins that you see today.

In its prime, Kuaua was home to several thousand Tiwa Indians living in hundreds of two-story dwellings clustered around three rectangular plazas. Portions of the old pueblo have been excavated, and in one of the kivas, a ceremonial structure in the south plaza, archeologists found a glorious surprise: painted murals on the interior walls, including large images representing Kachinas, costumed dancers, and sacred animals, including a jackrabbit and an eagle. Such paintings are extremely rare, and they are seldom found in good condition, but the Kuaua murals were virtually intact; they are ranked among the finest examples of precontact Native American art ever found in North America. The originals were painstakingly removed from the walls of the ruined kiva, layer by delicate layer, then preserved in airtight frames; some are on display in the small museum here. The kiva itself was reconstructed, and the murals were reproduced on the interior walls; a tour of the **painted kiva** is included with entry to the museum.

Leaving Coronado Historic Site, head back to US 550, and turn right. Continue for about 22 miles, then turn right on NM 4, toward Jemez Pueblo. This state highway, also called the **Jemez Mountain Trail Scenic Byway,** travels up into the Jemez Mountains, following the Jemez River, a major tributary of the Rio Grande, as it descends through the red rocks of San Diego Canyon. About 7.5 miles from the start of this wonderfully curvy road you'll reach the **Walatowa Visitors Center**, which offers exhibits and information about Jemez Pueblo, which has been home to the Jemez Indians since the late 1600s.

Ten miles beyond the visitors center you'll reach Jemez Springs, where there are several natural thermal pools, including **Jemez Hot Springs**, known as the "giggling springs," a lovely spot to soak away your worries

Opposite: NM 4, Jemez Valley, New Mexico

and woes. Just past the springs is **Jemez Historic Site**, another New Mexico state park. At this one, you can see the ruins of an early 17th-century Spanish mission, San José de los Jemez, alongside the ruins of the pueblo that it was built to serve; both were abandoned in 1680, during the chaos of the Pueblo Revolt *(see sidebar, page 336)*. A mile or so beyond the state park, pull over on the right side of the road and check out the **Jemez Soda Dam**, a large travertine formation in the Jemez River. Seven miles beyond the soda dam, you'll reach the intersection with NM 126.

Here you have a decision to make. You can either continue along the route as presented—including 110 miles of a beautiful road that takes you to the home of Georgia O'Keeffe—or you can take a shortcut, which saves you about 3 hours and takes you through the Jemez Mountains past the remains of a supervolcano (see sidebar).

Fall color in the Jemez Valley, New Mexico

Valles Caldera National Preserve

A Shortcut via Valles Caldera

To take the shortcut, continue straight on NM 4. You'll soon be looping south, then heading east through the mountains. This section of the Jemez Mountain Trail Scenic Byway passes by **Valles Caldera**, the ancient crater of the Jemez "supervolcano," which blew up 1.2 million years ago in one of the most powerful volcanic eruptions in the history of the planet.

A supervolcano is created when a massive pool of molten rock from deep inside the earth rises toward the surface under tremendous pressure, but finds no outlet. Caught between the rock and a very hot place, the magma literally explodes through the earth's crust in an eruption a thousand times more powerful than any in modern history. The quantity of material ejected during one of these cataclysmic super-eruptions is measured in cubic miles. There's no colossal cone-shaped mountain left behind to mark the passing of one of these giants; instead, there's a colossal crater.

All that's left of the Jemez crater, known as Valles Caldera, is a circular depression 13.7 miles across, comprising 89,000 acres. The once fiery landscape has weathered over the eons into a huge alpine meadow dotted with fumaroles and extinct volcanic domes that look like tree-covered hills. The meadows, steams, and surrounding forest are teeming with wildlife, including large herds of elk.

Valles Caldera National Preserve offers hiking and horseback trails, hunting, fishing, and educational programs, as well as a limited number of backcountry vehicle permits in summer.

Leaving the preserve, NM 4 will take you all the way to **Bandelier National Monument** (see below) and then, after 16 miles, to an intersection with NM 502; from that intersection, **Los Alamos** (see below) is 5 miles west, and US 285, the road to Santa Fe, is 16 miles east. **Note:** *This alternate route may be closed in winter.*

Valles Caldera National Preserve
Mile marker 39.2, NM 4, Jemez Springs, NM 87025
(575) 829-4100
nps.gov/vall

JEMEZ TO ABIQUIU

If you're not taking the shortcut, bear left at the intersection onto NM 126 and tighten your seat belt. This next stretch of road is a twisting, turning snake of a highway that takes you up, down, and around the rugged western flanks of the Jemez Mountains. After about 10 miles you'll come to **Fenton Lake State Park**, a popular spot for camping and fishing at a cool 7,900 feet. About 30 miles beyond the lake, you'll reach the small town of **Cuba**, where you'll rejoin US 550. Follow US 550 north for just under 5 miles to NM 96; turn right, toward La Jara, and follow that beautiful state highway through the foothills of the Jemez Mountains.

NM 96, east of Gallina, New Mexico

Traveling north on NM 96, you'll cross through a stunning landscape shaped by the region's violent geological past. The highway gains elevation as it crowds in closer to the mountains; stunted piñons give way to stands of majestic Ponderosa pines, and you'll feel a chill in the air, even in summer. The road runs north-northwest for 13 miles through the tiny farming communities of **La Jara** and **Regina** before curving east and climbing higher. Continue driving through **Gallina**, into increasingly dramatic countryside.

Pull over every now and again, to take in

the gorgeous views in every direction. You'll pass through red rock hills near **Coyote**, then about 12 miles farther on you'll see **Abiquiu Reservoir** on your left, a magnificent sky-blue lake formed by an impoundment of the Chama River; the lake provides all the usual recreational opportunities. An overlook beside the highway offers a fantastic view, with the red rocks of the surrounding hills beautifully reflected in the surface of the water. Just beyond the reservoir, the highway crosses the Chama River as it continues on its way south below Abiquiu Dam. A couple of miles past the lake, NM 96 ends at an intersection with US 84. Turn right here, and drive 7 miles south, following the Chama to the quaint little town of **Abiquiu**.

Georgia O'Keeffe, the groundbreaking artist who embodied the feminine side of American modernist painting through most of the 20th century, lived and worked in this village for more than 40 years. Her studio

Abiquiu Reservoir, New Mexico

Rio Chama, near Abiquiu, New Mexico

overlooked the same Chama River Valley you have just come through; its earth-toned landscape of ever-changing light and shadow inspired much of the artist's work in her later years. Tours of the **Georgia O'Keeffe Home and Studio** are available seasonally, from March to November; reservations strongly suggested. Tours leave from the Abiquiu Inn, a nice place to stay if you'd like to stop here. *(For more on Georgia O'Keeffe and Abiquiu, see* **Scenic Side Trip 25***)*.

ABIQUIU TO SANTA FE

Leaving Abiquiu, drive south on US 84, following the shallow valley of the Chama River. After about 15 miles, US 84 merges with US 285; five miles farther on, the Rio Grande sweeps in from the northeast, following a canyon of its own, and absorbs the Chama.

Jemez to Abiquiu Highlights

Fenton Lake State Park
455 Fenton Lake Road, Jemez Springs, NM 87025
(575) 829-3630

Georgia O'Keeffe Home and Studio
12 Palvadera Road, Abiquiu, NM 87510
(505) 685-4539
okeeffemuseum.org/tickets-and-tours

Abiquiu Inn
21120 US 84, Abiquiu, NM 87510
(505) 685-4378
abiquiuinn.com

Keep going into **Española**, and after about 3 miles you'll reach the intersection with NM 30, the Los Alamos Highway. Take that road south; you'll be following the Rio Grande, a ribbon of green off to your left. After 9 miles, you'll reach the intersection with NM 502. Bear right, toward Los Alamos, and after about 3 miles bear right again, then follow the curve around to your left, onto NM 4, toward White Rock, to begin a clockwise loop that will take you to Bandelier National Monument and then on to Los Alamos.

Stay on NM 4 until you reach White Rock, a modern town built to house employees of the government labs at Los Alamos. On your right, in the middle of the town, you'll find the **White Rock Visitors Center**. You must stop here if you want to visit Bandelier during peak season, from mid-May until mid-October. During those months, the Park Service offers free shuttles between the visitors center and the monument, leaving every 30 minutes. *Between 9 a.m. and 3 p.m. you must take the shuttle*; the rest of the day, and the rest of the year, you can drive your own vehicle down to the monument.

From White Rock, the road drops though a series of switchbacks for 9 miles to the entrance road for **Bandelier National Monument**, which sits at the bottom of Frijoles Canyon. The entrance road itself is a beautiful drive, with several scenic overlooks. Down you go, for about 3 miles, into the ravine; at the bottom, Frijoles Creek is lined with tall cottonwoods

Frijoles Canyon, Bandelier National Monument, New Mexico

interspersed with pines—a cool oasis in a mostly arid countryside. Ancestral Puebloan people settled here around AD 1100 and began farming and building. The volcanic "tuff" that predominates in the cliffs here proved to be a fabulous building material, easily carved into blocks and easy to tunnel into. Over almost 500 years in this idyllic spot, thousands of structures were built here, ranging from homes for one or two families to massive buildings with as many as 600 rooms.

If you have as much as an hour to spend here, watch the film in the visitors center, and then walk Main Loop Trail, an easy 1.2-mile hike that takes you past two sets of wonderful cliff dwellings and the ruins of **Tyuonyi**, one of the larger structures. What you see today is the circular foundation of a building that was originally two stories tall, with nearly 400 rooms, most of them granaries. If you have more time to spend, check out the **Alcove House**. It's not for everyone: you have to climb 140 feet straight up, using a series of ladders, to reach the picturesque ruin, which is built in a shallow cave. A

Cliff ruins, Bandelier National Monument, NM

longer trail leads to a pair of good-sized waterfalls. In all, there are 70 miles of trails in this national monument, three quarters of which is designated wilderness.

Foundations and fall color, Bandelier National Monument

Leaving Bandelier, head back up to NM 4, and turn left (west). Drive about 6 miles to the intersection with NM 501, and bear right, to Los Alamos, the site of the

Abiquiu to Santa Fe Highlights

White Rock Visitors Center (Bandelier shuttles)
115 NM 4, White Rock, NM 87544
(505) 672-3183

Bandelier National Monument
15 Entrance Road, Los Alamos, NM 87544
(505) 672-3861
nps.gov/band

Los Alamos Visitors Center
109 Central Park Square, Los Alamos, NM 87544
(505) 662-8105
visitlosalamos.org

Bradbury Science Museum
1350 Central Ave., Los Alamos, NM 87544
(505) 667-4444
lanl.gov/museum

La Fonda on the Plaza
100 E. San Francisco St., Santa Fe, NM 87501
(505) 982-5511
lafondasantafe.com

secret government lab where the first atomic bomb was developed, during World War II, under the codename Manhattan Project. It's still the site of a secure facility involved with nuclear research, but the town itself is no longer off-limits to the public. There are checkpoints on the roads leading in, but nothing heavy-handed; it's the sort of security we've grown accustomed to seeing at places like dams, power plants, and airports. The **Los Alamos Visitors Center** is on the square in the middle of town, and there's a great museum right down the block: the **Bradbury Science Museum**, which serves as the public face of Los Alamos National Laboratory. The museum houses artifacts related to the Manhattan Project and other world-altering research that has gone on here.

Leaving Los Alamos, make your way south through town to Trinity Drive, NM 502, and head east. Drive a bit more than 17 miles to get back on US 285, which will take you south, about 20 miles, to Santa Fe. This stretch of highway is casino row; there are several resort casinos on tribal land directly adjacent to the highway, with hotels and restaurants and all the amenities. If that's not of interest, keep driving: you'll be in Santa Fe in a matter of minutes; US 285 runs right into Interstate 25, and the end of this route. A good place to stay in Santa Fe is **La Fonda on the Plaza**, an elegant hotel right on the central plaza of this historic city.

BEYOND SANTA FE

From Santa Fe, **Scenic Side Trip 23** leads you up to Taos on the River Road, and **Scenic Side Trip 24** brings you back again, by way of the Enchanted Circle and the High Road. **Scenic Side Trip 25** takes you to Las Vegas (New Mexico, not Nevada) through the magnificent Sangre de Cristo Mountains.

Santa Fe/Taos Loop, Part A:

The Low Road to Taos

96 miles, **3** hours for drive time, more for optional routes, stops, and sightseeing

You take the High Road, and I'll take the Low Road, and I'll be in Taos afore ye ...

IF YOU'VE EVER WONDERED WHY NEW MEXICO IS CALLED THE Land of Enchantment, this two-part odyssey through the Sangre de Cristo Mountains will give you a pretty good idea. The route is structured differently from the others in this book. It is a loop from Santa Fe to Taos and back again—one of the most popular excursions in all of New Mexico—but because there's so much to see, the route spans two full chapters. This section of the loop (Part A) leads you north from Santa Fe on the **Low Road**, also known as the River Road, and then pauses in Taos. The second section of the loop (Part B, described in **Scenic Side Trip 24**), takes you back to Santa Fe on the **High Road**, after first making a circuit of Wheeler Peak, New Mexico's tallest mountain, on a beautiful series of roads known as the **Enchanted Circle**.   ➡➡

You can easily combine the Low Road and the High Road into a single day's drive, with or without the Enchanted Circle, but if you have more time, you should take it. Stay the night in Taos and spread this loop across two days. Enchantment is a rare and elusive perception, a little different for each of us.

If you hurry through this adventure, you'll never find it, but if you slow things down, it just might find you.

SANTA FE TO ESPAÑOLA

From Interstate 25, or from anywhere in Santa Fe, find St. Francis Drive (Exit 282A/B, US 285), and head north. St. Francis is the only major road that passes all the way through the city,

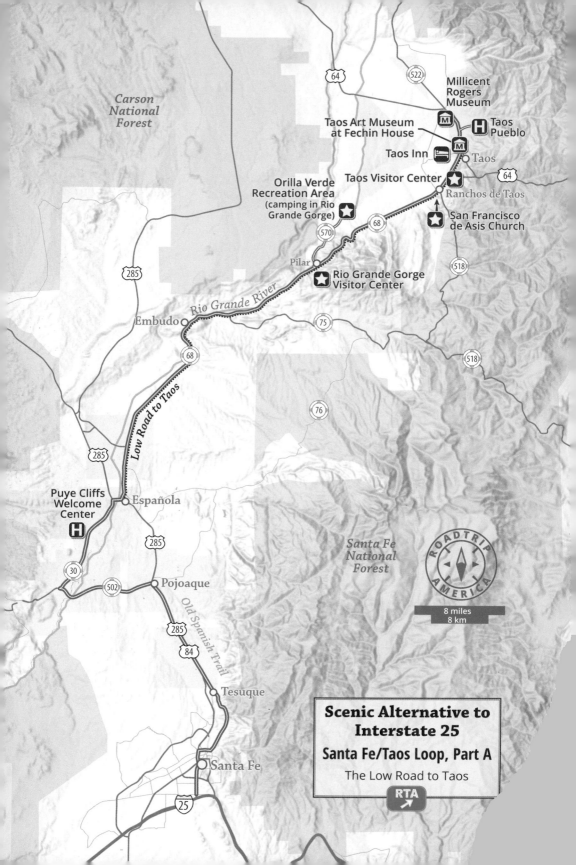

Carson
National
Forest

⑥④ ⑤②②

Millicent
Rogers
Museum

Taos Art Museum
at Fechin House

Ⓜ Ⓗ Taos
Pueblo

Taos Inn 🛏 Ⓜ

Taos Visitor Center Taos

Orilla Verde
Recreation Area
(camping in Rio
Grande Gorge) ★ ⑥⑧ Ranchos de Taos US ⑥④

★ San Francisco
de Asis Church

⑤⑦⓪

Pilar ⑤①⑧

★ Rio Grande Gorge
Visitor Center

Rio Grande River

Embudo ⑦⑤

US ②⑧⑤ ⑤①⑧

⑥⑧

⑦⑥

Low Road to Taos

US ②⑧⑤

Puye Cliffs
Welcome
Center

Española

Ⓗ

US ②⑧⑤

Santa Fe
National
Forest

ROADTRIP
AMERICA

③⓪

8 miles
8 km

⑤⓪② Pojoaque

US ②⑧⑤

Old Spanish Trail

⑧④

Tesuque

Santa Fe

I ②⑤

**Scenic Alternative to
Interstate 25**

Santa Fe/Taos Loop, Part A

The Low Road to Taos

RTA ↗

running half a mile or so west of the historic plaza and the old city center.

Santa Fe was founded in 1607, which makes it one of the oldest colonial towns in all of North America. It's pleasing to the eye, with plenty of Spanish Pueblo Revival architecture, especially in the historic areas: flat roofs, adobe walls, rounded corners, parapets, and projecting wooden roof beams called *vigas*. Upper floors are stepped, with blocky rooflines reminiscent of traditional Native American structures still in use in places like Taos Pueblo. Everything, everywhere, is painted in earth tones, and the uniformity is no accident: the city passed an ordinance in the 1950s making "adobe style" architecture a legal requirement for all new construction, including renovations, in most parts of town. Newer buildings aren't really adobe; they're just stuccoed to look that way (local folks call it "faux-dobey"). The goal was to give the city a unique ambience that would appeal to tourists, and it worked. Tourism became, and remains, one of Santa Fe's most important industries.

Santa Fe Suburbs; Historic Santa Fe neighborhood

Sculpture, Santa Fe, New Mexico

The city sits at 7,200 feet, in a shallow valley at the foot of the Sangre de Cristos ("Blood of Christ") mountains, the southernmost subrange of the Rockies and New Mexico's loftiest peaks. Some say the name comes from the reddish glow that's reflected by the range at sunrise and sunset; others that these were the dying words of a Spanish priest killed by Indians. Both explanations are plausible, and the ambiguity is pure New Mexico.

Leaving Santa Fe, take US 285 to Paseo de Peralta. Turn right (east), and drive to Bishop's Lodge Road, NM 590, which runs roughly parallel to the main highway and is a good bit more scenic. Follow the winding route north through the hills on the eastern edge of the city; just beyond the small town of Tesuque, NM 590 will merge back into US 285. The highway follows the course of a 19th-century pack train route called the **Old Spanish Trail**, descending a very gradual slope toward the Rio Grande, which lies a dozen miles to the west and 1,500 feet below. Most of the territory beyond the city limits belongs to one or another of the eight Northern Pueblos of New Mexico. Between Santa Fe and Española you'll pass through five of them: Tesuque, Nambe, Pojoaque, San Ildefonso, and Santa Clara. Each features a fancy resort-style casino, which makes this stretch of US 285 look a bit like the Las Vegas Strip; it's quite a bit more spread out, but there are plenty of bright lights.

When you reach Pojoaque, turn left at the intersection with NM 502, which follows the course of the Pojoaque River toward San Ildefonso Pueblo. The road crosses the Rio Grande at Los Alamos Canyon; nothing dramatic, just a pretty stretch of road. Beyond the river you'll come to a

fork, where you'll bear right onto NM
30 toward Española. After about 5
miles, watch for the **Puye Cliffs Welcome Center** on your left. The **Puye
Cliff Dwellings**, a National Historic
Landmark, are located just off the
road here. The site, which stretches
out for about a mile along a dun-colored mesa, features
two tiers of cliff dwellings that date to around AD 1400,
some built of masonry, others carved into the volcanic
tuff, like caves. There are more ruins at the base of the
mesa, and up top, a reconstructed community house.

From 900 to about 1580, a flourishing community
of farmers, artisans, and traders lived here—as many
as 1,500 people. Pressured by drought, they abandoned
the pueblo and cliff dwellings shortly before the first
Spanish colonists arrived in this area, moving a few
miles downriver to a place with a more dependable
water supply. There they built a new village, Santa Clara

*Murals, Española,
New Mexico*

**Santa Fe to
Española
Highlights**

Old Spanish Trail
nps.gov/olsp

**Puye Cliffs
Welcome Center**
300 NM 30,
Española, NM 87532
(505) 901-0681
puyecliffs.com

Pueblo, where their descendants have continued to live for more than 400 years. The tour guides at Puye are all from Santa Clara; these ruins were the homes of their own ancestors, and the history they relate is the history of their own people. That's a unique perspective, and it adds an extra dimension to the tours. Tickets are available at the Welcome Center; allow at least an hour to see the highlights.

ESPAÑOLA TO RANCHOS DE TAOS

Leaving Puye, drive north on NM 30 into Española. At Santa Clara Bridge Road, turn right, and drive across the river to Riverside Drive, NM 68. Bear left, and follow that highway north and east, running roughly parallel to the river, which is clad in a wide ribbon of green trees, a mile or so west of the road. After about 15 miles you'll pass through the small town of **Velarde**, and at that point the Rio Grande sweeps in right alongside the road. Here, it's a medium-sized river flowing at a leisurely pace, and the drive along this stretch is lovely; in the fall,

Rio Grande in the fall, off NM 68, the Low Road to Taos

the cottonwoods along the river go out with a bang, an explosion of yellow and gold that fills the whole valley with vibrant color. A mile or so beyond Velarde you'll pass through **Embudo**, which means "funnel" in Spanish, named for a point where the river is "funneled" between two conical knolls. As you travel upstream, the valley sharpens, with the river and the road running along the bottom of a narrow basin walled in by rumpled hills. Ten miles beyond Embudo you'll reach **Pilar**, where the Bureau of Land Management has established its **Rio Grande Gorge Visitor Center**.

The **Rio Grande Gorge**, which lies just ahead, was formed 29 million years ago when two tectonic plates split asunder, leaving a jagged crack in the earth as much as 800 feet deep, running from southern Colorado to a spot just north of Pilar. For a distance of almost 50 miles the Rio Grande is channeled through that chasm—a wild, fast-flowing river squeezed between sheer cliffs, with Class III and Class IV white-water rapids.

Rio Grande near Embudo (above); Rio Grande near Pilar (below)

During the spring runoff, the rapids in the Upper Gorge can swell into Class V monsters, standing waves of boiling froth that challenge even the most unflappable adrenaline junkies. Some of the companies that run rafting trips through the Lower Gorge use the parking lot of the visitors center as a staging area.

Upstream from Pilar, NM 68 veers away to the east, but another road,

NM 570, takes you north, staying close to the river as it flows down out of the gorge. The **Orilla Verde Recreation Area**, the southernmost section of **Rio Grande del Norte National Monument**, is just 3 miles up that road, and there are several well-maintained campgrounds where you can camp, or have a picnic, and watch the rafters float by. This is a great area for wildlife viewing, everything from bighorn sheep and mule deer to eagles, hawks, and migrating waterfowl. It's worth driving a few miles up NM 570, even if you don't plan to camp or picnic by the riverside. *(Another access point to this national monument is described in* **Scenic Side Trip 24**.*)*

Return to NM 68 and turn left. Beyond Pilar, the Low Road starts to rise up and away from the river, back into the foothills of the Sangre de Cristos. Like Santa Fe, Taos is nestled in a high valley along the western flanks of that majestic range of mountains, at an altitude of around 7,000 feet. Pilar is 1,000 feet lower, and the climb happens all at once, over the course of a single mile. You power your way up a long grade, round a curve at the top, and *whammo!* The Gorge of the Rio Grande smacks you right between the eyes, a jagged gash in the earth that looks like a wide lightning bolt and runs all the way to the horizon. The road makes a big U and then comes back around; the second viewpoint, slightly higher up, is even better than the first.

The rest of the ride to Taos crosses a high plain edged by higher mountains. The first cluster of civilization is **Ranchos de Taos**, a separate town, founded in the early 1700s by Spanish settlers. A favorite stop here is **San Francisco de Asis Church**, built in 1770, with adobe walls that are 4 feet thick. Pull into the lot just off NM 68 and walk around to the front of the building. Bring your camera! Here's your chance to take your own picture of one of the most photographed churches in the entire Southwest, a favorite subject of famed photographer Ansel Adams.

IN AND AROUND TAOS

The Taos area has been occupied for well over a thousand years. The Spanish, who first passed through here as early as 1540, found a thriving community in Taos Pueblo. By 1617, they'd built a small settlement and a church, the first step toward their mission to convert the Native Americans, but in Taos, the Native Americans wanted nothing to do with any of that. They asked the Spanish mission priest to gather his people and leave. The padre surrounded himself with guards and refused. Warriors from Taos killed the guards, and then killed the priest; that pretty well set the tone for relations between Taos Pueblo and New Spain. Bad blood simmered for almost half a century, until it finally boiled over in a mass uprising known as the Pueblo Revolt *(see sidebar)*.

Taos itself is just up the road from Ranchos de Taos. As you drive into town, look for the historic central plaza and park near it, if you can. Be prepared to circle the block, perhaps more than once; Taos is an extremely popular tourist destination and it can be crowded, especially on summer weekends.

At one time, Taos was a frontier town with a bawdy reputation, a place where trappers and mountain men came to cash in their pelts, buy some supplies, and spend whatever was left on "Taos Lightning" and dance hall girls. Times have changed. Today Taos is an upscale haven for artists and writers and avant-garde

Española to Ranchos De Taos Highlights

Rio Grande Gorge Visitor Center
NM 68, Peñasco, NM 87553
(575) 751-4899
blm.gov/visit/orilla-verde-recreation-area

Orilla Verde Recreation Area (camping in Rio Grande Gorge)
NM 570, Taos, NM 87571
(575) 758-8851

San Francisco de Asis Church
60 St. Francis Plaza, Ranchos de Taos, NM 87557
(575) 758-2754
san-francisco-de-asis.org

Sculpture, Taos, New Mexico

The Pueblo Revolt

By 1680, Spanish colonists had spread throughout the pueblo region, from the Hopi mesas in northern Arizona to north-central New Mexico. The Spaniards were spread thin; their only town of any size was Santa Fe, so they had no large force of men-at-arms, and that proved their undoing. From the beginning, their treatment of the Pueblo Indians was reprehensible. Innocent men, women, and children were slaughtered, maimed, and burned alive in places like Acoma and the central Rio Grande Valley; entire populations had been enslaved under the *encomienda* system, which gave Spanish colonists the right to conscript the labor of natives living on the huge blocks of land that Spain had appropriated. The Pueblo Indians were farmers—historically, a peaceful people—but the Spanish pushed them beyond their limit.

In the late 1670s, the Indians of Taos Pueblo, under the leadership of a Tewa medicine man named Popé, devised a grand plan to rid their territory of the unwelcome intruders. Sending couriers back and forth among widely separated villages, Popé and his coconspirators mustered the support of 46 other pueblos. On August 10, 1680, all but a handful of the tribes in New Mexico rose up in unison against the Spanish settlements. This coordinated rebellion was a decisive blow; the Spanish and their allies were driven all the way back to El Paso.

It was a glorious victory for the indigenous peoples, but alas, it didn't last. The pueblos had always been independent entities, and the coalition forged by Popé soon crumbled. In 1692, the Spanish returned and reclaimed their lost territory; the Indians, no longer unified, gave it up without a fight, but their struggle wasn't all for nothing. Before the Pueblo Revolt, Spanish authorities had gone to great lengths to eradicate the native culture, especially the Pueblo religion, which they saw as a threat to their mission. After the revolt, the Church loosened its grip. As a direct result, many aspects of traditional Pueblo culture have survived, despite the passage of centuries and the pervasive corrupting influence of modern society.

types—not to mention the throngs of tourists, most of them up from Santa Fe for the day. The picturesque storefronts are occupied by galleries, boutiques, and souvenir shops. There are several excellent museums, including the **Millicent Rogers Museum**, located 4 miles north of town, and the **Taos Art Museum**, near the plaza. A nice place to stay is the historic **Taos Inn**, right on US 64. Taos is a great town for wandering, with a lot of public art, beautiful views of the surrounding mountains, and a palpable sense of history, including relatively modern history, when this enchanting town, surrounded by beautiful mountains streaked with magical light, inspired the likes of writer D. H. Lawrence, painter Georgia O'Keeffe, and photographer Ansel Adams.

Opposite: Taos Pueblo

Taos Pueblo, the original, is just a mile or two up the road. As at most American Indian pueblos, nonresidents are not permitted to wander around unaccompanied *(see sidebar, Hopi Etiquette, page 229)*, so if you'd like a closer look, you'll have to join a tour. The pueblo, which is built to five stories in places, is by far the best-preserved living pueblo in the Southwest. It has been continuously occupied for hundreds of years; about 150 people live there still, despite the lack of electricity and running water. Tours are offered daily except during certain festivals and other observances. Photography is allowed

Ledoux Street and mural, Taos, New Mexico

on the tours, with some restrictions.

LEAVING TAOS

Returning to Santa Fe, you can either go back the way you came, on the Low Road along the river, or you can take the High Road, described in **Scenic Side Trip 24.** If you are headed on to Colorado, see **Scenic Side Trip 25** for a nice way to reconnect with Interstate 25.

Art gallery, Taos, New Mexico

Taos Highlights

Taos Visitor Center
1139 Paseo del Pueblo Sur, Taos, NM 87571
(575) 758-3873
taos.org/visitor-center

Taos Inn
125 Paseo del Pueblo Norte, Taos, New Mexico
87571
(844) 276-8598
taosinn.com

Millicent Rogers Museum
1504 Millicent Rogers Road, Taos, NM 87571
(575) 758-2462
millicentrogers.org

Taos Art Museum at Fechin House
227 Paseo del Pueblo Norte, Taos, NM 87571
(575) 758-2690
taosartmuseum.org

Taos Pueblo
120 Veterans Hwy., Taos, NM 87571
(575) 758-1028
taospueblo.com

Santa Fe/Taos Loop, Part B:

Enchanted Circle and the High Road

170 miles, **5** hours for drive time, more for optional routes, stops, and sightseeing

It's the Circle that's High, and the Road that's Enchanting, but it all evens out in the end

THIS IS THE ONLY ROUTE IN THIS BOOK THAT DOES NOT BEGIN AT an exit off an Interstate Highway. It's the continuation of the Santa Fe/Taos Loop that started in **Scenic Side Trip 23**, so it picks up where that one leaves off, in the middle of Taos. This side trip has two components. The first is a succession of roads known as the **Enchanted Circle**, a 360-degree circuit of Wheeler Peak, New Mexico's highest mountain, with several optional detours. The second part of the route is the **High Road to Taos Scenic Byway**, a wonderful series of roads that runs between Taos and Santa Fe, taking in some of the most delightfully picturesque countryside in the state. ➡➡

This route comes with two caveats. If you start your drive much later than noon, you'll probably want to skip the optional detours on the Enchanted Circle, to avoid running out of daylight on the High Road. If you make the drive in winter, you'll need to check road conditions on the NMDOT website (nmroads.com) before setting out, to avoid running into an unplowed highway at 9,000 feet; you might also review the list of "Seasonal Considerations" on page xviii.)

THE ENCHANTED CIRCLE

Even if you're only passing through, you should take a moment in Taos. There's a special beauty in the landscape and in the quality of light here. On the surface, the vibe is Santa Fe chic, but there's an undercurrent of Third World funk as well, left over from several earlier eras. Taos isn't one of those places that puts on Southwest style for the benefit of tourists. Taos is the original, and its multicultural roots run a thousand years deep. Walk around

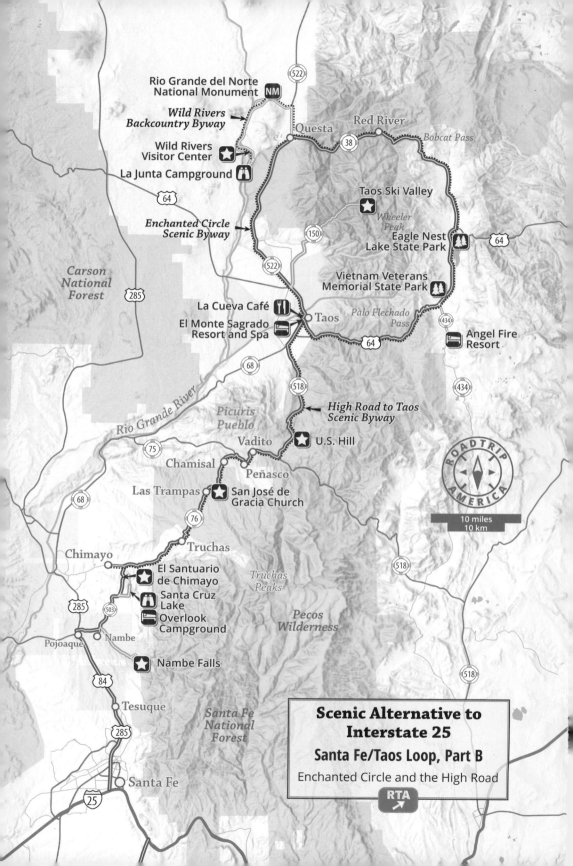

Rio Grande del Norte
National Monument **NM**

*Wild Rivers
Backcountry Byway*

Wild Rivers
Visitor Center

La Junta Campground

522

Questa

Red River

38

Bobcat Pass

Taos Ski Valley

*Wheeler
Peak*

Eagle Nest
Lake State Park

64

*Enchanted Circle
Scenic Byway*

64

150

Vietnam Veterans
Memorial State Park

522

Angel Fire
Resort

*Carson
National
Forest*

285

La Cueva Café

El Monte Sagrado
Resort and Spa

Taos

*Palo Flechado
Pass*

64

434

434

68

518

Rio Grande River

*Picuris
Pueblo*

Vadito

*High Road to Taos
Scenic Byway*

U.S. Hill

75

Chamisal

Peñasco

ROADTRIP
AMERICA

68

Las Trampas

San José de
Gracia Church

76

518

10 miles
10 km

Chimayo

285

503

Truchas

El Santuario
de Chimayo

Santa Cruz
Lake

Overlook
Campground

Nambe

*Truchas
Peaks*

*Pecos
Wilderness*

518

Pojoaque

Nambe Falls

84

Tesuque

285

*Santa Fe
National
Forest*

Scenic Alternative to
Interstate 25
Santa Fe/Taos Loop, Part B
Enchanted Circle and the High Road

RTA

Santa Fe

25

town with that in mind. Take a deep breath of the clean, mountain air. Hang out in the plaza, check out a gallery, buy a postcard, and if it's time for lunch, try the green chile at **La Cueva Café.**

NM 38, the Enchanted Circle, near Questa, New Mexico

Leaving Taos, drive north on US 64 (Paseo del Pueblo Norte). Three miles outside of town, you'll come to a three-way intersection with NM 522 and NM 150; the latter is the road up Wheeler Peak, the 13,159-foot centerpiece of the Enchanted Circle. If you'd like to take a look at **Taos Ski Valley,** one of New Mexico's most popular winter resorts, the drive up and back will take you about an hour. From the top of the road, at 9,320 feet, you can take the ski lift even higher; in summer, you can hike a popular trail that leads all the way to the summit, the highest point in the state.

Beyond the intersection with NM 150, US 64 curves away to the west, while the main route of the Enchanted

Circle continues northward, switching allegiance to a different highway. Now it follows NM 522, dipping and flowing through the creases and folds of the foothills along the thinly forested western flanks of the Sangre de Cristos. After about 20 miles, you'll reach the outskirts of **Questa**, a small farming and mining town. You're about to switch highways again, but before you do, consider another 1-hour detour, this time to see a spectacular portion of the recently created **Rio Grande del Norte National Monument** (see sidebar).

In Questa, turn off NM 522 onto NM 38, and follow that highway east out of town. After about 5 miles, you'll see that much of the mountainside north of the road has been scraped away. For 94 years, this was a molybdenum mine, Questa's largest employer until it ceased operations in 2014. Now it's an EPA Superfund site, under orders to clean up the mess that moly mining

The Coolest View of All

Rio Grande del Norte National Monument preserves a wild and scenic stretch of the Rio Grande and the impressive gorge through which it flows on its journey south from the Colorado Rockies. This is the same gorge you may have seen in **Scenic Side Trip 23**, but this time you'll be approaching it from the north, following the **Wild Rivers Backcountry Byway**. This detour, a 33-mile round-trip from Questa, provides a completely different perspective on this natural wonder, well worth the extra hour or so of driving.

At the turnoff to Questa, stay on NM 522 for another 2.5 miles until you reach NM 378/387. Turn left, and stay with the state highway as it curves right, then left. Drive west for 4 miles, until the road curves south again and swings in alongside the eastern rim of the Rio Grande Gorge. There are many pullouts along this stretch, with fabulous views of the gorge and the surrounding volcanic plain; a dozen trails, most starting from the campgrounds located along the rim, offer 22 miles of hiking along the edge of the chasm, to cold-water springs and petroglyphs, and down 800 feet to the river.

Seven miles beyond the first overlook, you'll reach the last and best one, La Junta Point, on a promontory above the confluence of the Rio Grande and the Red River, arguably the most spectacular view in New Mexico. The road loops back to the north here, first passing the **Wild Rivers Visitor Center**, a good place to stop for a break (open in summer only). Finish the loop and retrace your route back to Questa, with the gorge on your left this time.

Wild Rivers Visitor Center
1120 Cerro Road, Cerro, NM 87519
(575) 586-1150

made of the local environment. Beyond the mine, the road starts climbing, and the terrain becomes a bit more rugged as the highway snakes between steep, forested mountainsides. Eleven miles beyond Questa you'll come to **Red River**, a tourist town with a historic district dating back to the Old West. There's skiing here in the winter, and gold panning, zip-lining, mountain biking, and hiking in the warmer months.

Eagle Nest Lake, Enchanted Circle

Leaving Red River, the Circle gets serious! Stick with NM 38 as it climbs to 9,820 feet at **Bobcat Pass,** where the mountain views, up and over, are spectacular. You'll drop down the other side almost as quickly as you ascended; by the time you reach **Eagle Nest**, just 17 miles beyond Red River, the elevation is back to a mere 8,200 feet. The main attraction here is **Eagle Nest Lake**, a sky-blue,

2,400-acre reservoir backed up behind a dam on the Cimarron River. The fishing in this alpine lake is said to be excellent for trout, bass, perch, catfish, and kokanee salmon.

NM 38 ends here, at an intersection with US 64. Turn right onto the highway to continue the Enchanted Circle to the south, through the rolling grasslands of the broad Moreno Valley. After about 7 miles the road curves slightly west, and a couple of miles beyond that point you'll see a white, sail-like structure off the road on the right. This is **Vietnam Veterans Memorial State Park**, a monument and chapel dedicated to the men and women who lost their lives in the Vietnam War. Built in 1971, it was the nation's first major Vietnam War memorial, a solemn and quite beautiful place, well worth a stop and a moment of reflection for those who made that sacrifice. Less than a mile beyond the memorial, you'll come to the intersection with NM 434, which can take you to **Angel Fire**, the other Taos-area ski resort and popular all-season playground, just a few miles down that road.

Back on US 64, the highway climbs out of the Moreno Valley following tight, steep switchbacks on the way

Enchanted Circle Highlights

La Cueva Café
135 Paseo del Pueblo Sur, Taos, NM 87571
(575) 758-7001
lacuevacafe.com

Enchanted Circle
enchantedcircle.org

Eagle Nest Lake State Park
42 Marina Way, Eagle Nest, NM 87718
(575) 377-1594

Vietnam Veterans Memorial State Park
34 Country Club Road, Angel Fire, NM 87710
(575) 377-6900
vietnamveteransmemorial.org

Angel Fire Resort
10 Miller Lane, Angel Fire, NM 87710
(575) 377-4499
angelfireresort.com

El Monte Sagrado Resort and Spa
317 Kit Carson Road, Taos, NM 87571
(575) 758-3502
elmontesagrado.com

up to **Palo Flechado Pass**, at 9,109 feet. Again, you'll descend almost as quickly; from the bottom, you'll follow the highway down along the shallow drainage of the Rio Fernando de Taos, passing side canyons like Mondragon, Casias, and Cortado. Eighteen miles beyond the pass, you'll emerge from the Sangre de Cristos into Taos itself, closing the loop on your tour of the Enchanted Circle.

Angel Fire, New Mexico

Before you start the next leg of this route, check your time; it's only 85 miles to Santa Fe, but the High Road is slow by its nature, and when there's traffic (especially on summer weekends), it's slower still. If it's already late in the day, consider staying the night in Taos and finishing the route in the morning. In the mood for a splurge? Consider **El Monte Sagrado Resort and Spa**, a high-end option that checks all the boxes.

THE HIGH ROAD TO TAOS SCENIC BYWAY

Leaving Taos, drive south on Paseo del Pueblo Sur, NM 68. Follow that road all the way through town to **Ranchos de Taos** (*see* **Scenic Side Trip 23**) and the intersection with NM 518, where you'll turn left, toward Picuris Pueblo. Just past the intersection, look for the first sign marking the **High Road to Taos Scenic Byway**; remember that sign, white letters on brown, because this route makes many changes from one state highway to another. The two-lane paved road follows the shallow drainage of the Rio Grande del Rancho on a gradual upward slope for about 8 miles, then it starts climbing in earnest, twisting and turning through a series of switchbacks and curves

on a densely forested mountainside; the views, especially to the east, are amazing. The road tops out at a pass called **U.S. Hill**, about 12.5 miles from the start of NM 518; the broad, gently sloping clearing to the west of the highway near that high point is a popular sledding spot in winter.

Beyond the top of the hill, the highway flows down the mountain in long, graceful curves for 3.5 miles. At the bottom of the slope, watch for signs for the junction with NM 75; you'll bear right, then make what amounts to a sharp U-turn, putting you onto NM 75 headed west toward Peñasco. The road will take you through the valley of the Rio Pueblo to the tiny town of **Vadito** before swinging south, up and over a forested ridge, and into the larger valley of the Rio Santa Barbara. You'll pass through the small farming town of **Peñasco**; after a couple of miles, just before you enter **Picuris Pueblo**, follow the Scenic Byway signs and make a left turn onto NM 76. Follow the new road west, then south through **Chamisal**.

Most of these rural villages, like others you will pass through along this road, have been occupied by people of the same lineage for many generations; the area is isolated culturally as well as geographically. It is almost like another country, with a heritage more closely allied with Old Mexico than with New Mexico. The language of choice tends to be Spanish, and time seems to have been suspended, or at least slowed down, floating somewhere between the 1930s and the modern era. That's changing, of course, as the red-hot real estate market in Santa Fe and Taos attracts investors eager to restore and modernize these old adobe homesteads, then sell them at a hefty profit for use as artists' studios or summer homes for wealthy retirees. The sea that surrounds this vanishing island in time is the **Pecos Wilderness**, close to a

Opposite: NM 518, the High Road to Taos

Opposite: Truchas, NM 76, the High Road to Taos

quarter million acres of pristine peaks and rocky canyons lying directly northeast of New Mexico's capital city.

From Chamisal, drive south on NM 76 across a low range of forested hills to the next valley over, where you'll find the village of **Las Trampas** surrounded by a patchwork of small, irrigated fields that have been producing crops here since the town was founded, in 1751. On your left as you enter the town you'll see **San José de Gracia Church**, a fine old adobe church with walls that are 4 feet thick. The building has been reverently maintained by the people of this close-knit community for more than 250 years, making it one of the best-preserved examples of Spanish Colonial architecture in New Mexico.

As you drive south from Las Trampas, the highway rises, falls, twists, and turns along the weathered flanks of the Sangre de Cristos. After about 7 miles, you come round a curve, and there they are: the **Truchas Peaks**, North and South, both higher than 13,000 feet and clad in snow more often than not. The ridge that includes the peaks sits at the heart of the Pecos Wilderness and separates the watershed of the Rio Grande from that of the Pecos. The highway winds through the old hilltop town of **Truchas**, one of the prettiest in the region, with that gorgeous mountain backdrop to the east and an expansive view of the Rio Grande Valley to the west. It might even look familiar. Robert Redford used Truchas as the shooting location for his film *The Milagro*

San José de Gracia Church; Las Trampas, High Road to Taos

Sanctuary of Chimayo, High Road to Taos

Beanfield War, based on the novel by John Nichols, a longtime resident of Taos.

The road has been dropping in elevation, so by the time you get to Truchas, you'll be out of the woods. Keep driving south on NM 76 through the familiar piñon-and-juniper scrub that predominates below 6,000 feet; your field of view bursts wide open here, with mountains to your left and high desert spread beyond the horizon on your right. After about 6 miles you'll come to the outskirts of **Chimayo**, in the valley of the Santa Cruz River, and after another 2 miles you'll be in

the center of this wonderful little town, founded by Spanish settlers in the late 1600s on the site of an abandoned Tewa pueblo. For more than 200 years, Chimayo has been famous for its weavers, and there are artisans' shops in the town where you can buy beautiful traditional weavings, wood carvings, and metalwork.

Ofrenda, traditional altar, Santuario de Chimayo

The High Road continues south with a turn onto NM 98, which will lead you right past the area's biggest attraction: **El Santuario de Chimayo**, a Roman Catholic shrine called the "Lourdes of America" for the physical and spiritual healing power attributed to soil taken from the dirt floor of a back room in the chapel. The shrine attracts 300,000 worshippers every year, 30,000 of them during Easter Week. The sanctuary is a designated National Historic Site, and is one of the most important Catholic pilgrimage destinations in the U.S. The many *ofrendas* (offerings) and the altars decked in candles, rosaries, and photos

High Road to Taos Highlights

High Road
El Santuario de Chimayo
15 Santuario Drive, Chimayo, NM 87522
(505) 351-9961
elsantuariodechimayo.us

of loved ones is *puro* Latin America, and the beautifully landscaped grounds make for a lovely walk.

Beyond the sanctuary, drive south on NM 98 for 2.6 miles to the intersection with NM 503, Cundiyo Road. The High Road turns right, but if it's not too late in the day, consider turning left instead, toward **Santa Cruz Lake**. Follow signs to the graded dirt road that runs north for about a mile to **Overlook Campground**. There's a stunning view of the beautiful mountain lake from the overlook at the end of the road. If you're equipped for camping, there is a lovely campground here, and it is rarely crowded. Otherwise, return to NM 503 and head west.

After about 5 miles on NM 503 you'll come to **Nambe Pueblo**. Stay on NM 503, now called Nambe Road, as it winds through the picturesque village. From here you can take an excursion to **Nambe Falls**, a series of waterfalls on the Rio Nambe that are accessible via a short hike. You can visit the falls during daylight hours from Thursday to Sunday during the warmer months; there's a fee for entry.

Leaving Nambe, continue west for about 3 miles on NM 503, to the intersection with US 285 and the end of the High Road to Taos. From there, drive 20 miles south on the divided highway to Santa Fe, Interstate 25, and the end of this remarkable route. For more on Santa Fe, including lodging options, see **Scenic Side Trips 22, 23, and 25**.

BEYOND SANTA FE

Headed north? **Scenic Side Trip 25** will take you to Raton, near the Colorado border, following some of the most dramatically scenic roads in the state. Headed south? Reverse the itinerary of **Scenic Side Trip 22** for an alternative route to Albuquerque that circles the Jemez supervolcano.

Opposite: Near Nambe Pueblo, High Road to Taos

Next page: Ristra of chile peppers

Santa Fe to Raton

via Abiquiu, Brazos Summit, Taos, and Cimarron

274 miles, **6** hours **45** minutes for drive time, more for optional routes, stops, and sightseeing

There's a Low Road, and there's a High Road. We call this one the Whoa! Road

Beyond Santa Fe, Interstate 25 turns south, and then east, curving around the southern end of the Sangre de Cristos before finally heading north again, following the course of the historic Santa Fe Trail to Raton, our final destination. This is a pleasant 176-mile journey that takes about 3 hours, but if you have a full day, consider this scenic alternative, which takes a wide swing to the west. ➨

The route takes you to Abiquiu and the Ghost Ranch before climbing up and over Brazos Summit, where the views are beyond breathtaking. You'll cross the Rio Grande on one of the highest bridges in the U.S. Then, after a quick stop in Taos, you'll travel the southern section of the Enchanted Circle Scenic Byway, up and over Palo Flechado Pass to Eagle Nest. As a finale, the route descends the entire length of Cimarron Canyon to the once wicked town of Cimarron, finally ending in Raton, where the vast expanse of the Great Plains meets the great chain of the Rockies, on the border between New Mexico and Colorado.

Santa Fe to Tierra Amarilla

If you only have time to do one thing while you're in Santa Fe, drive to **Santa Fe Plaza** in the center of town. Find a place to park and take a stroll. The plaza was established in this spot when the city was founded in 1610; the **Palace of the Governors**, which fronts the plaza along the north side, is the oldest public building in the United States. The **Cathedral Basilica of Saint Francis of Assisi**, the mother church of the Archdiocese of Santa Fe, is located one block east down Palace Avenue—a beautiful building, dedicated in 1887. Walk the grounds and check out the statuary, which includes a sculpture of Kateri Tekakwitha, the first Native American woman to attain sainthood. When the bells toll in the tower of the

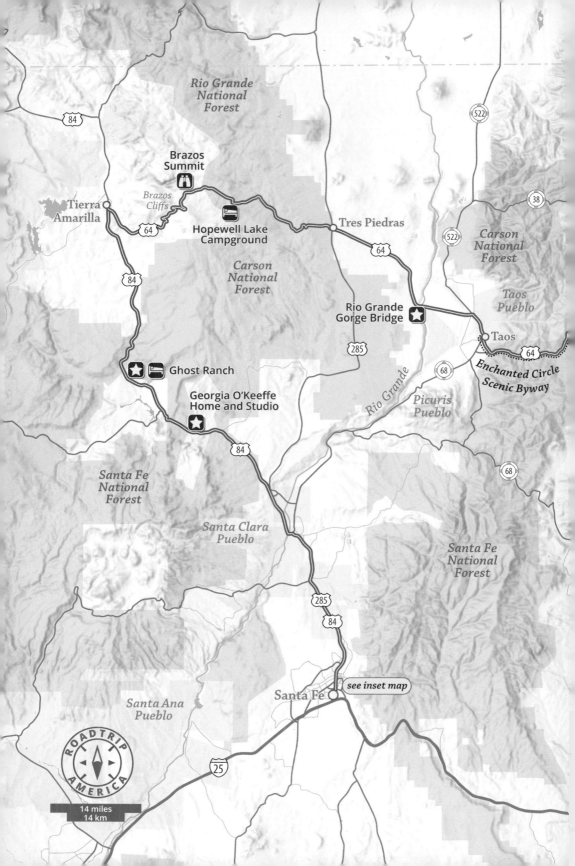

84

Rio Grande
National
Forest

Brazos
Summit

Brazos
Cliffs

Tierra
Amarilla

64

Hopewell Lake
Campground

Carson
National
Forest

Tres Piedras

522

522

38

Carson
National
Forest

Taos
Pueblo

84

Rio Grande
Gorge Bridge

64

Taos

Ghost Ranch

285

68

Enchanted Circle
Scenic Byway

64

Georgia O'Keeffe
Home and Studio

Rio Grande

Picuris
Pueblo

84

68

Santa Fe
National
Forest

Santa Clara
Pueblo

Santa Fe
National
Forest

285

84

Santa Fe

see inset map

Santa Ana
Pueblo

ROADTRIP
AMERICA

25

14 miles
14 km

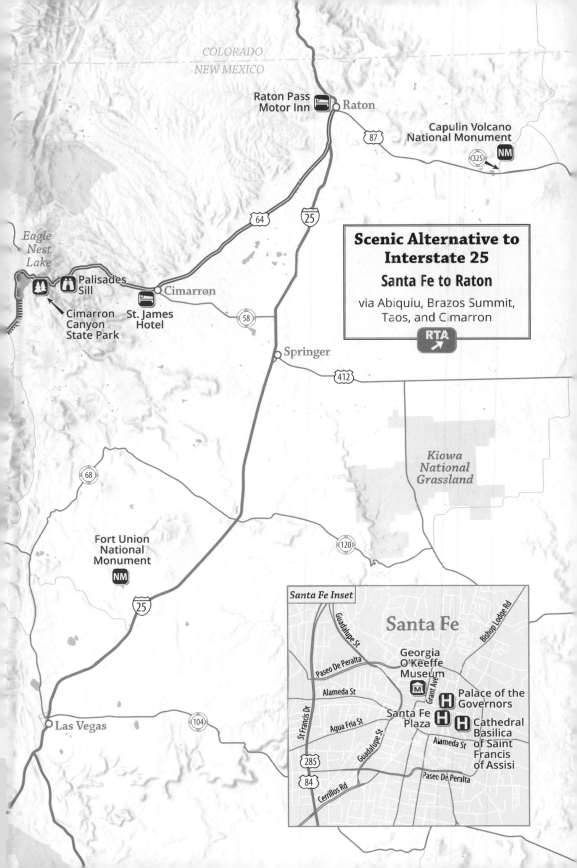

Cathedral Basilica of St. Francis of Assisi, Santa Fe, New Mexico

church, you can feel it as well as hear it. Three blocks away you'll find the **Georgia O'Keeffe Museum**. The world-renowned painter, who died in 1986 at the age of 98, is practically synonymous with New Mexico, and this small but quite elegant museum houses a beautiful collection. Not an art lover? Stop in anyway. O'Keeffe's paintings are powerful—she might just make you a convert.

Leaving Santa Fe, drive north on US 285 to **Española**; see **Scenic Side Trip 23** for a description of that stretch of road. In Española, stay on US 285 as it crosses the Rio Grande on the Santa Clara Bridge and heads off to the northwest, following the river. Eight miles beyond the bridge, US 285 veers off toward Ojo Caliente. Go straight past that intersection and switch to US 84, which follows the shallow valley of the Chama River toward **Abiquiu**, 13 miles farther along. Like the Rio Grande, which merges

Saint Thomas the Apostle Church, Abiquiu, New Mexico

with the Chama just north of Española, the river's course is marked by trees and a patchwork of small, irrigated fields edged by arid, dun-colored hills that are speckled with piñon and juniper scrub. There's plenty of life in this bone-dry landscape. You just have to add a little water.

The picturesque village of Abiquiu is quite spread out, with a population density of just one person per square mile. That's a whole lot of elbow room, which was doubtless part of the appeal to Georgia O'Keeffe, the artist, who lived here for 40 years, beginning in the mid-1940s. The play of light over the surrounding landscape was her constant inspiration. If you found her museum in Santa Fe of interest, consider a visit to the **Georgia O'Keeffe Home and Studio**, near the middle of this seemingly sleepy, scenic town. Abiquiu once had a very different reputation, as a den of sin and sorcery; in one of the more complicated episodes in Spanish-American history,

Opposite: US 84, north of Abiquiu, New Mexico

Spanish authorities held witch trials here in the 1760s. For more on Abiquiu, including information on lodging and tours of O'Keeffe's studio, see **Scenic Side Trip 22**.

Leaving Abiquiu, stay on US 84 as it crosses to the other side of the Chama on a short bridge. Northwest of the village, the road starts climbing up into the foothills of the Tusas Mountains, an extension of the San Juan Range of the Colorado Rockies. After about 10 miles, the road rounds a curve into an area of weathered red sandstone mesas and buttes, which are layered with pale tans, grays, and sun-bleached purple. Just down the road you'll see signs and a large gate—the entrance to **Ghost Ranch**, a 21,000-acre property with a history going back 200 million years. In the late Triassic period, when the climate and terrain were much different, a herd of dinosaurs got themselves stuck in a bog. The unfortunate creatures died there, and eventually became fossils.

Georgia O'Keeffe home and studio, Abiquiu, New Mexico

Fast-forward to the late 19th century, when the valley became the hideout for the Archuleta brothers, notorious

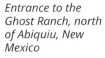

Entrance to the Ghost Ranch, north of Abiquiu, New Mexico

cattle rustlers with a reputation for robbing and murdering travelers. To keep neighbors from poking around, they spread stories about flying cows, 30-foot-long snakes, and red hairy monsters they called "earth babies." In the end, one brother killed the other in a dispute over buried gold; the remaining brother was hanged from a cottonwood tree by vigilantes. The spirits of all those violently departed, both victims and perpetrators, are said to haunt the canyon still: the ghosts of Ghost Ranch.

In 1947, a paleontologist poking around in the weathered hills discovered the fossilized skeletons of those hapless Triassic dinosaurs, and the Ghost Ranch gained fame as one of the richest sources of early dinosaur fossils ever discovered. In 1955, the ranch was bequeathed to the Presbyterian Church, which now uses it as a retreat and conference center. Tours are available, which include entry to two museums on the property: the **Florence Hawley Ellis Museum of Anthropology** and the **Ruth Hall Museum of Paleontology**, both featuring exhibits related to the area. Rustic accommodations are also available. It's a terrific place to hang out, unplug, and just relax for a while.

About 4 miles beyond Ghost Ranch on US 84, you'll come to the **Echo Amphitheater** on the west side of the highway. Here a towering, multicolored sandstone cliff has been hollowed by wind and water, forming a natural alcove with smooth, curving sides. A short trail leads to the base of the cliff, where the natural acoustics are such that the slightest sound creates a perfect echo, reverberating back from the alcove. The site has hiking trails, a picnic area, and a campground maintained by

Carson National Forest.

The highway rises and falls with the landscape, flowing across the flanks of the mountains through pine forest and hardscrabble ranchland. After about 26 miles, you'll reach the outskirts of Tierra Amarilla, "Yellow Earth," population 750, a farming, ranching, and timber town founded in 1832. There's not much to see in Tierra Amarillo, which lies east of the highway. If you need gas or a rest room, continue down US 84 a bit past the turnoff to US 64 to a small cluster of service stations; otherwise, make a sharp right onto US 64, which will lead you back south again.

TIERRA AMARILLA TO RATON

Remember that highway sign, US 64, because you'll be staying with it for the next 170 memorable miles. The first stretch of road, between Tierra Amarilla and Tres Piedras, crosses Brazos Summit at 10,507 feet, the highest point on any through highway in New Mexico, and there is little traffic. This is said to be one of the finest motorcycle routes *anywhere*, climbing to the heights and descending again in a series of wide, graceful curves that are an absolute joy to drive—on two wheels, or four.

Driving up, you'll pass through dense pine forest and huge stands of aspens that turn the mountainsides gold in early fall, one of the finest displays of autumn color in the state. After about 20 miles you'll reach the top. There's a small parking area on the left side of the road where you can pause for a look at the **Brazos Cliffs**, soaring more than 2,000 feet above the surrounding plain. The ridge you're driving along falls away steeply here, opening an expansive view to the west that seems to go on forever. That monolithic block of Precambrian quartzite rising up directly before you is part of a ridge so tall that it affects weather, diverting wind and storms

Santa Fe to Tierra Amarilla

Cathedral Basilica of Saint Francis of Assisi
131 Cathedral Place, Santa Fe, NM 87501
(505) 982-5619
cbsfa.org

Georgia O'Keeffe Museum
217 Johnson St., Santa Fe, NM 87501
(505) 946-1000
okeeffemuseum.org

Ghost Ranch
280 Private Drive 1708 (1709A US 84), Abiquiu, NM 87510
(505) 685-1000
ghostranch.org

Brazos Cliffs, from US 64 east of Tierra Amarilla

as they move across the Great Plains. At the height of the spring snow-melt, waterfalls spring from the cliffs and cascade down the mountain in braided streams.

Keep going as the highway flows back down the other side of the summit. You'll pass through forest and broad expanses of meadow that are alive with wildflowers in spring and summer. About 8 miles farther along you'll pass **Hopewell Lake**, where you'll find a basic campground, good fishing, and abundant wildlife, including beavers that chew down aspens to build their lodges. The highway rolls and flows for another 5 miles or so, climbing up and over a ridge before dropping into the valley of the Rio Tusas. You'll pass by isolated ranches and hayfields as you descend the gentle slope, then you'll climb up and over one more pine-clad ridge before you reach Tres Piedras, "Three Stones," another small timber town, frigid in winter at an altitude of 8,000 feet.

US 64 intersects US 285 here; go straight through that intersection and head toward Taos. Tres Piedras sits at the edge of the scrubby plain of piñon and creosote that borders the Rio Grande Gorge, dead ahead about 20 miles. When you get there, pull over in the lot on the right, just before the vertigo-inducing **Rio Grande Gorge Bridge**. This suspension bridge crosses the chasm 565 feet above the river. When it was built, in 1965, it was the second-highest bridge in the world; it lost that ranking some years back, but it's still an awesome structure, in a very impressive setting.

Below: Rio Grande Gorge and Bridge, US 64, west of Taos, New Mexico

Twelve miles beyond the bridge, you'll reach Taos. Stop for lunch and take a stroll around the plaza of this beautiful adobe town. Better yet, stay the night; there's a lot of history here, and plenty to see. *(For information about Taos, including lodging options and much more about the remarkable Rio Grande Gorge, see* **Scenic Side Trips 23** *and* **24***.)*

Leaving Taos, continue on US 64 as it travels east up the drainage of the Rio Fernando de Taos, then climbs up and over Palo Flechado Pass, at 9,109 feet. You'll travel through rugged mountains for about 20 miles, winding your way down to the broad, grassy plain of the high-altitude Moreno Valley. Ten miles farther along you'll reach Eagle Nest, along-side **Eagle Nest Lake**, the sparkling blue 2,400-acre reservoir created by a

dam on the Cimarron River. This section of US 64 is part of the famous scenic byway known as the **Enchanted Circle**, which is an adventure in its own right (*see* **Scenic Side Trip 24**; *the direction of travel between Taos and Eagle Nest will be reversed in that route description*).

US 64 travels east from Eagle Nest toward Cimarron. The road climbs a low ridge that offers splendid views of the lake to the south, then rounds a curve and drops down the other side into **Cimarron Canyon State Park**, which begins just below the dam. This is a popular recreation area in summer, with campgrounds, hiking trails, abundant wildlife, and excellent fly fishing. The park extends along an 8-mile stretch of Cimarron Canyon and includes the **Palisades Sill**, a formation of igneous rock that creates a spectacular cliff above the wild, fast-flowing river toward the eastern edge of the park.

Another dozen miles downriver, you'll be in the town of **Cimarron**. The name is derived from a Spanish word for "wild," referring to an animal, a place, or a free-spirited person—a maverick. There's not much of old Cimarron left to look at, but back in the day it was wild, all right. Before it became a town, it was the headquarters of one of the largest ranches in U.S. history, the 1.7 million-acre Maxwell Land Grant. The owner of that spread, one Lucien Maxwell, built an opulent mansion there that included a hotel, a casino, and a brothel, and he lived like a feudal lord. The town that grew up around Maxwell's place was a popular stop on the Santa Fe Trail, chockablock with saloons and frequented by the likes of Kit Carson, Annie Oakley, and Buffalo Bill Cody, who organized the original version of his Wild West Show in Cimarron.

Opposite: Cimarron River, US 64, Cimarron Canyon

St. James Hotel, Cimarron; "Everything is quiet in Cimarron. Nobody has been killed for three days."

The Maxwell Mansion is long gone, but the **St. James Hotel**, which was built across the street from it in 1872, is still standing—and still operating. In its heyday, the St. James was particularly popular with outlaws, including Jesse James himself, and murder and mayhem were common occurrences. At least 26 deadly shootings happened right in the hotel, and additional flooring was added to the upstairs rooms to protect guests from bullets shot through the ceiling of the bar downstairs. The newspaper in Las Vegas, New Mexico, once reported: "Everything is quiet in Cimarron. Nobody has been killed for three days."

Leaving Cimarron, follow US 64 for 34 more miles to reconnect with Interstate 25. The first exit for Raton, which marks the end of this route, is about

Tierra Amarilla to Raton Highlights

Hopewell Lake Campground
US 64, Tres Piedras, NM 87577
(435) 245-6521
recreation.gov (reservations)

Cimarron Canyon State Park
28869 US 64, Eagle Nest, NM 87718
(575) 377-6271

St. James Hotel
617 S. Collison Ave.,
Cimarron, New Mexico 87714
(575) 376-2664
exstjames.com

Raton Pass Inn
308 Canyon Drive, Raton, NM 87740
(575) 445-3641
ratonpassinn.com

Santa Fe Trail

Before there were roads of any kind in the American West, there were trails. Tracks in the dirt, mostly, leading from ports on the Mississippi River west to the new frontier. There was the Oregon Trail, the California Trail, and the Mormon Trail, but perhaps the most famous, and the most economically important, was the Santa Fe Trail.

First established as a trade route in 1821, the Santa Fe Trail ran 834 miles from Independence, Missouri, to Santa Fe, the capital of the northernmost province of the newly independent Republic of Mexico and a connecting point to the Camino Real, the "Royal Road," which led south all the way to Mexico City. Manufactured goods from the East Coast had enormous value in the remote Mexican provinces, and traders made overnight fortunes that attracted more traders. The wagonloads of goods and all those teams of horses and mules attracted Comanche raiders, who saw the wagon trains as easy pickings on wheels. Soon, the traders were organizing armed caravans of a hundred wagons at a time, traveling four abreast and hauling artillery.

When New Mexico became a U.S. territory, following the Mexican-American War, which ended in 1848, settlers with wagonloads of household goods joined the traders on the trail. The wagon trains rolled west at such a steady pace that they disrupted the migration of buffalo across the plains, possibly hastening the demise of those mighty herds. A typical crossing of the Santa Fe Trail took as long as three months. The record was held by Francis X. Aubrey, the "Skimmer of the Plains," who rode from Santa Fe to Independence in 5 days, 16 hours, using fresh horses staged along the way—an incredible feat that has never been matched for sheer endurance.

The trail became obsolete when the railroad reached Santa Fe in 1880. In 1987, it was declared a National Historic Trail; there are markers and interpretive signs at various places between Raton and Santa Fe, including Fort Union National Monument, Las Vegas, and Cimarron.

Santa Fe National Historic Trail
nps.gov/safe

3 miles farther north. The **Raton Pass Inn,** at the north end of town, is a low-key, friendly motel if you need a place to stay the night.

BEYOND RATON

If you're headed north, the Colorado border is about 7 miles farther along on I-25. Heading south, there are some wonderful back roads and things to see between Raton and Santa Fe. Take NM 72 east from Raton up across **Johnson Mesa**, then NM 325 south to **Capulin Volcano National Monument**. Other attractions include **Fort Union National Monument** and historic **Las Vegas, New Mexico**.

Acknowledgements

This book would not have been possible without the support—and the interminable patience—of Mark Sedenquist and Megan Edwards of Imbrifex Books. I'd like to thank my editor, Nancy Zerbey, for her encouragement and her insight. *Arizona and New Mexico: 25 Scenic Side Trips* was a journey we took together, and it's a far better book for her perceptive influence. Many thanks as well to book designer Sue Campbell for her consummate skill in assembling all the bits and pieces into a truly beautiful package, and to Chris Erichsen for his wonderful maps. A special thanks to Joe Day of Tsakurshovi Trading Post, for recommending Navajo Route 13 over the Lukachukai Mountains (not to mention that tasty 'Signature Soup' at the La Posada Inn in Winslow). The rotating crew of compañeros who rode along with me whilst I road-tested these particular road trips included Carl Duisberg, Alex Witzeman, and Rick Obermiller. Thanks to all, and a special thanks to my wife Jill, for patiently putting up with me through the whole long process.

Index

A

AAA membership xviii
Abiquiu Inn, Abiquiu, NM 322
Abiquiu, NM 321–322, 359–360
Abiquiu Reservoir 321
Abo ruins (mission) 292–294, 296
Abyss, The (Grand Canyon) 214
Acoma Pueblo, NM 269–271, 336
Adams, Ansel 335, 337
"adobe style" architecture 329
Aerospace Maintenance and
     Regeneration Group
     (AMARG) 110
Agua Prieta, Mexico 77, 81
Ailman House. See Silver City
     Museum
Akimel O'odham Indians 125
Alamogordo, NM 33–34
Albuquerque International Balloon
     Fiesta 305
Albuquerque, NM 273–274,
     301–305
Alcove House (Bandelier National
     Monument) 324–325
Algodones, NM 305–306
Allen, Rex 62
Alpine, AZ 54–55
AMARG (Aerospace Maintenance
     and Regeneration
     Group) 110
America the Beautiful Annual
     Pass xx, 191
Anasazi culture 238–239,
     255–256, 258–259
Anderson Scenic Overlook 43

Angel Fire Resort, Angel Fire,
     NM 344
Angel's Landing (Zion National
     Park) 193
Angel's Window (Grand
     Canyon) 196
Antelope Canyon 200, 202
Apache Gold Casino 66, 67
Apache Indians. See also Indian
     Wars
  Chiricahua Apaches 75–78
  Mescalero Apache
     Reservation 33
  San Carlos Apache
     Reservation 66
  Spanish missions and 99,
     293–294, 295, 296
Apache Lake, AZ 162
Apache Sunrise Resort, Greer,
     AZ 57
Apache Trail Historic
     Road 159–162
archaeological sites. See pueblo
     ruins
Archuleta brothers (outlaws) 362
Arcosanti 154
Arizona Biltmore Hotel, Phoenix,
     AZ 73, 74
Arizona Canyon Jeep Tours 241
Arizona Capitol Museum 72, 74
Arizona Inn, Tucson, AZ 115
Arizona (movie) 113
Arizona Snowbowl 217–218
Arizona-Sonora Desert
     Museum 113, 115
Armstrong, Lance 104

Ash Fork, AZ 187
atomic testing 36, 326
Atsinna Pueblo (ruins) 267–268
Aubrey, Francis X. 369
auto insurance xviii
Aztec Ruins National
     Monument 255–256, 259

B

Bajada Loop (Saguaro National
     Park) 114
Bandelier National
     Monument 323–325
Bandera Volcano 268
Bear Creek Motel & Cabins, Pinos
     Altos, NM 46, 47
Bebb willows 216
Bell Rock (Sedona) 139, 156
Bernalillo, NM 313
Besh-Ba-Gowah Archaeological
     Park 67–68
Best Western Territorial Inn,
     Bloomfield, NM 254
Bezos, Jeff 23
Big Lake, AZ 57
Big Room (Carlsbad
     Caverns) 26–27
Billy the Kid 31
Billy the Kid Trail 30–33
Biosphere 2 117–120
Bird Cage Theatre 85–86
bird watching
  Bitter Lake National Wildlife
     Refuge 30
  Bosque del Apache National
     Wildlife Refuge 282–285

Hassayampa River
    Preserve 132
Lake Roberts 43
Orilla Verde Recreation
    Area 334
Patagonia-Sonoita Creek
    Preserve 96, 97
Ramsey Canyon
    Preserve 92–93
Sevilleta National Wildlife
    Refuge 290
Bisbee, AZ 81, 83–84
Bisbee Mining and Historical
    Museum 84
Bisti Badlands 249, 252–254
Bisti/De-Na-Zin
    Wilderness 252–254
Bitter Lake National Wildlife
    Refuge 30
Black Mountains
    (Arizona) 176–177
Black Range (Sierra Diablo, New
    Mexico) 42–43
Blue Origin 23–24, 25
Blue Range Primitive Area 58
Blue Vista Overlook 58
Bobcat Pass (Enchanted Circle
    Scenic Byway) 343
Boca Negra Canyon (Petroglyph
    National Monument) 304
Bogart, Humphrey 219
"Boneyard, The" (Aerospace
    Maintenance and
    Regeneration Group) 110
Bonita Canyon Scenic Drive 80
Boot Hill Graveyard
    (Tombstone) 86
Bosque del Apache National
    Wildlife Refuge 282–285
botanical gardens

Arizona-Sonora Desert
    Museum 113, 115
Boyce Thompson
    Arboretum 68, 70
Desert Botanical Garden 73, 74
Living Desert State Park 28
Boyce Thompson Arboretum 68,
    70
Bradbury Science Museum 325,
    326
Brantley Lake State Park 28, 29
Brazos Cliffs 363–364
Brazos Summit 363
Bright Angel viewpoint (Grand
    Canyon) 195
Browne, Jackson 231
Buckhorn Saloon and Opera
    House 46
"Buffalo Bill" Cody 366
Buffalo Pass (Lukachukai
    Mountains) 246
Burma-Shave signs 186–187
Butterfield Stage Coach 78
Bylas, AZ 66

C

Caballo Lake State Park 42
Call of the Canyon (picnic area,
    Oak Creek Canyon) 141
Camelback Mountain 73, 74
Cameron, AZ 209, 225
Cameron Trading Post 207–210
Camp Verde, AZ 150
Canyon de Chelly National
    Monument 235–241
Canyon del Muerto (Canyon de
    Chelly) 233
Canyon Lake, AZ 160–161
Cape Royal overlook (Grand
    Canyon) 195–196
Capitan, NM 31–32

Capulin Volcano National
    Monument 369
Carlsbad Caverns National
    Park 26–28, 29
Cars (movie) 180
Carson, Kit 366
Casablanca (movie) 219
Casa Grande Ruins National
    Monument 124–125
Casas de Suenos Old Town
    Historic Inn, Albuquerque,
    NM 274
Castle Butte 230
Catalina Highway 104–106
Cathedral Basilica of Saint Francis
    of Assisi 355, 363
Catwalk National Recreation
    Trail 52, 54
caverns
    Carlsbad Caverns National
        Park 26–23
    Grand Canyon Caverns 185,
        188
    Kartchner Caverns State
        Park 89–91
cell phone coverage xvii
Chaco Culture National Historical
    Park 257–259
Chaco roads 259
Chama River Valley 321–322, 358
Chamisal, NM 347
Chapel of the Holy Cross
    (Sedona) 139, 140, 156
Chihuahuan Desert 28
children and travel xviii
chile peppers 40
Chimayo, NM 350–351
Chimney Butte 230
Chinle, AZ 241
Chino Copper Mine 48
Chiricahua Apaches 75–78, 80

Chiricahua Mountains 75–77
Chiricahua National
        Monument 77, 78–80
cholla cacti xix, 122
Cibola National Forest 299
Cimarron Canyon State
        Park 366–367, 368
Cimarron, NM 366–367
City of Rocks State Park 48
Clarkdale, AZ 137–138
Clifton, AZ 59–60
Clifton Cliff Jail 61
Clifton Townsite Historic
        District 61
climate change research 120
Cloudcroft 33
Coal Mine Canyon 225–227
Cochise 77
Coconino National Forest 55, 141
"code talkers," Navajo 251
Cody, "Buffalo Bill" 366
Cold War 100
Colorado River 183
Colorado River and Trail
        Expeditions 184
Colter, Mary Jane 231
conquistadores 292–293
Continental Divide 43, 268
Cooley, Corydon 169
copper mining
    active open pit mines 48,
        50–52, 59
    Bisbee mineworkers strike 81
    effect of copper prices 50–52,
        67, 81
    environmental destruction
        caused by 67
    Jerome, Arizona 135–137
    Superior, Arizona 69
Copper Queen Hotel, Bisbee,
        AZ 84

Cornville, AZ 138
Coronado, Francisco Vásquez
        de 55, 93, 265, 315
Coronado Historic Site 315–316,
        320
Coronado National Memorial 93,
        95
Coronado Trail Scenic Byway 55–
        56, 58–61
Corrales, NM 305
Cottage Bed and Breakfast,
        Safford, AZ 60, 62
Crescent Moon Picnic
        Area 138–139
Crook, George 168
Crystal Palace Saloon
        (Tombstone) 85, 86

D

Datil Mountains 279
Davis-Monthan Air Force
        Base 109
Day, Joe and Janice 228–229
Death Valley Days (TV series) 113
Debbie's Hide A Way, Page,
        AZ 206
Delaware North Company 215
Delgadillo, Angel 185
Delgadillo's Snow Cap
        Drive-In 186, 188
Desert Botanical Garden
        (Phoenix) 73, 74
Desert Caballeros Western
        Museum 132
desert travel xix
desert varnish 238, 303
Desert View (Grand
        Canyon) 211–212
Desert View Watchtower (Grand
        Canyon) 211

Devil's Canyon, Pinal County,
        AZ 68
"Devil's Highway" (US Route
        666) 56, 58–59
Diamond Creek Rapid (Colorado
        River) 184
Dixie Ellis' Lower Antelope Canyon
        Tours 206
Douglas, AZ 81–82
Douglas, James "Rawhide
        Jimmy" 137
Dreamy Draw (Piestewa
        Peak) 143–144
dude ranches 131–132
Duncan, AZ 63–64
Duquesne House, Patagonia,
        AZ 96, 97

E

Eagle Nest Lake State Park 343–
        344, 365
Eagle Nest, NM 343
Eagles (band) 232
Earp, Wyatt 84, 133
Echo Amphitheater 362
Echo Canyon Recreation Area 73,
        74
Eisenhower, Dwight 198
El Malpais National
        Monument 269, 271,
        275–278
El Monte Sagrado Resort and Spa,
        Taos, NM 344, 345
El Morro National
        Monument 266–267
El Rancho Hotel, Gallup,
        NM 248, 251
El Santuario de
        Chimayo 351–352
El Tovar Hotel, Grand Canyon
        Village, AZ 214, 215

Embudo, NM 333
emergency preparedness xvii
Emory Pass 43
Enchanted Circle Scenic
    Byway 339–345
encomienda labor system 336
Esplendor Resort, Rio Rico, AZ 97,
    98
Estancia Basin 294

F

Farmington, NM 254
Fenton Lake State Park 320, 322
Fish Creek Hill (road) 157,
    161–162
Flagstaff, AZ 187–188, 218–219
Flagstaff Visitors Center 188,
    219, 220
floods xviii
Florence, AZ 122–124
Florence Hawley Ellis Museum of
    Anthropology 362
flying saucers 29–30, 279, 280
"fly-out" (Bosque del Apache
    National Wildlife
    Refuge) 283
Ford, John 241–242, 244
Fort Bowie National Historic
    Site 77–78
Fort Huachuca 92
Fort Selden State Historic
    Site 37–38
Fort Union National
    Monument 369
Fort Verde State Historic
    Park 150–151, 153
fossils 37, 169, 360–361
Fountain Hills, AZ 146–147
Fountain Park 147

Fourth of July Campground
    (Cibola National
    Forest) 299
four-wheel drive xvii
Franklin Mountains State Park 23
Frey, Glenn 232

G

Gadsden Hotel, Douglas,
    AZ 81–82, 84
Gallo Campground (Chaco
    Canyon) 259
Gallup Chamber of
    Commerce 251
Gallup Cultural Center 261, 265
Gallup, NM 249–250, 261, 264
Garden of Allah 131–132
Gates Pass (Tucson
    Mountains) 115
General Hitchcock
    Highway (Catalina
    Highway) 104–106
Georgia O'Keeffe Home and
    Studio 322, 359
Georgia O'Keeffe Museum 358,
    363
Geronimo 77, 150, 168
Geronimo Trail Scenic
    Byway 42–43
Ghost Ranch 360–361, 363
Giganticus Headicus 177–179
Gila Cliff Dwellings National
    Monument 42–45, 46
Gila Hot Springs 44, 46
Gila-Pinal Scenic Road 68
Gila River Indian Reservation 125
Glen Canyon Dam 198
Glen Canyon National Recreation
    Area 198
Globe, AZ 67, 165
Golden, NM 310

Goldfield Ghost Town 160, 165
gold mining 131
Goulding's Lodge, Oljato-
    Monument Valley, UT 242,
    244
Goulding's Trading Post 244
Grand Canyon Caverns 185, 188
Grand Canyon (Diamond
    Creek) 181–184
Grand Canyon Lodge, North Rim,
    AZ 196
Grand Canyon Lodges 214–215
Grand Canyon National Park
    North Rim 194–195
    South Rim 210–215
    watching sunrise at 212
Grand Canyon Railway 187, 188
Grand Canyon Village,
    AZ 213–214
Grand Staircase–
    Escalante National
    Monument 196–197
Grandview Point (Grand
    Canyon) 213
Granite Mountain Hotshots,
    deaths of 133
Gran Quivira ruins (mission) 294,
    296
Grants, NM 260, 275
Grapes of Wrath, The
    (Steinbeck) 173
Grey, Zane 143
Guadalupe Mountains National
    Park 24
Guadalupe Peak 24–25
Gunfight at the O.K. Corral 85, 86

H

Haak'u Museum 271
Hackberry General Store 179,
    180

Hannagan Meadow 56
Hannagan Meadow Lodge,
        Alpine, AZ 55–56
Hart Prairie Preserve 216, 217
Harvey, Fred 231
Hassayampa Inn, Prescott, AZ 134
Hassayampa River Preserve 132
Hatch Chile Festival 40
Hatch, NM 40
Hawikku (pueblo) 265
Heard, Dwight 72
Heard Museum 72, 74
Hermit Road (Grand
        Canyon) 214
High Road to Taos Scenic
        Byway 339, 345
Highway 60 165–168
highway system 165, 173
Historic Route 66. *See* Route 66
        (highway)
hogans (Navajo dwelling) 252
Hohokam 74, 125, 151
Holbrook, AZ 169
Holden, William 113
Hole in the Rock (Papago
        Park) 73
Holiday Inn Canyon de Chelly,
        Chinle, AZ 241
Holliday, Doc 84, 133
hoodoos 78–80, 226, 307
Holy Trinity Monastery 87–88
Hopewell Lake 364
Hopewell Lake Campground 368
Hopi Cultural Center 228, 230
Hopi guides 227
Hopi Point (Grand Canyon) 214
Hopi Reservation 221, 227–230
Horse Mesa Dam 162
Horseshoe Bend 200, 204–205
hot air balloons 305

Hotel El Capitan, Van Horn,
        TX 23, 25
Hotel Encanto de Las Cruces, Las
        Cruces, NM 35, 36
Hotel Monte Vista, Flagstaff,
        AZ 219, 220
Hotel San Carlos, Phoenix, AZ 74
hotels and lodging
    Abiquiu, NM 322
    Albuquerque, NM 274
    Alpine, AZ 55–56
    Angel Fire, NM 344
    Bisbee, AZ 84
    Bloomfield, NM 254
    Carlsbad, NM 29
    Chinle, AZ 241
    Cloudcroft, NM 33
    Douglas, AZ 81–82, 84
    Flagstaff, AZ 219, 220
    Gallup, NM 248, 264
    Grand Canyon, AZ 215
    Grand Canyon Village, AZ 214,
        215
    Greer, AZ 57
    Jerome, AZ 137
    Kanab, UT 194
    Las Cruces, NM 35, 36
    Lordsburg, NM 49
    North Rim, AZ 196
    Oljato-Monument Valley,
        UT 242, 244
    Page, AZ 205–206
    Patagonia, AZ 96, 97
    Payson, AZ 149, 150
    Phoenix, AZ 73, 74, 128
    Pinos Altos, NM 46, 47
    Prescott, AZ 134
    Rio Rico, AZ 97, 98
    Safford, AZ 60, 62
    Santa Fe, NM 325, 326
    Scottsdale, AZ 128

Sedona, AZ 140
Silver City, NM 43, 46, 48, 49
Springdale, UT 193, 194
Taos, NM 337, 338, 344, 345
Tombstone, AZ 86
Truth or Consequences, NM 42
Tucson, AZ 115
Van Horn, TX 23, 25
Winslow, AZ 231
Hotel Valley Ho, Scottsdale,
        AZ 128
Hotevilla, AZ 227
hot springs
    Gila Hot Springs 44, 46
    Jemez Hot Springs 317–318,
        320
    La Paloma Hot Springs and
        Spa 42
    Riverbend Hot Springs 42
house-boating 198–199
Huachuca mountains 92–93
Hualapai Indian Reservation 180
Hualapai Lodge 182, 184
Hubbard Museum of the
        American West 32–33
hummingbirds 23, 114
Hunts Mesa (Monument
        Valley) 243

I

Ice Cave and Bandera
        Volcano 268, 271
icy roads xix
IMAX theater (Grand
        Canyon) 215
Indian lands, etiquette on xx, 229
Indian Pueblo Cultural
        Center 301, 304
Indian Route 6 (road) 182
Indian Wars 37, 77–78,
        150–151, 166–168

Inn on Broadway, The, Silver City, NM 48, 49
Inscription Rock Trail 267
insurance, auto xviii
International UFO Museum and Research Center 30

J

James, Jesse 368
Jemez Historic Site 318, 320
Jemez Hot Springs 317–318, 320
Jemez Mountains 317, 320
Jemez Mountain Trail Scenic Byway 317–319
Jemez Pueblo 317
Jemez Soda Dam 318
Jerome, AZ 135–137
Jerome Grand Hotel, Jerome, AZ 137
Jerome State Historic Park 137
Johnson Mesa 369

K

Kanab, UT 194
Kartchner Caverns State Park 89–91
Kartchner, James and Lois 91
Kasha-Katuwe Tent Rocks National Monument 306–307
Keepers of the Wild Nature Park 179–180
Kino, Eusebio Francisco 98, 99, 111
kivas (Anasazi building) 256, 258, 296, 317
Kohl's Ranch Lodge, Payson, AZ 149, 150
Kuaua Pueblo (Coronado Historic Site) 315–316
Kykotsmovi, AZ 228

L

La Cueva Café, Taos, NM 341, 344
La Fonda on the Plaza, Santa Fe, NM 325, 326
Laguna Pueblo 272
La Junta Point (Wild Rivers Recreation Area) 342
Lake Pleasant Regional Park 131
Lake Powell 198
Lake Roberts Cabins & General Store, Silver City, NM 46
Lake Roberts (Silver City, NM) 43, 46
Landmark Lookout Lodge, Tombstone, AZ 86
La Paloma Hot Springs and Spa, Truth or Consequences, NM 42
La Posada Hotel, Winslow, AZ 231
La Roca Restaurant (Mexico) 97
Las Cruces, NM 36, 37
Las Trampas, NM 348
Las Vegas, NM 369
Laughlin, NV 177
lava dikes 247
La Ventana Arch (El Malpais) 277–278
Lawrence, D. H. 337
Lazy B (ranch) 63
Lee's Ferry 198
lightning storms xix
Lincoln County War 31
Lincoln Historic Site 31, 33
Lipan Point (Grand Canyon) 213
Little Colorado River Gorge 210
Little Painted Desert County Park 230–231
Living Desert State Park 28, 29

Lodge, The, Cloudcroft, NM 33
lodging. *See* hotels and lodging
Lordsburg, NM 49
Los Alamos, NM 325–326
Los Alamos Visitors Center 325, 326
Los Cerrillos, NM 307–308
Los Lunas, NM 273
Lost Dutchman's Mine 159
Lost Dutchman State Park 160, 165
Lowell Observatory 219, 220
Lower Granite Gorge (Grand Canyon) 184
Low Road to Taos 327, 334
Lukachukai Mountains 244–245

M

Madrid, NM 308–309
Magma Mine (Superior, AZ) 69
Majestic View Lodge, Springdale, UT 193, 194
Manhattan Project 326
Manzano Mountains 292, 298
Mather Point (Grand Canyon) 212, 214
Maxwell, Lucien 356
Mazatzal Mountains 147
McGinn's Pistachio Tree Ranch 33, 35
McKittrick Canyon 24–25
mercury mining 143
Mesa Arizona Temple (Mormon) 126
Mesa AZ 126
Mescalero Apache Reservation 33
Mexican border, travel advice xix–xx, 77
Milagro Beanfield War, The (movie) 348–350

Millicent Rogers Museum 337, 338

Mimbres pottery 47

Mingus Mountain 135–136

Mishongnovi, AZ 230

missions, Spanish

    Abo ruins 292–294, 296

    Apache Indians and 99, 293–294, 295, 296

    details on 99

    Gran Quivira ruins 294, 296

    Nuestra Señora de Perpetuo Socorro 289

    Quarai ruins 296

    Salinas Pueblo Missions National Monument 292–294, 296

    San José de los Jemez 318

    San Miguel de Socorro 290

    San Xavier del Bac 99, 111–113

Mix, Tom 122

Moenkopi Legacy Inn, Tuba City, AZ 227

Mogollon culture 44–45

Mogollon (ghost town) 54

Mogollon Range 43

Mogollon Rim 56–57, 148–149

molybdenum mining 342–343

"monsoon season" xviii, 21, 108, 129, 171, 202, 235, 249

Montezuma Canyon Road 94

Montezuma Castle National Monument 151–152, 153

Monument Valley 241–244, 242

Moran Point (Grand Canyon) 213

Morenci, AZ 59, 60

Mormons 126

Mountainair, NM 294

Mount Baldy (White Mountains) 57

Mount Graham (Pinaleño Mountains) 61, 65

Mount Graham Red Squirrel 66

Mount Lemmon 66, 104

Mount Lemmon Ski Valley 107

Mt. Lemmon Science Tour (smartphone app) 105–106

Mummy Cave Ruin (Canyon de Chelly) 238

murals (Coronado Historic Site) 317

Murray Hotel, Silver City, NM 48, 49

Museum of Nature and Science (Las Cruces, NM) 37

Museum of Northern Arizona 218–219, 220

Mystery Valley (Monument Valley) 243

N

Nambe Falls 353

Nambe Pueblo, NM 330, 353

Narrows, The (Zion National Park) 193

National Geographic Visitor Center (Grand Canyon) 215

National Park passes xx, 191

native American cultures, ancient. *See also* pueblo ruins

    Anasazi culture 238–239, 255–256, 258–259

    Hohokam 74, 125, 151

    Mogollon culture 44–45

    Salado culture 67–68, 164

    Sinagua culture 137, 153, 221–222

Western New Mexico University Museum 47, 49

Navajo backcountry permits 225, 227

Navajo Nation 207–210, 233, 252

Navajo Point (Grand Canyon) 213

Navajo Spirit Tours 242, 243

Navajo Tours (Upper Antelope Canyon) 206

New Age movement 139

New Mexico Mining Museum 275, 278

Nichols, John 350

Niza, Marcos de 265

Nogales, AZ 97

Nogales, Mexico 77, 97

Northern Arizona University 219

North Rim Drive (Canyon de Chelly) 238–239

North Rim, Grand Canyon National Park 194–196

Nuestra Señora de Perpetuo Socorro (mission) 289

O

Oak Creek Canyon 140–141

Oakley, Annie 366

Oatman, AZ 177

O'Connor, Sandra Day 63–64

O'Keeffe, Georgia 321–322, 337, 358, 359

Old Oraibi, AZ 227–228

Old Spanish Trail 330, 331

Old Time Fiddlers Contest 149

Old Town Plaza (Albuquerque) 274

Old Town Scottsdale 127

Old Tucson (movie studio) 113, 115

Oraibi, AZ 227–228
Orilla Verde Recreation Area 334, 335
Out of Africa Wildlife Park 153

P

Page, AZ 198, 205–206
Paintec Desert 169
painted kiva (Coronado Historic Site) 317
Palace Hotel, The, Silver City, NM 48, 49
Palace of the Governors 355
Palace Restaurant and Saloon, The 133–134
Palisades Sill (Cimarron Canyon) 366
Palo Flechado Pass (Enchanted Circle Scenic Byway) 345, 365
Papago Indians. *See* Tohono O'odham Indians
Papago Park 73, 74
Parker Canyon Lake 95
Parry Lodge, Kanab, UT 194
Patagonia, AZ 96
Patagonia Lake State Park 96
Patagonia-Sonoita Creek Preserve 96, 97
Payson, AZ 147–149
Peach Springs, AZ 180
Peñasco, NM 347
Pecos Wilderness 347–348
Petrified Forest National Park 169–170
Petroglyph National Monument 301–304
petroglyph sites
  Canyon de Chelly 237
  Inscription Rock Trail 267

Petroglyph National Monument 301–304
  Three Rivers Petroglyph Site 35
Phantom Ranch (Grand Canyon) 215
Phelps Dodge Corporation 50–51
Phoenix, AZ 70–74, 126–128, 143
Phoenix Mountains Preserve 143
Phoenix Zoo 73, 74
Picuris Pueblo, NM 347
Piedras Marcadas Canyon (Petroglyph National Monument) 304
Pie-O-Neer Pies, Pie Town, NM 278
Piestewa Peak 143
Piestewa Peak Park 72–73, 74
Pie Town Cafe 278
Pie Town, NM 278
Pilar, NM 333
pilgrimage sites 112, 351
Pima Air & Space Museum 110
Pima Indians 99, 125
Pimería Alta 99
Pinal County Courthouse 123–124
Pinal County Historical Society & Museum 121, 124
Pinaleño Mountains 61
Pinal Pioneer Parkway 120–122
Pine, AZ 150
Pinetop-Lakeside, AZ 168
Pink Jeep Tour (Sedona) 140
Pinos Altos, NM 47
pistachio, world's largest 33, 35
Plains of San Agustin 279–280
Point Imperial (Grand Canyon) 195
Pojoaque Pueblo 330

Prehistoric Trackways National Monument 37
Prescott, AZ 133–134
Prescott, W. H. 133
prisons, in Arizona 123
Prohibition era 82
pronghorn antelope 281
Pueblo Bonito (Chaco Canyon) 258
Pueblo Grande Museum and Archaeological Park 73–74
Pueblo Revolt of 1680 289, 318, 335, 336
pueblo ruins
  Asinna Pueblo 267–268
  Aztec Ruins National Monument 255–256, 259
  Bandelier National Monument 323–325
  Besh-Ba-Gowah Archaeological Park 67–68
  Canyon de Chelly National Monument 235–241
  Casa Grande Ruins National Monument 125
  Chaco Culture National Historical Park 257–259, 259
  Gila Cliff Dwellings National Monument 42–45
  Montezuma Castle National Monument 151–152, 153
  Pueblo Grande Museum and Archaeological Park 73–74
  Salinas Pueblo Missions National Monument 292–294, 296

Three Rivers Petroglyph Site 35
Tonto National
    Monument 162–163,
    165
Tuzigoot National
    Monument 137, 138
Walnut Canyon National
    Monument 221–222,
    225
Wupatki National
    Monument 207, 210,
    223, 224–225
Puye Cliff Dwellings 331–332
Puye Cliffs Welcome Center 331

Q
Quarai ruins (mission) 296
Queen Creek Canyon 68–69
Queen Mine (Bisbee, AZ) 84
Questa, NM 342

R
Radium Springs, NM 37–38
Rainbow Forest Museum 169
Ramsey Canyon Preserve 92–93,
    95
Ranchos de Taos, NM 334–335
Raton Pass Inn, Raton, NM 368,
    369
Redford, Robert 348
red maples 299
Red Mountain 215–216
Red River, NM 343
Red Rock Pass 139, 156
Red Rock State Park 138, 140
rental vehicles xvi
Rex Allen Days 62
Rex Allen Museum 60, 62
Riders of the Purple Sage
    (Grey) 148

Riggs Flat Lake 65–66
Rim Country Museum 148, 150
Rinconada Canyon (Petroglyph
    National Monument) 304
Rio Bravo (movie) 113
Rio Grande del Norte National
    Monument 334, 342
Rio Grande Gorge 333, 334, 342
Rio Grande Gorge
    Bridge 364–365
Rio Grande Gorge Visitor
    Center 333, 335
Rio Grande (river) 273
Riverbend Hot Springs, Truth or
    Consequences, NM 42
River People 125
River Road to Taos. *See* Low Road
    to Taos
road conditions xvi
roadside assistance xviii
roadside attractions 178
roadtrip advice xiii–xx
RoadTrip America xx
rodeos 149
Roosevelt Dam. *See* Theodore
    Roosevelt Dam
Roosevelt Lake, AZ 162
Rosemont Talus Snail 66
Roswell Incident 29–30
Roswell, NM 29–30
Route 66 (highway) 173,
    176–180, 185–188
Route 66 (song) 178
Route 66 (television series) 178
Route 666, US. *See* US Route 666
    ("Devil's Highway")
Ruidoso Downs 32
Ruidoso, NM 32–33
ruins, pueblo. *See* pueblo ruins
Ruth, Adolph 159

Ruth Hall Museum of
    Paleontology 362

S
Sabino Canyon 101–105
Sabino Canyon Visitors
    Center 101
Safford, AZ 65
Safford Ranger District Office 66
saguaro cacti 107, 108
Saguaro National Park 107–108,
    114, 115
Salado culture 67–68, 164
Salinas Pueblo Missions National
    Monument 292–294, 296
Salt Mission Trail Scenic
    Byway 289, 298
Salt River Canyon 165–167
Salt River Wilderness Area 166
salt trade 294
San Carlos Apache
    Reservation 66
sandhill cranes 284–285
Sandia Crest 311–312
Sandia Crest House 311, 312
Sandia Mountains 299–300,
    311–312
Sandia Peak Tramway 299–300
Sandstone Bluffs overlook (El
    Malpais) 277–278
San Felipe de Neri Church 274
San Francisco de Asis
    Church 334–335
San Francisco Peaks 215
Sangre de Cristos
    mountains 330, 334
San Ildefonso Pueblo 330
San José de Gracia Church 348
San José de los Jemez
    (mission) 318

San Jose Mission Church (Laguna Pueblo) 272–273

San Miguel de Socorro (mission) 290

Santa Catalina Mountains 101–105

Santa Clara Pueblo 330, 331–332

Santa Cruz Lake Recreation Area 353

Santa Fe National Historic Trail 369

Santa Fe, NM 329–330

Santa Fe Plaza 355

Santa Rita Mountains 66

San Xavier del Bac (mission) 99, 111–113

San Ysidro Church (Corrales) 305

Schnebly Hill Road 156

Scottsdale, AZ 127–128

Second Mesa (Hopi Reservation) 228

Sedona Airport 139

Sedona Airport Vortex 139

Sedona, AZ 138–140, 156

Sedona Chamber of Commerce 139, 140

Seligman, AZ 185–187

Seven Falls (Sabino Canyon) 103–104

Sevilleta National Wildlife Refuge 290, 291

Sharlot Hall Museum 134

Shiprock 246–248

Show Low, AZ 168–169

Sierra Blanca mountains 32

Sierra Diablo (Black Range, New Mexico) 42–43

Sierra Vista, AZ 92

Silver City Museum 47, 49

Silver City, NM 47–48

Silver King Mine 123

Sinagua culture 137, 153, 221–222

singing cowboys (movies) 62

Sipaulovi, AZ 230

Sitting Bull Falls 28–29

Sky City (Acoma Pueblo) 269–271

Sky City Cultural Center 271

Sky Island Parkway (Catalina Highway) 104–106

sky islands 61, 65, 66, 75, 92–93, 104

Sky Ranch Lodge, Sedona, AZ 140

sledding 347

Slide Rock State Park 141

Smokey Bear 32

Smokey Bear's Gravesite 32, 33

snow xix

Socorro Heritage & Visitors Center 290, 291

Socorro, NM 289–290

Soleri Bells 154

Soleri, Paolo 154

Sonoita, AZ 96

Sonoran desert 66

Sonoran Desert people, ancient. *See* Hohokam

South Mountain Park 71–72, 74

South Rim Drive (Canyon de Chelly) 235–238

South Rim, Grand Canyon National Park 210–215

Space Biospheres Ventures 119

space observation

  Lowell Observatory 219, 220

  Very Large Array (VLA) 279–280, 283

Spaceport America 42

space travel

  Biosphere 2 117–120

Blue Origin 23–24, 25

  Spaceport America 42

Spider Rock (Canyon de Chelly) 235

Springdale, UT 194

Springerville volcanic field 57

Squaw Peak Park 72–73

Stagecoach (movie) 241

Standin' on the Corner Park 231–232

stargazing 219

St. David, AZ 37

Steeple Rock 63

Steinbeck, John 173

St. James Hotel, Cimarron, NM 368

Strawberry, AZ 150

Strawberry Schoolhouse 150

Subway, The (Zion National Park) 193

Summerhaven, AZ 107

Sunset Crater Volcano National Monument 207, 210, 223–224, 225

Superfund sites 342–343

Superior, AZ 69

Superstition Mountains 157–158

Superstition Wilderness Area 159

supervolcanos 319

T

"Take It Easy" (song; Eagles) 231–232

Taliesin West 145–146, 147

Taos Art Museum 337, 338

Taos Inn, Taos, NM 337, 338

Taos, NM 335, 337, 339–341, 345

Taos Pueblo 335, 337–338, 338

Taos Ski Valley 341

Taos Visitor Center 338

Tekakwitha, Kateri (saint) 111–112, 355

Tempe, AZ 126

Tempe Town Lake 126

Tesuque Pueblo 330

Texas madrones 25

Theodore Roosevelt Dam 160–161, 162

Third Mesa (Hopi Reservation) 227–228

Thompson, William Boyce 70

Three Rivers Petroglyph Site 35

Tierra Amarilla, NM 363

Tiguex War 315

Tijeras, NM 299

time zones xvii

Tinkertown Museum 310, 312

Titan Missile Museum 99–100, 100

Tiwa Indians 317

Tohono O'odham Indians 108, 111

Tombaugh, Clyde 219

Tombstone, AZ 84–86

Tombstone Courthouse State Historic Park 85, 86

Tombstone Epitaph, The 85

Tom Mix Memorial 122

Tonto National Monument 162–163, 165

Tonto Natural Bridge State Park 149–150

Top-of-the-World, AZ 68

Tortilla Flat, AZ 161, 165

trading posts 209–210

traffic 117, 129

Trailer Village RV Park, Grand Canyon, AZ 215

Trail of the Mountain Spirits Scenic Byway 43

travertine 149, 318

Tres Piedras, NM 364

Trinity Hotel, Carlsbad, NM 29

Trinity site 36

Truchas, NM 348–349

Truchas Peaks 348

Truth or Consequences, NM 42

Tsakurshovi Trading Post 228–229, 230

Tubac, AZ 99

Tubac Presidio State Historic Park 99, 100

Tucson, AZ 101–116

 Aeronautics Corridor 109–111

 Arizona-Sonora Desert Museum 113, 115

 Catalina Highway 104–106

 Gates Pass (Tucson Mountains) 115

 Old Tucson (movie studio) 113, 115

 Sabino Canyon 101–105

 Saguaro National Park 107–108, 114, 115

 San Xavier del Bac (mission) 99, 111–113

Tucson Mountains 115

tuff 307

Tumacacori 98, 100

Tumacácori National Historical Park 98, 100

turquoise 307–308

Turquoise Trail National Scenic Byway 307–310, 308

Tusas Mountains 360

Tusayan, AZ 215

Tuzigoot National Monument 137, 138

Tyrone Copper and Gold Mine 50–51, 54

Tyrone (ghost town) 50–51

Tyuonyi (Bandelier National Monument) 324

U

UFOs 29–30, 279, 280

uranium mining 275

U.S. Highway system 165, 173

U.S. Hill, High Road to Taos Scenic Byway 347

US Route 666 ("Devil's Highway") 56, 58–59

V

Vadito, NM 347

Valentine, AZ 179

Valles Caldera National Preserve 319

Van Horn, TX 23, 25

vehicle maintenance checklist xvi

Verde Canyon Railroad 137, 138

Verde Valley, AZ 137–138

Vermilion Cliffs 196

Very Large Array (VLA) 279–280, 283

Vietnam Veterans Memorial State Park 344

Village of Corrales 305

Vishnu Temple (Grand Canyon) 213

VLA (Very Large Array) 279–280, 283

volcanic geology 43

 El Malpais National Monument 269, 271, 275–278

 Ice Cave and Bandera Volcano 268

 Kasha-Katuwe Tent Rocks National Monument 306–307

lava dikes 247
Red Mountain 215–216
Shiprock 246–248
Springerville volcanic field 57
Sunset Crater Volcano National
        Monument 207, 210,
        223–224, 225
supervolcanos 319
tuff 307
Valles Caldera National
        Preserve 319
Volcanoes Day Use Area,
        Petroglyph National
        Monument 304
Volcanoes Day Use Area,
        Petroglyph National
        Monument 304
"vortex" sites (Sedona) 139
Vulture Mine Tours 131, 132

W

Wahweap Marina (houseboat
        rentals) 206
Walatowa Visitors Center 317,
        320
Wallow Fire (2011) 55, 57
Walnut Canyon National
        Monument 221–222, 225
Walnut Grove dam collapse 133
Waltz, Jacob 159
Watson Lake Park 134
Wayne, John 113, 241, 244
Weaver Mountains 132
Western New Mexico University
        Museum 47, 49
Westerns (movies) 62, 113, 122,
        241–242, 244, 251, 264
West Fork Trail (Oak Creek
        Canyon) 141
Wheeler Peak, NM 341

Whetstone Mountains 89
Whiskey Row (Prescott,
        AZ) 133–134
White Dove of the Desert.
        See San Xavier del Bac
        (mission)
White House Ruin (Canyon de
        Chelly) 238
White House Trail (Canyon de
        Chelly) 235, 238
White Mountains 55–56, 57
White Rock, NM 323
White Rock Visitors Center 323,
        325
White Sands Missile Range
        Museum 35–36
White Sands National
        Monument 33–34
White Spar Highway 132
Whitewater Canyon, NM 52
Wickenburg, AZ 131–132
Wickenburg, Henry 131
Wigwam Motel, Holbrook,
        AZ 169, 170
wildlife xix
Wild Rivers Backcountry
        Byway 342
Wild Rivers Visitor Center 342
Wild West Show (Buffalo
        Bill's) 366
Willcox, AZ 61–62
Williams, AZ 187
Williams Valley, AZ 57
wine country 96, 138
Winslow, AZ 231–232
World's Oldest Continuous
        Rodeo 149
World's Smallest Museum 68,
        69

Wotan's Throne (Grand
        Canyon) 213
Wright, Frank Lloyd 145–146
Wupatki National
        Monument 207, 210, 223,
        224–225

Y

Yaki Point (Grand Canyon) 212
Yarnell, AZ 133
Yarnell Hill 133
Yavapai County Courthouse 133
Yavapai Lodge, Grand Canyon,
        AZ 215
Yavapai Point (Grand
        Canyon) 214

Z

Zane Grey Cabin 148, 150
Zion Canyon 191
Zion Canyon Scenic
        Road 191–192
Zion–Mount Carmel Tunnel 193
Zion National Park 189–194
Zion National Park Lodge,
        Springdale, UT 193, 194
zoos
    Arizona-Sonora Desert
        Museum 113, 115
    Keepers of the Wild Nature
        Park 179–180
    Living Desert State Park 28
    Out of Africa Wildlife Park 153
    Phoenix Zoo 73, 74
Zuni Mountains 266
Zuni Pueblo 264, 265–266
Zuni Visitors Center 265

Check out these other travel and outdoor guides from Imbrifex Books

Base Camp Las Vegas: 101 Hikes in the Southwest
by Deborah Wall
Expanded 2nd Edition with 40 New Hikes!
ISBN: 9780997236941 (print)
ISBN: 9780997236989 (e-book)
BaseCampGuides.com

Base Camp Denver
(coming in winter of 2018)

Base Camp Denver: 101 Hikes Along Colorado's Front Range
by Pete KJ
Scenic and exciting hikes within a few miles of Denver!
ISBN: 978-1945501135 (print)
(also in e-book)
BaseCampGuides.com

THE LOCAL ANGLER
Fly Fishing Austin
(coming in spring of 2019)

THE LOCAL ANGLER Fly Fishing Austin: 55 Wades in Central Texas
by Aaron Reed
Great fishing spots in and around the Texas capital!
ISBN: 978-1945501241 (print)
(also in e-book)
TheLocalAngler.com